W9-AYB-529

Best wishes!

Steve Splaine

The Web Testing Handbook

Steven Splaine
Stefan P. Jaskiel

STQE Publishing

The Web Testing Handbook

Published by
STQE Publishing

A Division of Software Quality Engineering, Inc.
330 Corporate Way, Suite 300
Orange Park, Florida 32073
USA
www.sqe.com

Copyright © 2001 by
STQE Publishing

International Standard Book Number: 0-9704363-0-0

Printed in the United States of America

First Printing: January 2001

Second Printing: August 2001

Trademarks

All terms mentioned in this book that are known to be trademarks or service marks have been appropriately capitalized. STQE Publishing cannot attest to the accuracy of this information. Use of a term in this book should not be regarded as affecting the validity of any trademark or service mark.

Warning and Disclaimer

Every effort has been made to make this book as complete and accurate as possible, but no warranty or fitness is implied. The information provided is on an "as is" basis. The authors and the publisher shall have neither liability nor responsibility to any person or entity with respect to any loss or damages arising from the information contained in this book.

Book

Advisors & Reviewers
Jennifer Brock
Eric Brown
Lee Copeland
Rick Craig
Dan Crawford
Dave Gelperin
Robin Goldsmith
Laura and Jon Hagar
Jim Hobert
Jeff Jones
Amanda McCrary
Wayne Middleton
Dale Perry
Alberto Savoia
Karen Sullivan
Bill Tuccio
Greg Turner
Laurie F. White
Pamela Young

Cover Designer
Jamie Borders

Indexer
Bill Graham

Companion Web Site

Designer & Tester
Steven Splaine

Developers
Adrian S. Johnson
Kevin Shallow
Tom Stock

Graphic Designer
Jamie Borders

Webmaster
Mickey Epperson

From Steven,

■■■■■■■■■■■■■■■■

To my wife, Darlene, and our son, Jack –
the joy of our lives. You've given my life
both meaning and purpose. I love you
both more than words can say.

~

To my parents, John and Muriel Splaine.
Thank you for all of the encouragement
and support that you've provided me
throughout my life.

From Stefan,

■■■■■■■■■■■■■■■■

To my parents, Maria and Walter Jaskiel,
for teaching me how to choose the best
road to follow among life's many choices.

~

To my friend and colleague, Michele Rimes,
for always listening and helping me find
meaning in my life and work.

Table of Contents

Chapter 3 – Compatibility 51

Chapter 4 – Navigation 83

Chapter 5 – User Interaction 111

Chapter 10 – Emerging Technologies 315

Chapter 11 – Post Implementation... 343

Foreword

The thorough testing of Web sites and Web applications is not an easy task. The breadth of knowledge and range of skills required to succeed are greater than ever before. But for those with the drive and determination to acquire that knowledge and practice those skills, the rewards are also greater than ever before.

In a few short years, the Internet has managed to have a huge and long-lasting impact in a number of areas, and software testing is definitely one of them. The Internet has made software testing more important than ever *and* more complex than ever. In the pre-Internet days, when release cycles were measured in months, the impact of poor software quality took time to surface, to spread, and to get fixed. With enough marketing support, a software company could become a market leader, even if their products suffered from inferior quality; simply because by the time the product was purchased, installed, understood, and finally used, the cost of switching to another product was too high. In the world of Web sites and Web applications, on the other hand, the impact of poor quality is almost immediate and switching costs are minimal. If users find the functionality, performance, or usability of a Web site not to their liking, a competitive site is just a mouse-click away and the business loss due to poor quality is immediate.

In addition to making software testing more important than ever, the Internet has also made it more complex and demanding than ever. First of all, the range of components and technologies used by Web applications is extremely broad and heterogeneous. Ten years ago, the typical testing assignment involved testing one application written in one language and running on one operating system/hardware platform. Today, to thoroughly test a Web application, an engineer might need to know and understand a fair amount of HTML, XML, JavaScript, Visual Basic, SQL, Java, and C^{++}, just to name a few, as well as various flavors of UNIX and Windows. In order to be effective, the engineer would also need to know the system's architecture and hardware, and understand how components like gateways, routers, and load-balancers participate in the site's overall functionality and performance and how they should be tested. The categories of tests that have to be performed have also increased dramatically for Web applications. The huge number of potential users, for example, has made scalability testing a key requirement. Similarly, the broad range of software and hardware configurations that will be used by a Web site's visitors makes compatibility testing more complicated and more necessary than ever, while the easy accessibility of competitors' Web sites has made usability testing, previously a rather rare consideration, an absolute necessity. Few companies can afford to have one, or more, specialists in each of these areas of testing. But in the greatest majority of cases, the testing responsibility for an entire Web site or application will rest on the shoulders of a small team or even a single individual who will also be responsible for dealing with the more traditional types of tests, such as functionality.

Besides adding significant complexity to the testing tasks, the Internet has also accelerated the pace of all activities related to it. The software development cycle has definitely switched to *Web Time*, and so we find ourselves in a situation where we need to know and do more than ever before, and we need to do it faster than ever before.

Fortunately, the unprecedented testing challenges created, or magnified, by the Internet have been balanced by an equally unprecedented focus on testing solutions. New companies have been formed to develop and market innovative technology, tools, and services specifically for Web testing, while many existing companies have switched their focus and revised their products to address more directly the testing needs created by the Internet. The sales of software testing tools and services are at an all time high, which indicates not only that many companies have realized the importance of testing, but they are also ready to make the investment necessary to do it right.

On the other hand, there is one area that has, so far, failed to keep up with challenges, demands, and opportunities presented by Web testing: the availability of dedicated software testing professionals with the knowledge and expertise required to design and implement an effective and successful Web testing effort. While there are large numbers of people whose primary job responsibility is Web testing, many of them lack the training and experience required to do the work thoroughly and effectively. Without prior experience or guidance, these Web testers have no choice but to improvise, re-invent the wheel over and over again, and learn lessons the hard way, all under tremendous time pressure. This is where this very well researched, very well written, and very timely book comes in.

Steven Splaine and Stefan P. Jaskiel have done a wonderful job of condensing the major areas of knowledge required for Web testing in a very effective format. As you will be able to tell by just looking at a few pages of this book, they chose concreteness over abstraction and practicality over philosophy. It is clear that their knowledge was not acquired in some ivory tower, but in the front lines of the Internet revolution, harvested through their own experiences and by talking to, and learning from, other leading practitioners.

I had the pleasure of attending one of Steven Splaine's first courses on Web testing. The course was sold-out, the room was full, and people were furiously taking notes. I realized then and there that the course material would make a book that would be immensely useful, make that indispensable, to anyone involved in testing Web sites and Web applications. I have been successfully involved with Internet and Web site testing for many years now, and some people even considered me something of an authority on Web load testing. However, I still walked out of Steven's course with a binder full of notes and ideas to improve my own techniques and approaches.

As I said at the very beginning, Web testing presents great challenges; but the personal, professional, and financial rewards will also be great for those who choose to accept those challenges and arm themselves with the knowledge required to overcome them. If you study and practice the material in this book, you will definitely become part of an elite group of professionals whose skills and contributions are going to be in great demands for years to come. I wish you the best of luck in your career.

Alberto Savoia
Chief Technologist
Keynote Systems Inc.

Preface

Except for the simplest of Web sites, it quickly becomes apparent that some sort of test planning is needed. All too often, the initial number of bugs found from ad-hoc testing is large enough that not all of them are fixed the first time they're detected. This puts an additional burden on the people who test the Web site or application. Not only must they conjure up imaginative new tests, but they must also remember how previous tests were executed in order to reliably re-test the Web site/application, and ensure that known bugs have been removed and no new bugs have been introduced. Quite frankly, "post-its" are not an adequate solution.

In our experience, the easiest way to plan (or design) the testing of a Web site/application is to develop a series of Test Plans. These plans help ensure that the Web site/application is comprehensively tested and can be reliably re-tested. Each test plan is focused on a different phase of the testing process (e.g., unit testing, system testing, or post-implementation testing), while the individual test cases within each test plan are grouped into categories that focus on a single aspect of testing (e.g., usability, compatibility, performance, etc.) A by-product of this approach is that several teams can work in parallel, which provides a significant advantage when working in "Web Time." Additionally, having several documented and well-scoped groups of test cases makes outsourcing some or all of the testing effort much more controllable.

This book has been designed with this strategy in mind. The intention being that each chapter focuses on a different aspect of testing a Web site/application. Each of the chapters can be read individually or in any sequence, however, we recommend you read the *Introduction* chapter first. The checklist(s) at the end of each section can be used as a set of candidate test cases, and the tools that are referenced in each chapter provide a method for automating many of these test cases.

Of course, at test execution time, there's nothing to prevent you from scheduling test cases from different categories and executing them together. You may consider, for example, running some of the functional integrity checks while the Web site is also being stress tested. Some test cases in one category may actually be duplicates of test cases in another category, but from a test design perspective, this is perfectly acceptable. It's better to have 120% test coverage than 80% test coverage. Obviously, from a test execution perspective, running duplicate tests is less than optimal. A Master Test Plan is a common approach taken to reduce this problem and provide a framework for coordinating all of the various activities defined in the individual test plans. In addition, a master test plan can be used to help identify many of the planning risks associated with testing Web sites/applications and subsequently document the potential contingencies that could be employed to mitigate each risk, thereby reducing the overall risk of the project.

■■■■■■■■■■■■■■■■■■

A Master Test Plan ties together all the separate test plans into a single cohesive effort.

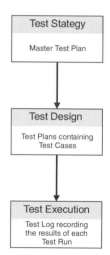

This book seeks to help developers and testers who are making the transition from testing traditional client/server, PC, and/or mainframe systems to testing rapidly changing Web sites and applications. This book explains the technologies that are typically used to build these Web sites/applications and suggests test cases and techniques that can be included in a Web site's test plans to ensure that the technology has been implemented correctly. However, this book stops short of recommending a formal high-level testing strategy such as a process or methodology, as this topic alone could easily form the basis of an entire book.

Rather than restrict ourselves to the content that we could include in the pages of this book, we decided to provide the reader with two additional resources. The first resource is a Web site, which has been designed and built for the specific purpose of providing our readers with the opportunity to practice the testing tips and techniques covered in this book, thereby gaining real-world hands-on Web testing experience. The second resource is a series of test plans, developed for the companion Web site using the information covered in this book and the IEEE 829-1998 software-testing standard. The purpose of these test plans is to provide examples of how the information in this book can be used to develop a set of test plans for a specific Web site. These test plans are not intended to be the perfect test suite for all Web sites/applications, nor do they attempt to drive down to the low-level details of platform specific test execution (e.g., how to turn off JavaScript on browser X or the latest performance quirks of Web server Y). Any examples covering such a rapidly changing subject would most likely be out of date before this book could be published. Instead, we hope that our readers will extrapolate and customize these documents based on their own individual and unique needs.

Finally, we welcome any comments or suggestions from the readers of this book or visitors of the companion Web site. One thing is certain about the Web – it will grow not only in terms of numbers, but also in terms of technology and complexity and, consequently, will require even more rigorous testing. We hope that the combined resources of this book and companion Web site will place our readers in a good position to meet the challenges of testing whatever new technology the wizards of Silicon Valley come up with next.

Steven Splaine
Tampa, Florida
Steve@Splaine.net

■■■■■■■■■■■■■■■■■

The companion Web site and associated test plans can be found at:

sqe.com/bdonline/

■■■■■■■■■■■■■■■■■

The Institute of Electric and Electronics Engineers (IEEE.org) provides more information on the 829 standard.

Acknowledgements

The rapid pace of changing technology makes it difficult – if not impossible – for a single person to understand every aspect of software engineering. While each of us plays a vital role in our specific area of expertise, the technology arena is so vast and dynamic that we must rely heavily on our colleagues to help us disseminate our ideas and extend our own knowledge and understanding. This book is not the result of the effort of any individual. It is the result of a concerted effort of an entire team. A project such as this could not be successful without the contributions of many people.

"No man's knowledge here can go beyond his experience."

- John Locke

We would like to thank everyone who helped develop and review SQE's Web/E-Business Testing Course, which provided much of the structure and content for this book. Many of SQE's students and clients also provided suggestions for improvements to the training course, which were included in this book. Many thanks to the team of advisors and reviewers who spent many hours of their "free time" reviewing this book. Perhaps the most valuable contributions, however, came from the people who developed the tools to test the technology that we're writing about in this book. Without these tools, it's doubtful that we would have had enough free time to write this book. Special thanks to the staff at the companies who provided many of the tools that we used and shared their technical expertise with us.

Empirix (formerly RSW Software)
Envive
Keynote Systems
Mercury Interactive

RadView Software
Segue Software
Watchfire

Chapter 1 – Introduction

We're living in the age of convergence, and technology is the catalyst that's bringing us all together. Traditional business models, distribution channels, and competitors are changing more rapidly than ever before. The proverbial "wolf at our doorstep" no longer exists because the playing field has completely changed. Shopping malls, for example, that were once concerned with competition in the same neighborhood are now concerned about competitors around the world. Technology and the Internet have enabled consumers to place orders from the comfort of their own homes for anything and everything that they want or need, bypassing physical storefronts completely.

The Internet is still experiencing significant growth and is emerging as a global medium for communications and commerce. The number of Web users worldwide is estimated to increase from 97 million at the end of 1998 to 320 million by the end of 2002, a 35% compounded annual growth rate.[1] The number of Web users in the U.S. will increase from 52 million at the end of 1998 to 136 million by the end of 2002, a 27% compounded annual growth rate.[1] During the same period, the number of business Web sites in the U.S. is projected to increase from 650,000 to 2.6 million, a 41% compounded annual growth rate[2]. Like it or not, the e-commerce revolution has begun and we're all part of it.

■■■■■■■■■■■■■■■■

[1] Estimated by International Data Corporation (IDC.com)

■■■■■■■■■■■■■■■■

[2] Estimated by Forrester Research (forrester.com)

We've all experienced firsthand how the e-commerce revolution impacts us as consumers, but how does it affect us behind the scenes? What aspects of e-commerce should your organization be concerned with? What steps can you take to ensure that your organization's e-commerce solutions meet (or exceed) your business requirements? Which tools are available to help you test your organization's Web site against these requirements? These are just a few of the questions that this book will try to answer.

The e-commerce revolution has taken us by storm and many of us who test the software have become the casualties. While technology has improved exponentially, education in the field of Web testing has been neglected by comparison. Web projects typically have fewer documented requirements than traditional software projects. If neither the design/development team nor the project sponsor specifies any requirements, then how can you effectively test a Web site to ensure that it meets your organization's requirements? If you only check the items that have been specifically identified, then who checks the other items? The responsibility still rests with the person assigned to test the Web site – you?

It's important to remember that there are always requirements: performance, usability, navigation, and many others. Some of these requirements may be explicitly stated through a formal document, while others are implied or assumed. Correct spelling, for example, is expected but rarely explicitly stated as a requirement. Since organizations and individuals often perceive Web site requirements differently, the challenge lies in identifying all of the implicit requirements for your specific project. Personalities, budgets, schedules, skill levels, and corporate strategy are all variables. The only common factor in the equation – although not constant – is the *technology*. If you can understand the technology used to develop a Web site, then you'll gain the insight necessary to create reasonable requirements that you can use to design your test cases. Therein lies the premise behind this book.

The primary focus of this book is testing Web technology and the critical issues that surround that technology. This book

■■■■■■■■■■■■■■■■■

You should test your Web site for:

* code quality
* compatibility
* navigation
* user interaction
* usability and accessibility
* performance
* scalability
* reliability and availability
* post implementation

■■■■■■■■■■■■■■■■■

Requirements fall into two main categories:

* explicit
* implicit

Understanding the *technology* is the key to identifying the implicit requirements.

assumes that you already have some basic software testing experience and have used the Internet to some extent. Consequently, this book does not cover generic testing processes and techniques. There are already a number of fine books that cover this knowledge domain, many of which are listed in the *Further Reading* section. This book explains the principles of Web testing using a high-level horizontal approach as illustrated in Figure 1-1.

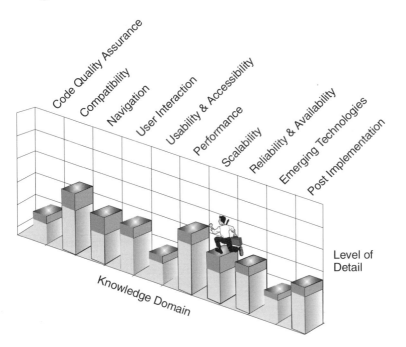

■■■■■■■■■■■■■■■■■■
Figure 1-1

Scope of this
Book

This book provides a foundation in many areas rather than focusing on a single aspect of Web testing in great detail, since each of these topics could contain enough information to fill an entire book. The intent is to help you gain enough knowledge to develop a comprehensive set of test cases, which you can then use to test your organization's Web sites and applications efficiently and effectively.

For the benefit of those who are new to the Web, the next few sections of this chapter provide a brief history of the Internet and an overview of how it works. Those of you who are familiar with this background information may want to skip the next few sections and go directly to the section that explains the case study.

Internet vs. Web ■ ■ ■ ■ ■

In 1969, two computers, one at the University of California Los Angeles (UCLA) and the other at Stanford Research Institute (SRI), were connected together via the Advanced Research Projects Agency Network (ARPANet) using a 50 Kbps network. Over the past thirty years, this event has been the catalyst for the development of the complex network of servers, routers, and switches that form the backbone of our Internet today. An idea that began as a research tool for the government and universities has ultimately affected the way millions of people interact with each other every day. Indeed, it could be said that the Internet is changing our very society.

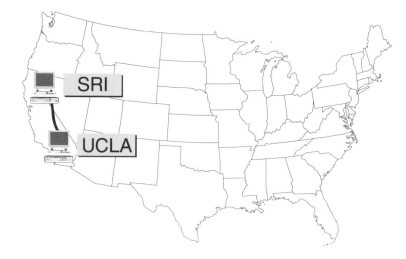

■■■■■■■■■■■■■■■■■

Figure 1-2

ARPANet was formed in 1969 in the United States. The network had grown to 23 nodes by 1971, and went International in 1973.

In order to effectively and efficiently test Web-based applications, you need to understand the basics of how the Internet works. The Internet is *not* the same as the Web, although these terms are often erroneously used interchangeably. The Internet is a network of physical connections of fiber optics, copper wire, routers, hubs, switches, and other components that provides an infrastructure for worldwide communications between computers. The World Wide Web (WWW) is just one of the many applications that utilize the infrastructure of the Internet. It consists of software that allows hyperlink access to textual and graphical information (i.e., Web pages) on host computers connected to the Internet. The Web can thus integrate a company's marketing and transaction processing mechanisms via an electronic commerce system, which allows businesses to advertise and sell their products and services to consumers and other businesses via the Internet.

■■■■■■■■■■■■■■
What's the difference between the Web and the Internet?

■■■■■■■■■■■■■■
The World Wide Web Consortium (W3C.org) provides an overview of the history of the Web.

Internet Applications

The Internet is utilized by a number of applications, each using a different high-level network protocol but all using the same lower-level network protocol IP (Internet Protocol) to handle network communications. Six of the more common applications are illustrated in Figure 1-3. Web servers transfer documents (e.g., Web pages) to each other using the HyperText Transfer Protocol (HTTP). HTTP is a communications protocol that allows computers in a network to interact with each other by sending and receiving requests for documents. There are several different variations of HTTP that Web browsers may use. Unfortunately, the lack of modularity in the design of HTTP has made its evolution (i.e., new versions) difficult and caused problems for other Internet applications. A new generation of

■■■■■■■■■■■■■■
HTTP Implementations:

♦ HTTP 0.9, 1.0, and 1.1
♦ HTTP-NG (Next Generation)
♦ HTTPS (Secure HTTP)

HTTP (HTTP-NG) attempts to produce a simpler, but more capable and more flexible, protocol than the original version of HTTP. Another variation, HTTPS, uses an encryption technology to scramble HTTP information before it is sent over the Internet.

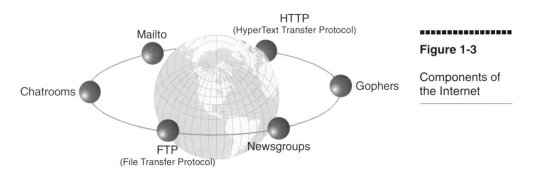

■■■■■■■■■■■■■■■■

Figure 1-3

Components of the Internet

File Transfer Protocol (FTP) is another communications format that has been optimized for transferring large files and is therefore often used to download (or upload) software products and patches.

Chat rooms and newsgroups are also significant components of the Internet. Chat rooms offer a convenient place where users can communicate with each other in real time. Newsgroups, also known as Usenets, are discussion forums where users with the same interests can exchange ideas by posting articles on a virtual bulletin board. Users can post their articles via e-mail and view various newsgroups directly through their Web browsers. Toshiba (toshiba.com) estimated that, by 1999, there were over 30,000 newsgroups across the Internet with topics on recreation, business, social, computers, and many other categories.

■■■■■■■■■■■■■■■■

The *Appendix* provides additional background information on the various network protocols used by the Internet and the Web.

Early in the evolution of the Internet, a search and retrieval tool called *Gopher* was used to locate specific information. Suppose, for example, you wanted to find information on classic cars. A gopher could run (in cyberspace, of course) to every connected server around the world searching for every bit of information on classic cars. In the early days of the Internet, the gopher's job was easy because there wasn't much information to search through. With the amount of information available today, however, those poor little gophers might never return from their search. Today, Gopher has been replaced by a myriad of powerful search and meta-search engines such as AltaVista, Dogpile, Lycos, and others.

Did you know...

Gopher was named for the University of Minnesota's mascot.

Internet e-mail uses various protocols to transfer messages from one e-mail system to another. Mailto is a gateway that provides a common connection between e-mail systems around the world. E-mail messages can be sent to people connected to online networks such as Prodigy, America Online (AOL), and CompuServe and also to people who are connected directly to the Internet.

Web Evolution

Many companies have experienced an evolution in their business models. When we think back and remember how businesses operated in the early 1990s, paper was the most convenient and widely used method for disseminating information. Although word processors and spreadsheets were used extensively to enter, manipulate, and store data, printed reports were usually distributed via postal mail or fax machine. Purchase orders, inventory lists, balance sheets, bank statements, and other business documents were used as the basis of most business processes. The advent of the Internet started a revolution that triggered an evolution in the way business is done. Volumes of paper-based books, manuals, folders, and memos that once filled rows of book shelves and file cabinets are being converted into electronic formats and stored on networks.

Did you know...

The term *Internet* was derived from *inter-network*, an interconnected set of networks.

Businesses have come to realize that this mass of information becomes knowledge *only when* the right people can access the right information at the right time. Otherwise, the information is just raw data that occupies disk space and loses meaning over time. As your company begins to recognize the value of information in the right people's hands, the evolution begins. As the evolution continues, the Web typically moves from an organization's periphery and eventually becomes a core part of the organization's structure. Figure 1-4 shows the progression of an organization's Web site from an extension of the Marketing department to a core business application.

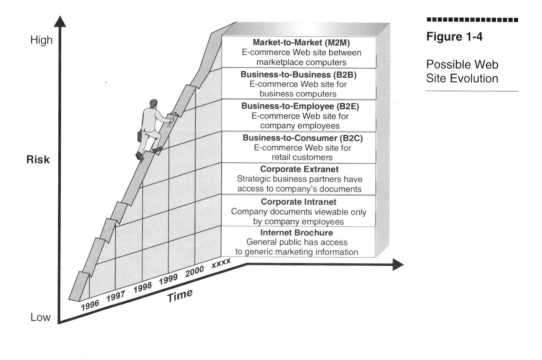

■■■■■■■■■■■■■■■■■

Figure 1-4

Possible Web
Site Evolution

Basic Internet Architecture

In the first step of evolution, the general public was given access to the Internet through home and work computers. Users were given access to a continually growing number of "Internet brochures" which advertised products or services offered by organizations. As the Internet evolved and more people gained access to the World Wide Web, individuals and groups began developing and implementing their own Web sites. People often used these Web sites to voice their opinions, beliefs, and ideas throughout the world. Figure 1-5 illustrates the basic architecture of the Internet. Office computers are typically connected to a proxy server that acts on the behalf of the real user. The proxy server intercepts clients' requests for specific services or applications, evaluates these requests, and determines which requests should be passed forward and which ones should be dropped. Proxy servers are beneficial to the client because they filter information and improve data security. The proxy server is connected to an Internet Service Provider (ISP), which provides the client with access to the Internet. Coming from the other side of Figure 1-5, a Web server provides the Web pages that the client has requested. Routers and switches provide the connectivity between the Web servers that comprise the backbone of the Internet. Home computers follow a similar path with the exception that a proxy server is typically not used. Instead, the home user is connected directly to an ISP.

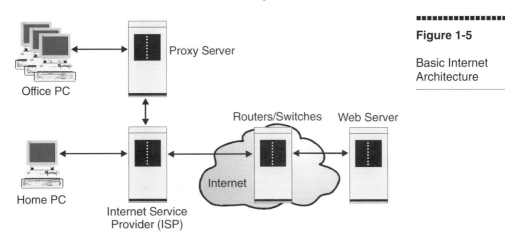

Figure 1-5

Basic Internet Architecture

Corporate Intranet

In the next step, organizations attempt to set up their own intranets (Figure 1-6) in order to facilitate collaborative efforts among their employees, integrate processes, and create a common interface (i.e., a browser) across multiple applications, thereby improving business efficiency. An intranet is a private computer network based on the same communication standards as the Internet. It's a smaller version of the Internet that only authorized members of an organization can access. An organization may build an intranet in order to have a manageable, secure version of the World Wide Web within the confines of their organization. An intranet Web site looks and acts just like any other Web site, but with the restriction that "outsiders" are unable to access the information stored on the site. Intranet Web sites are typically linked to internal systems for accounting, inventory, order entry, production scheduling, and other functions. Consequently, technical support engineers have access to online product documentation to help them answer calls quickly and accurately. Marketing managers have access to training course agendas, workbooks, and instructor guides in order to ensure their customers have adequate training on their products and services. The human resources department has access to payroll records. The possibilities for sharing information are unlimited.

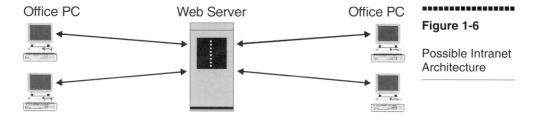

Office PC　　　　　　　　Web Server　　　　　　　Office PC

Figure 1-6

Possible Intranet Architecture

Internet Virtual Private Network

One implementation of the intranet is an Internet Virtual Private Network (IVPN), illustrated in Figure 1-7. IVPNs use the Internet to connect remote intra-organizational networks together. This allows network administrators to connect corporate branch offices and project teams to a common network via local and remote access. Organizations that choose to use IVPNs may need to make special arrangements through their Internet Service Providers (ISPs).

■■■■■■■■■■■■■■■■
Remember to check for adequate encryption when testing IVPNs.

In the acronym IVPN, the word "virtual" implies that the network is dynamic and connections are established in accordance with the specific needs of the organization at any given moment in time. Hence, the network is formed logically and its architecture is independent of the physical structure of the Internet. Unlike networks that are connected via dedicated lines, IVPNs do not need to maintain permanent connections through the Internet – connections are established and released as necessary. This releases bandwidth and network resources for other purposes, which consequently reduces costs.

■■■■■■■■■■■■■■■■
Broadwing (broadwing.com) and VeriSign (verisign.com) both provide additional information on using IVPNs.

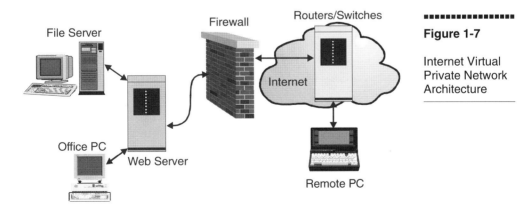

■■■■■■■■■■■■■■■■
Figure 1-7

Internet Virtual Private Network Architecture

IVPNs use encryption software loaded on client PCs that connect across the Internet to special software loaded on an organization's Web server. It's not enough, however, for an IVPN to offer its information to anyone who finds it interesting. This was the basis for the inception of the Internet, but an IVPN must take this concept a few steps further. Communications at both ends must be encrypted to prevent people outside of your intranet from understanding your information. Firewalls and secure applications help ensure that only authorized users are permitted to access corporate and remote office Web sites.

IVPNs must perform four critical functions in order to ensure data security: authentication, access control, confidentiality, and data integrity. Many commercial firewall vendors offer encrypted IP tunnel support for building distributed IVPNs over the public infrastructure. Tunneling is a technology that enables one network to send its data via another network's connections. In essence, the Internet acts as an inexpensive WAN component of the intranet.

■■■■■■■■■■■■■■■■■
Did you know...

A firewall is a set of programs located on a network server that protects the resources of a private network from users outside of the private network.

■■■■■■■■■■■■■■■■■
IVPNs must perform four critical functions to ensure data security:

◆ authentication
◆ access control
◆ confidentiality
◆ data integrity

Corporate Extranet

Extranets are designed to allow a select group of outside business partners (e.g., vendors, OEM accounts, accounting firms, etc.) direct access to an organization's Web site. This group may have access to areas such as inventory, purchasing, payroll, and other areas, depending on their specific requirements. The network may use the Internet or Internet technology built on a private physical network. Figure 1-8 shows the basic architecture for an extranet built on a private network. The outside client has direct access to the firewall via a dedicated connection. There are no routers or switches in this example of an extranet because the Internet is not used. A Web server provides the outside client with the Web pages that are requested. These pages may include business data that pertains to the daily operation of the organization. In this example, the extranet provides an exterior security boundary that protects the organization from the open Internet, but still allows sharing of information between business partners.

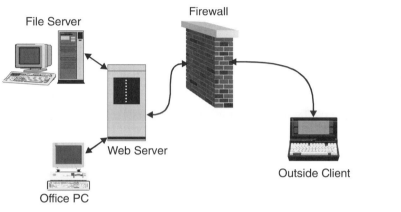

File Server

Firewall

Web Server

Office PC

Outside Client

Figure 1-8

Possible Extranet Architecture

Business-to-Consumer (B2C)

Business-to-Consumer (B2C) Web sites are designed specifically for advertising retail products and services directly to consumers and processing their orders over the Internet. Figure 1-5 (Basic Internet Architecture) illustrates a typical B2C architecture in which online merchants design the content and functionality of their Web sites specifically for retail customers. Dell Computer Corporation (dell.com), for example, is a leading manufacturer of custom-configured personal computers. Dell is different from many other computer manufacturers in that they sell their computers directly to consumers and businesses without going through retail stores or other traditional distribution channels.

Dell began as a mail-order company that advertised in the back of magazines and sold their computers over the phone. As of May 2000, Dell was selling approximately $14 million in equipment every day with approximately 25% of these transactions taking place over the Internet using the B2C business model.

Business-to-Employee (B2E)

Business-to-Employee (B2E) Web sites are similar to B2C sites with the exception that the person who is purchasing the product or service over the Internet is acting on behalf of another business. Consequently, the transaction amounts, the sequence of events, and potentially the degree of customer loyalty may differ. Each of these factors can affect the Web site's risk profile, thereby impacting the priorities of different categories of tests.

Business-to-Business (B2B)

Extranets are rapidly replacing the costly Electronic Data Interchange (EDI) applications that were popular a few years ago. In Business-to-Business (B2B) Web sites, humans are typically no longer part of the business transactions, as complex (and often expensive) X12 Electronic Data Interchanges (EDIs) that link the computers of two or more business partners are being replaced by generic TCP/IP communications. Extensible Markup Language (XML) is often used as the basis for defining the structure of the data that is exchanged. Figure 1-9 illustrates a typical B2B architecture.

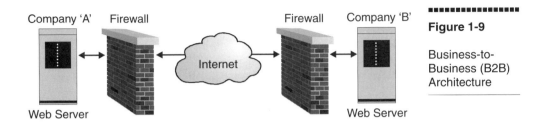

Company 'A'   Firewall   Firewall   Company 'B'

Internet

Web Server   Web Server

Figure 1-9

Business-to-
Business (B2B)
Architecture

Market-to-Market (M2M)

A B2B Web site typically connects just two businesses, a marketplace connects many businesses, and a Market-to-Market (M2M) hub allows numerous companies to compete against each other for business via a seemingly single marketplace.

Other Categories

At the time of publication, other categories of Web site were also in existence. These types include Business-to-Government (B2G), Consumer-to-Consumer (C2C), Business-to-Anyone (B2A), and Application-to-Application (A2A). Again, each category will have a slightly different risk profile and, as a result, may necessitate some tests being given a higher priority than others. Consider the following example. A Business-to-Consumer (B2C) Web site (e.g., Amazon.com) could be expected to have a large number of Web page requests from impatient customers with relatively little loyalty (there are plenty of other places to buy books). Therefore, this B2C Web site might consider performance and usability to be extremely important and assign the highest priority to the tests that check these attributes. A Market-to-Market (M2M) Web site, on the other hand, might not even have a user interface. A marketplace may consider maintaining live connections and up-to-date, fresh information with as many other Web sites as possible to be the most important criteria. In this case, reliability and availability might be the types of tests that should be given the highest priority.

Mitigating Risk ■ ■ ■ ■ ■

In theory, each of the various types of Web sites seeks to provide users with access to the information that they need. As a company progresses towards these higher levels in the evolution of Web sites, the overall risk to the company increases significantly. The risk of unauthorized employees accessing payroll information or sensitive technical data increases as more people are given access to various parts of an organization's network. Performance, scalability, and usability also become increasingly important issues to consider.

A traditional way of mitigating the risk of software failure is to test the software in a controlled test environment, thereby hopefully catching any defects before they make it into a production system. Web sites are becoming increasingly more complicated, and organizations are becoming more dependent on their successful operation. Consequently, these Web sites are also becoming more risky from a risk analysis perspective. It is because of this increase in risk, that many organizations are recognizing that they need to devote dedicated resources to testing their mission-critical Web sites and applications. Gone are the days when the Webmaster could give the new Web site the "once over" before promoting it into production. Unfortunately, in comparison to the mountains of information that have been written on how to build Web sites and Web applications, there is precious little information on how to test them. This book and its companion Web site hope to fill a significant part of this void.

Web testing is a journey along a continually changing road. The road (i.e., technology) has hills and curves, but the underlying principles of how to maneuver those curves stay the same. If you remember the principles described in this book and stay abreast of the latest changes in the technology, you'll know how to handle what lies ahead.

Brown & Donaldson Case Study ■ ■ ■ ■ ■

To make the information in this book easier to understand and apply, each of the topics illustrated in Figure 1-1 is explained using a case study approach. A fictitious online brokerage firm, Brown & Donaldson (B&D), and an associated Web application (BDOnline) are used to illustrate the Web testing principles and practices explained in this book. Numerous examples are provided for you to follow and subsequently apply to your own specific projects. B&D and its employees do not exist, but the scenarios presented within this case study are typically based on real-life experiences. We selected an online brokerage firm as the subject of our case study because online investing has gained tremendous popularity over the past few years, and it's familiar to a larger number of readers than most other categories of high-risk e-business applications.

■ ■ ■ ■ ■ ■ ■ ■ ■ ■
Case Study

The B&D Brokerage Firm will be used as a practical example throughout this book and can be found at:

sqe.com/bdonline/

This companion Web site also contains a number of example test plans that can be downloaded and viewed by the reader.

Consider the following scenario. One morning Donald Thump (Chief Executive Officer of B&D) calls Julie Sold (Vice President of Marketing) into his office to tell her about an article that he read in a popular business magazine. Donald explains how dramatically the world will change with the advent and growing popularity of the Internet. He tells Julie how important e-commerce will be for the future of B&D and directs her to develop a Web presence for B&D. Julie enthusiastically says, "What a great idea," and promises to have the Web site up and running by the end of the month.

After her meeting with Donald, Julie meets with Ivan Networkski (Director of Information Systems) and explains the details of her meeting. Julie says, "The only requirements are that the Web site looks cool and that it's up and running by the end of the month." Ivan assembles a team and puts *you* in charge of testing the Web site. There are no written requirements, no in-house Web-based testing tools, no one on your staff with Web testing experience, and very little time. Does this scenario sound familiar? If so, read on…

■■■■■■■■■■■■■■■■■

The Internet has opened new avenues for organizations, but the road is full of bumps and potholes. We'll explore these obstacles and provide solutions through a case study.

Useful URLs ■■■■■

Table 1-1 Useful Web Sites

Web Site URLs	Description of Services
developer.com, devguru.com, devx.com, enterprisedev.com, internet.com	Background information on Web technologies.
advisor.com, inquiry.com	Online assistance.
bbc.co.uk, learntheweb.com, sev.com.au, webreference.com	Basic tutorials and education on the Web and Internet.
webopedia.com, whatis.com	Web terms and definitions.
cnet.com, webreview.com	Reviews of hardware and software used on the Web.
betasoft.com, coyotevalley.com, dunhamsoftware.com, methods-tools.com, qacity.com, rstcorp.com, softwareqatest.com, sqa-test.com, stickyminds.com, and webreview.com	Testing resources such as forums, papers, links, and reviews of books and tools.
sqe.com/bdonline/	Case study Web site and downloadable test plans.

Chapter 2 – Code Quality Assurance

In a Web environment, developers and testers are subject to continually shrinking software schedules that are much more demanding than most mainframe, client/server, and PC project schedules of the past. Since Web sites provide customers with twenty-four-hour, seven-day-a-week access to products and information, scheduled downtime is usually extremely limited or non-existent. In addition, fierce competition throughout the Internet forces management to plan and execute Web-based solutions faster than ever before. Consequently, you're often given little or no time to develop, test, and maintain your organization's Web site. This constant push to immediately complete Web-based projects is often referred to as *Web Time* – a direct result of the dynamic characteristics of the Internet. Given the constraints of Web Time, how can you ensure that your organization's Web site will function and perform in an environment as dynamic and volatile as the Internet? Part of the solution lies in your organization's ability to implement an effective process to ensure the quality of the Web site(s) and then ensure that this process is understood and followed by everyone involved in the project.

Unfortunately, quality is a relative term that means different things to different people within an organization. Managers often argue over which requirements are most important based on personal bias and perception. Engineering may perceive that a quality product is one that implements source code and data structures efficiently and effectively. Marketing may perceive that a Web site meets quality standards if it attracts a large number of visitors. The quality assurance and/or testing departments are often held responsible for sorting through the

■■■■■■■■■■■■■■■■■■
Case Study

Review the following *Case Study Test Plans* to see an example of how the topics covered in this chapter can be utilized to test a Web site:

- Unit
- Code Q/A

Visit:
sqe.com/bdonline/

various perceptions of quality in order to uncover the "real" quality requirements for the Web-based project.

The first line of defense against a poor, low-quality Web site is Unit Testing. Unit testing consists of testing a single module of code, which in our case, might correlate to a single Web page or Java servlet. Unit testing has two main purposes. First and foremost, it ensures that each release of your organization's Web-based application meets or exceeds an expected level of quality. Second, it is used to detect code-level errors at the earliest stage in the development cycle. This is when software bugs are least time-consuming to find and least costly to fix.

■■■■■■■■■■■■■■■■

Unit testing has two main purposes:

- To ensure a consistent level of quality
- To detect errors early in development

Although conducting a unit-level test is often the responsibility of the developer who wrote the software component (or unit), development of a standard set of unit-level test cases (i.e., a unit testing checklist) should be a collaborative effort between the developers and the testers of the Web site or application. Many production software bugs could be avoided entirely, by providing the developer with a simple checklist of tests to run against each unit of code, prior to releasing it for inclusion in the next system build.

When implemented and enforced, a consistent, comprehensive, and easy-to-understand unit testing checklist can dramatically reduce the number of bugs found in subsequent testing efforts and the number of bugs that actually make it to production. This can significantly improve the quality of your Web site. To assist your organization in developing an initial checklist, each of the following sections in this chapter lists some basic checks that should be considered for inclusion in your Web site's unit testing checklist.

HTML Validation ■ ■ ■ ■ ■

Currently, most Web pages are written using the HyperText Markup Language (HTML). Although Web pages may contain graphics, sound, and video files with a variety of file extensions (e.g., GIF, JPEG, WAV, MPG, and others), the core description is still typically written in HTML. HTML is not a programming language such as C++ or Visual Basic. It is a standard coding system used to describe the format and composition of Web-based documents. A Web browser interprets the HTML code and displays it on your monitor or television (e.g., WebTV/AOLTV) according to its interpretation of the HTML standard.

HTML validation should be the first item on your unit testing checklist. This involves making sure that the HTML code in your Web application complies with World Wide Web Consortium (W3C) specifications. As the Internet continues to evolve and Web-based applications continue to be developed, HTML validation will become increasingly important in order to ensure document portability. The fundamental reason that HTML standards exist, is to ensure that Web page elements and structures can be understood by the widest range of Web clients. By adhering to these standards, you can maximize the accessibility of your work to the largest possible range of users.

Many authoring and validation tools are available to help you test HTML code for compliance with W3C standards. Some HTML authoring tools such as Dreamweaver from Macromedia (macromedia.com) and Hot Dog from Sausage Software (sausage.com) now include their own HTML validation tools. Dreamweaver even allows the developer to select which browser to validate the HTML code against. The tool then scans the

HTML specifications are published by the World Wide Web Consortium.

(www.w3c.org)

Several options are available for validating HTML code:

+ manually inspect the code
+ use a tool to scan and compare your code against a standard
+ use an online service to validate your code
+ use a browser that strictly adheres to the W3C standard

source code to determine whether or not the HTML is compliant for that particular version of the browser. In addition to authoring tools, there are now non-authoring tools, which have been designed purely to test and validate a Web site or application. Linkbot from Watchfire (watchfire.com), for example, allows a tester to decide which version of the W3C HTML specification a Web site should be validated against. The W3C offers a tool called Tidy that promises to clean up a Web site's HTML code free of charge. Finally, there are a number of online validation services that will check your site's HTML code (refer to Table 2-1). These services typically perform a limited number of basic checks free of charge, and offer more rigorous scans for a nominal fee.

Table 2-1 Sample Online HTML Validation Services

Web Site URL	Description of Services
anybrowser.com	◆ Identifies the majority of common HTML code errors. ◆ Includes an archive of older versions of various browsers. This allows you to actually "see" your Web site as it would appear in other browsers. ◆ Allows you to test your Web site using various screen resolutions. ◆ Includes an archive of older versions of the HTML standard that you can test your Web site against.
htmlworks.com	◆ Identifies the majority of common HTML code errors. ◆ Allows you to analyze your Web site for load times, bad links, and search engine rank and popularity. ◆ Optimizes your HTML code to improve performance.
netmechanic.com	◆ Identifies and fixes the majority of common HTML code errors and generates a repaired file for you to upload. ◆ Automatic testing of your site can be scheduled weekly, bi-weekly, or monthly. Notification of results is sent via e-mail. ◆ Testing is configurable. You can specify which tests you want to run and tailor their tools to meet your specific needs.
W3C.org	◆ The final word in HTML compliance

Opera is a browser developed by Opera Software of Norway (opera.com) that requires strict compliance to the W3C HTML standard. Poorly coded HTML tags that might work in Microsoft Internet Explorer (MS-IE) or Netscape Navigator will often fail in Opera. While this may not be a desirable feature for the average Web user, such a tool can be extremely valuable to someone who wants to test a Web page for compliance to W3C standards. Alternatively, you can use the View Source option in Netscape or MS-IE to manually inspect the HTML code that makes up a Web page. You should, however, be careful when selecting a tool for viewing and editing your Web sites source code. Certain products such as Microsoft FrontPage and Active Server Pages (ASP) can automatically include special extensions, which may restrict portability.

Of course, simply running your code through a validation tool is not enough to guarantee that it's well designed. Peer-level code inspections and reviews are often the best way to improve the quality of a Web page's structural and aesthetic design.

Web Browser Differences ■■■■■

While every Web browser on the market today can read and display HTML, each product (and version) displays the information in a slightly different way. Some browsers are more forgiving than others when syntax errors are encountered. And, some browsers have been enhanced to include additional features not currently specified in the W3C HTML standards. There are tags that some browsers will understand that others won't. Netscape and Microsoft have both implemented a number of features that are not included in industry standards. Web pages created using these features may appear correctly when viewed through one brand of Web browser, but when using another brand or an older version of the same brand may cause problems. Tables, floating images, frames, background colors, and font colors are just some of the features that are supported differently by different brands and versions of Web browsers. Consequently, it is extremely important to determine at project startup which version(s) or dialect(s) of HTML your Web site is going to be developed with. Some organizations choose to use the lowest-common-denominator approach. That is, they only use features that are supported by all versions of the major browsers. Alternatively, some organizations choose to use the most recent versions and extensions in an effort to be on the "bleeding edge" of technology. Whichever approach you choose to use, it's advisable to explicitly state which standards were followed during its development. Additionally, each unit should be tested to confirm compliance to these standards.

Since most Web browser manufacturers now build their browsers to support the W3C HTML standard, source code written to W3C HTML version X should work with any browser released after version X was ratified. In the event that a particular Web browser does not render W3C compliant HTML code correctly, this may be reflective of a bug in the Web browser itself rather than the actual Web page being tested. Using a tool or service to scan a Web page's HTML and compare it against the selected W3C HTML standard provides a consistent approach for validating your HTML code, rather than trying to manually test your Web page via numerous browsers.

Table 2-2 lists some of B&D's test cases for validating their Web site's HTML code.

■■■■■■■■■■■■■■■■■
Did you know...

There are hundreds of different Web browsers, each of which has one or more different versions.

An extensive archive of Web browsers is available at:

browsers.evolt.org

NOTE: Do not precede this URL with www.

Table 2-2 B&D's HTML Checklist

		HTML Validation
Pass	Fail	Description
☐	☐	Any exceptions to W3C HTML v4.0 standards have been approved and documented.
☐	☐	HTML code is W3C HTML v4.0 compliant (barring any approved exceptions).
☐	☐	Web page renders correctly when viewed with Opera 5.0 browser.
☐	☐	Comments and change control logs are not included in the HTML sent to the client.

Image Validation

Diagrams, photographs, and maps – often called *images* – are critical to the functionality and appearance of Web pages, yet they can be extremely costly in terms of download time. An under-compressed image can add several percentage points to a Web page's abandonment rate. For this reason alone, it's worth paying particular attention to the number and size of images, and the formatting options used to render them on your Web page. There is a trade-off between adding more graphics to help keep a reader's attention or transforming raw data into usable information, and the loss of attention due to longer download times.

Image File Formats

Image files are stored in many different electronic formats, each with unique characteristics, advantages, and disadvantages. Image file formats vary significantly, depending on which application is used to create the image and the purpose for which the image will be used. Different compression algorithms used to create these files can affect load time, resolution, and quality. Table 2-3 lists some of the most common image file formats used in Web pages and provides a description of each.

Table 2-3 Common Web Page Image File Formats

File Extension	Developer / Name	Advantages and Disadvantages
BMP	**Microsoft** Bitmap	◆ Not recommended for use on Web pages. ◆ Commonly used and widely supported in the Windows operating system. ◆ Poorly supported under most other operating systems. ◆ One of the first file formats developed for storing images.
GIF	**CompuServe** Graphics Interchange Format	◆ Suitable for simple Web page graphics with few colors. Can be interlaced and be made transparent. Logos and buttons are typically stored as GIF images. ◆ Software developers must pay patent and license fees to implement the GIF algorithms. ◆ This format is most likely to be viewable in older versions of browsers.

(Continued)

Table 2-3 (*Continued*)

File Extension	Developer / Name	Advantages and Disadvantages
JPEG (JPG)	**Joint Photographic Experts Group** Joint Photographic Experts Group	◆ <u>Best format for</u> photographs and complex color graphics on Web pages. ◆ Uses a "lossy" compression algorithm that discards parts of an image to save space. ◆ Allows the creator to make decisions regarding image quality and file size. ◆ In general, the quality of the image decreases as the file size decreases. ◆ Progressive, opacity control, gamma correction, and true-color and gray scale palettes are supported. ◆ May not be viewable in older versions of some browsers.
PNG	**W3C** Portable Network Graphic	◆ <u>May eventually replace</u> GIF format for simple Web images. ◆ Patent-free and license-free development. ◆ "Lossless" algorithm doesn't allow adjustments in image quality and file size. ◆ All image quality is restored when the file is decompressed for viewing. ◆ Transparent colors, opacity control, gamma correction, and true-color and gray-scale palettes are supported.
TIFF (TIF)	**Aldus** Tagged Image File Format	◆ <u>Not recommended for</u> use on Web sites. ◆ Transparent colors, opacity control, gamma correction, and true-color and gray-scale palettes are supported. ◆ Commonly used and widely supported in the Windows and Macintosh operating systems. ◆ Extremely large file size. ◆ Typically used for complex color images in professionally produced publications and brochures.

In general, JPEG is the best format for photographs or images with complex color gradations because it can store up to 16.7 million colors. GIF files are best suited for simple graphics like logos, buttons, and other images that are not likely to contain a large number of different colors. GIF files can store a maximum of 256 colors, which isn't enough to adequately display most photographs. However, GIF files have been around longer than JPEG files and are therefore more likely to be viewable in older versions of browsers. GIF files allow the image to be interlaced. This allows a rough version of the image to be displayed almost immediately, giving the visitor something to look at while waiting for the entire image to load. Figure 2-1 shows an example of a JPEG versus BMP image. Based on file size alone, the JPEG image is the best choice for Web-based applications.

■■■■■■■■■■■■■■■■■
Did you know...

The more colors used by an image, the larger the file size.

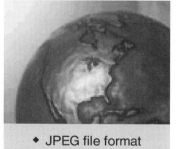 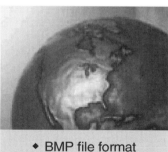

• JPEG file format
• 4 KB file size

• BMP file format
• 295 KB file size

■■■■■■■■■■■■■■■■■
Figure 2-1

Sample JPEG versus BMP Image

GIF images are downloaded in 8x8 pixel blocks. Therefore, for optimal performance, a Web site should only use GIF images that are sized in multiples of eight (8) pixels. A graphic that occupies 32x16 pixels, for example, will download using eight (4x2) blocks of data. Conversely, a graphic that occupies 33x17 pixels will need fifteen (5x3) blocks of data in order to download the image and will take nearly twice as long to download.

Using the WIDTH and HEIGHT tags to specify an image's size will allow a browser to start displaying the image before it has finished downloading the entire Web page. There are many utilities that you can download over the Internet that will analyze your images and, if necessary, resave them in a more compressed format. GIF Lube from websitegarage.com and SmartSaver from ulead.com are examples of some of the utilities that are available.

Animated GIF's consist of several images stored in the same file. These images are displayed sequentially to make the image appear to be animated – this creates the illusion of motion. Obviously, a file that contains several images is going to take longer to download than a file that contains a single image. Figure 2-2 shows an example of the components of an animated GIF file. In this example, each frame of the animation sequence is stored in a single file called *bd-scroll.gif*.

■■■■■■■■■■■■■■■■■■

Shareware Web sites offer a wide variety of image creation and validation utilities. An extensive collection of shareware is available at:

acme.com
download.com
freeware32.com
netscape.com
shareware.com
softseek.com
tucows.com

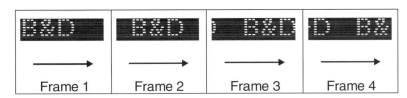

| Frame 1 | Frame 2 | Frame 3 | Frame 4 |

■■■■■■■■■■■■■■■■■■

Figure 2-2

Components of a Sample Animated GIF File

Downloading four images as shown in Figure 2-2 is likely to take four times as long as downloading a single image, even though all four images are stored in the same file. Consequently, animations should be used sparingly and only when necessary. Many Web sites only use animations if they directly generate revenue for the site or if they link to a business partner with a reciprocal agreement.

Alternative Graphics Text

ALT tags (i.e., ALT="...") should be used to provide descriptive information to Web visitors who don't want to or can't view images through their browsers. The ALT attribute should contain a replacement for the information content of the image (i.e., a description of the image).

ALT tags can also improve search engine recognition. One of the most important readers of your Web page is an indexing robot. Unfortunately, an indexing robot is blind and can't understand your images. ALT tags provide a means by which the robot can "see" your images and ensure that your Web site is indexed properly. The same is true for audio browsers such as Home Reader from IBM (IBM.com), which can read the textual content of a Web page aloud.

Image Maps

An image map is a graphic that, when clicked, takes the visitor to one of several different URLs. A good example of an image map is the B&D Office Locations picture shown in Figure 2-3. This picture shows an image of the United States, with B&D office locations highlighted. By clicking on the appropriate city on the image map, the visitor is redirected to the Web page containing the street address and telephone number for that particular office.

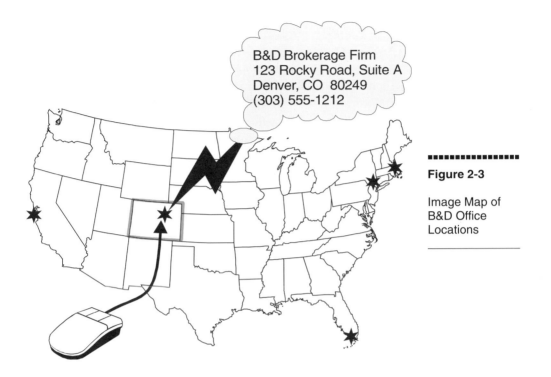

Figure 2-3

Image Map of
B&D Office
Locations

There are two types of image maps: client-side and server-side. With a client-side image map, the information required to create the appropriate link is downloaded to the client (browser) when the page is initially accessed. This allows the link to be established quickly, but requires more data to be initially downloaded to the client. With a server-side image map, the information required to create the link resides on the Web server and is only accessed when needed. This can cause a longer delay between the user selecting an image and the browser navigating to the desired link than with an equivalent client-side image.

Each online development tool, monitor resolution, platform, and combination of these factors supports only certain image file formats. Each file format compresses in a different way,

■■■■■■■■■■■■■■■■

Did you know...

A single Image Map file may download much faster than a corresponding set of single-image files.

responds to resizing differently, handles colors differently, and so forth. It's unreasonable to expect the quality assurance (Q/A) or testing team to check every graphic image; this should be the job of the artist or developer who created the graphic. However, an independent Q/A analyst may want to perform random quality assurance checks in order to ensure that each image adheres to the department's formatting guidelines. Table 2-4 lists some basic image validation checks that could be included in a unit testing checklist.

Table 2-4   B&D's Image Checklist

		Image Validation
Pass	Fail	Description
☐	☐	This image adds value to this Web site.
☐	☐	If this image is animated, it links to an approved business partner or it's directly related to B&D's marketing campaign.
☐	☐	This image is stored in the most appropriate format (e.g., GIF files for buttons and JPG files for photos).
☐	☐	If a GIF file, the image size is a multiple of 8 pixels.
☐	☐	The visual size of this image is appropriate for the size of the viewable screen (i.e., it does not occupy too much or too little screen real estate).
☐	☐	The physical file size of this image is as small as possible without compromising the quality of the image (i.e., the file was saved using the optimum compression ratio).
☐	☐	An appropriate ALT tag is included with this image.
☐	☐	The WIDTH and HEIGHT (expressed as page % and not absolute pixel sizes) tags have been specified for this image.
☐	☐	B&D has a legal right to use this image on a Web site (e.g., it is not trademarked or copyrighted by someone else, unless they have granted B&D explicit permission to use this image).

(Continued)

Table 2-4 (*Continued*)

Image Validation

Pass	Fail	Description
☐	☐	The total size of all of the images on this Web page does not exceed 50 Kbytes.
☐	☐	There is not more than one animated image on this Web page.
☐	☐	Photographic images aside (e.g., JPG images), no more than 256 total colors are used on this Web page.
☐	☐	Any image maps used are client side (as opposed to server side).

Font Validation

Specifying fonts (and sizes) for use on the Web is a difficult process. Thousands of fonts are available through various desktop applications, but only a limited number and specific types of fonts are typically installed on a client system. It's important to remember that new clients are emerging every day. Internet PCs, WebTV/AOLTV, Personal Digital Assistants (PDAs), and other intelligent devices should be considered when specifying fonts for your Web site. If you specify a font that is not installed on one of these clients, the text will be displayed in the client's default font with possibly unpredictable results.

Most browsers and operating systems probably won't have your desired font installed as default. In some cases, however, default fonts may exist as slight variations of your font. Arial in Windows, for example, exists as Helvetica on the Mac operating system. The default fonts for most Netscape Navigator users are Times (proportional) and Courier (fixed). Internet Explorer, on the other hand, uses Helvetica (proportional) and Carrier (fixed) as its defaults. The typical solution for determining which font(s) to standardize on is to identify your intended audience

Web-based statistics tools can help you gather a variety of information about your Web site's visitors.

For more details, visit:

accrue.com
ilux.com
netgen.com
sane.com
webtrends.com

and select a font that meets the needs of the majority of your intended users and then specify two or three alternate fonts as backups. Web-based statistics tools can help you determine which browsers and operating systems most of your clients use.

As a general rule, avoid using stylized, cursive, or decorative fonts. The resolution of most computer screens renders subtle font characteristics invisible or makes the text difficult to read. Instead, consider using sans serif fonts (i.e., without decorative curves) like Arial, Avant Garde, and Helvetica for your Web-based applications.

Embedded Fonts

Embedded font technology allows the fonts used in the creation of a Web page to travel with that document. Both Navigator 4.0 (and higher) and Internet Explorer 4.0 (and higher) support embedded font technology, enabling them to render Web pages exactly the way the developer wanted them to be displayed. Technically, the font information is not embedded in the Web page, but transmitted to the browser in a separate file. Unfortunately, in addition to taking a considerable amount of time to download over a modem, there are two competing standards for embedded font technology: Netscape versus Microsoft.

In 1997, Netscape partnered with Bitstream to incorporate TrueDoc dynamic font capabilities into Netscape's browser software. The combination resulted in a Web browser capable of recognizing and displaying portable fonts in HTML documents. In this case, font portability means that Netscape users are able to create Web documents using any TrueType or PostScript fonts and be assured that the fonts will be displayed correctly – regardless of which fonts are installed on the client's system.

■■■■■■■■■■■■■■■■■

HexMac Software Systems offers a standalone product and Microsoft FrontPage plug-ins that allow developers to create custom embedded fonts.

For more details, visit:

hexmac.com

In a similar effort to achieve font portability, Microsoft partnered with Adobe to incorporate OpenType font capabilities into Internet Explorer. Unfortunately, OpenType font technology differs from TrueDoc technology in both file format and extension. This means that users (and developers) can't just download a font file and copy it into their local font directory.

Recently, Microsoft developed a library of new TrueType fonts (Windows and Mac O/S) designed especially for use on the Web. These fonts are specifically designed to enhance a character's legibility when viewed via a browser. These fonts can currently be downloaded free of charge from the typography section of Microsoft's Web site (microsoft.com/typography). Today, TrueDoc technology is better supported than OpenType technology, but as with everything on the Web, that can change quickly.

Symbol Fonts

Symbol fonts are very different from ordinary text fonts. Most symbol fonts don't have the conventional letter shapes of regular text fonts. Instead they are collections of symbols packaged in the form of a font. This means you can use them in word processors, graphic design programs, and most other applications that can handle traditional text. Unfortunately, Web-based applications often experience problems displaying symbol fonts. In order to avoid these problems, Web developers can map their symbol fonts to the "private use area" of their Unicode. Unicode is covered in more detail in the *Usability and Accessibility* chapter. Symbols can be referenced in HTML by &#nnnnn, where nnnnn is a value between 65280 and 65535.

■■■■■■■■■■■■■■■■■■
Did you know...

If you see blank boxes in your Web page, you may have a problem with the symbol fonts that you're using.

Proportional vs. Fixed-Width Fonts

Proportional (or variable-width) fonts use varying amounts of space between each character. A capital "W," for example, uses more horizontal line space than a lower case "i." On the other hand, fixed-width (or constant-width or monospace) fonts use the same amount of horizontal space for each character. Courier is the most commonly available fixed-width font. Figure 2-4 illustrates the visual differences between proportional and fixed-width fonts.

| Times New Roman is an example of a proportional-width font. |
| Courier is an example of a fixed-width font. |

■■■■■■■■■■■■■■■■■■

Figure 2-4

Proportional versus Fixed-Width Fonts

Using standard fonts is an important aspect of good Web page presentation. The fonts that you select are directly related to the overall appearance and functionality of your Web site. If your fonts aren't displayed properly, graphics and links can become misaligned and the entire meaning and purpose of your Web site may be lost. Hence, it's important that your organization establishes and maintains a standard list of fonts that meets your customers' requirements. As an absolute minimum, your standard fonts should work well with standard installations of Navigator and MS-IE on Windows, Macintosh, and UNIX platforms. Defining and using a standard set of fonts can significantly reduce the amount of time you spend testing your Web site and checking for proper text formatting. Table 2-5 lists some basic font validation checks that can be included in your unit testing checklist.

■■■■■■■■■■■■■■■■■■

Remember, "image" is extremely important on the Web, so choose your fonts carefully.

Table 2-5 B&D's Font Checklist

		Font Validation
Pass	Fail	Description
☐	☐	The font is proportional.
☐	☐	The primary font is Verdana, with Arial and Sans-Serif specified as alternates.
☐	☐	The browser's base font size is not altered.
☐	☐	Only relative font sizes (e.g., small, medium, and large) are used, rather than specific point sizes.
☐	☐	No more than three (3) font sizes are used on the Web page.
☐	☐	Symbol fonts are used only when absolutely necessary.
☐	☐	If symbol fonts are used, they are properly mapped to the "private use area" of the developer's Unicode.
☐	☐	Browser default colors are not overridden.

Printer-Friendly Web Pages

Most printers and monitors don't display the same font in exactly the same way. Consequently, printed pages may appear different than the screen version. If exact formatting of a particular Web page is extremely important, a test page should be printed in order to ensure that it matches the browser's display. An online application form, for example, may allow the user to fill out the information online or print a blank form that can be mailed or faxed back. It's also important to check that a printed Web page fits appropriately on standard-sized paper. Many scrollable Web pages push one or two lines onto the last printed page when printed on U.S. "Letter" size or European "A4" size paper. If your Web pages experience printing problems, you may want to include printer-friendly versions of these pages, as illustrated in Figure 2-5.

Did you know...

Some browsers now come with print preview capabilities.

Dark backgrounds (especially black) and white text typically will not print correctly on plain white paper printers.

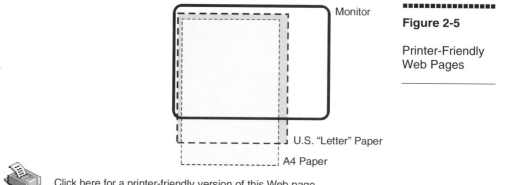

Click here for a printer-friendly version of this Web page.

B&D used the test cases listed in Table 2-6 to validate that their
Web pages were printer-friendly.

Table 2-6   B&D's Printer-Friendly Checklist

		Printer-Friendly Validation
Pass	Fail	Description
☐	☐	The test on the Web page is formatted correctly when printed via a 72-dpi printer using Letter and A4 paper sizes.
☐	☐	The content of the Web page is clearly readable when printed with a black and white printer.
☐	☐	The content of the Web page is clearly readable when printed with a color printer.
☐	☐	The background color of the Web page is white.
☐	☐	Only dark colors are used for the text on the Web page.

Style Guides ■ ■ ■ ■ ■

Many organizations have established standards that employees
must follow when developing paper-based documentation.
Some of the most common standards include detailed

instructions for the proper use of company logos, design of title pages, page design for printed manuals, acronyms, abbreviations, grammar, and writing style, among others. Unfortunately, all too often, the responsibility of developing and enforcing a set of development standards for online documents remains unassigned. Without a standard style guide to follow, Web developers can't help but incorporate their own style of presentation into their projects. Consequently, an organization's Web site will appear disjointed because it will contain as many different styles as there are developers on the project.

When properly implemented, style guides can yield many benefits. They enable a consistent look and feel and sharing of current best practices, which, in turn, promotes reusability of code and helps developers apply good GUI design principles. Style guides can help improve an organization's image, reduce the amount of formal and informal training that's required, and save testing time and money. The key to a good style guide is to keep it active – don't just print it and store it in a binder on a bookshelf for future reference. A good style guide is followed, continually referenced, and improved, while adherence is checked and enforced. A style guide may contain a series of rules that developers must follow along with detailed descriptions. Additionally, a style guide may contain information about the proper use of style sheets and templates.

■■■■■■■■■■■■■■
Does your company have and actively use a style guide?

■■■■■■■■■■■■■■
GUIguide.com sells a software-based GUI standard for Web applications.

Style Sheets ■■■■■

Style sheets allow Web developers to control the rendering of a Web page without complicating its structure. HTML style sheets can be used to control fonts, colors, leading, margins, typefaces, and other aspects of Web page presentation. Figure 2-6 shows an example of an HTML style sheet used to control general browser defaults for text and background colors, and fonts. Colors are represented in hexadecimal format (e.g., #ffffff represents white and #000000 represents black).

```
BODY        {

            background:     #ffffff;

            color:          #000000;

            font-family:    Verdana, Arial, Sans-Serif;

            }
```

Figure 2-6

Style Sheet for Setting General Browser Defaults

Style sheets work by separating style (as specified by the W3C CSS1 standard) and layout (CSS2 standard) from the structure and content of your Web page. Although style rules can be embedded inside a Web page, they are ideally stored in a separately referenced HTML document called a *style sheet*. It is this separation that gives style sheets their power. You can change the overall look of an entire page or even your entire Web site by changing one style rule or sheet.

Style sheets are engineered with the future in mind. As the Internet continues to evolve, devices other than browsers will enable viewing, hearing, and even feeling the Web. Style sheets' separation of style from structure makes it easier to adapt Web pages to different technologies and different ways of experiencing those technologies. The blind, for example, could have a special sound-oriented style sheet that specifies speech parameters, and reading style. WebTV could invoke special television-optimized style sheets that enlarge letters, shrink wide tables, and simplify layouts. The possibilities for the future are endless. Today, however, style sheets help ensure that Web developers working on the same project do things in a consistent manner, without too many personal touches. This helps ensure that your organization's Web site will have a uniform look and feel.

The World Wide Web Consortium (W3C) has recommended Cascading Style Sheets (Level 1) as an industry standard and provides an online service for validating CSS files.

Microsoft has a tool called StyleT, which can be used to check CSS files for errors.

Browsers that can't interpret style sheets will typically ignore them.

Cascading Style Sheets (CSS)

A Cascading Style Sheet (CSS) is a mechanism that allows developers and readers to attach multiple styles to the same HTML document. Browsers use a series of rules to determine which associated style sheet should take precedence over another.

Browsers typically adopt the following hierarchy or rules:
1. HTML tag attributes override all style sheets.
2. Inline style sheets are used to define a portion of a page.
3. Internal style sheets (i.e., embedded) are defined at the top of a page and apply to the entire page.
4. External style sheets (i.e., embedded or imported) are defined outside of a page. Often, a single external style sheet is used for an entire Web site, thereby giving the site a consistent look and feel.
5. External (i.e., style) sheets linked.
6. A viewer's custom browser settings.
7. A viewer's default browser settings.

When multiple style sheets within the same category contain conflicting rules, the rule that the browser reads last takes precedence over any previously read rules.

Other Style Sheets

There are several other categories of style sheets that you should be aware of. JavaScript Style Sheets (JSS) are almost functionally identical to Cascading Style Sheets (CSS). JSS, however, is specific to Netscape browsers, and while the features are very similar to CSS, the syntax is different. The naming conventions, for example, follow JavaScript standards. A Dynamic Cascading Style Sheet (DCSS) refers to the ability of some browsers to change the properties defined in a CSS dynamically. Netscape and Microsoft both started supporting CSS in their 4.x generation of browsers. Unfortunately, their implementations differ not only between the two brands, but also between different versions of the same brand.

Table 2-7 lists some of B&D's test cases for style sheets.

Table 2-7 B&D's Style Sheet Checklist

		Style Sheet Validation
Pass	Fail	Description
☐	☐	The style sheet is W3C CSS Level 1 compliant.
☐	☐	The style sheet is correctly interpreted by the 4.x generation of Web browsers.
☐	☐	The style sheet complies with B&D's printer-friendly standards.
☐	☐	The style sheet complies with B&D's font standards.
☐	☐	The style sheet is defined as an external CSS file.
☐	☐	Web pages do not modify the style sheet dynamically.
☐	☐	Web pages that use the style sheet provide acceptable rendering when viewed by browsers that do not support CSS or have CSS turned off by the client.

Table Validation ■ ■ ■ ■ ■

Tables provide developers with a large degree of flexibility and control over how information is formatted and displayed on a Web page. Tables help break up text and convey complicated ideas in a visual format. But, tables aren't limited to just formatting text. They can also be used to place images (along with text) in specific locations on a page. Tables may contain horizontal and vertical lines to separate rows and columns.

■ ■ ■ ■ ■ ■ ■ ■ ■ ■ ■ ■ ■ ■ ■ ■ ■
During development and/or testing, developers can "switch on" grid lines to help debug table formatting problems.

These lines may or may not be visible, depending on the design of the Web page. Web browsers handle tables differently, depending on how the visitor has configured his or her browser. Figure 2-7 shows a sample page from B&D's Web site as the developer had intended it to be displayed.

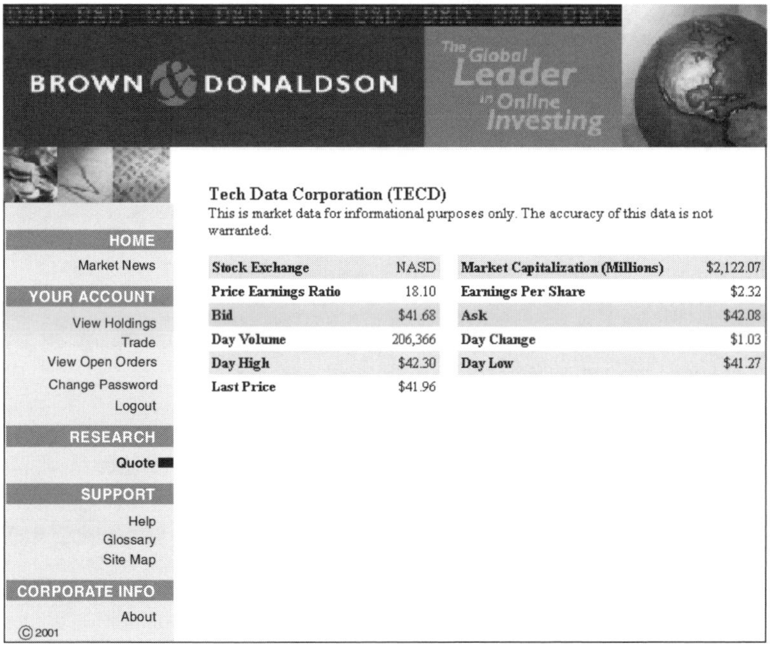

Figure 2-7

B&D's Quote Page Displayed Correctly Using a Default Font Size of 10 Points

Default fonts and color schemes can be controlled and set on the client-side based on personal preference. Suppose, however, that the visitor decides to change the default font or font size used by the Web browser. The results can range from a minor misalignment of text to major formatting problems such as overlapping text and images, displaced buttons, or dropped sentences. The list of possible consequences can be extremely long and depends on the design elements included in your Web site. Figure 2-8 shows some of the problems that occurred with B&D's Web page when the default font size on a client was changed from 10 to 16 points.

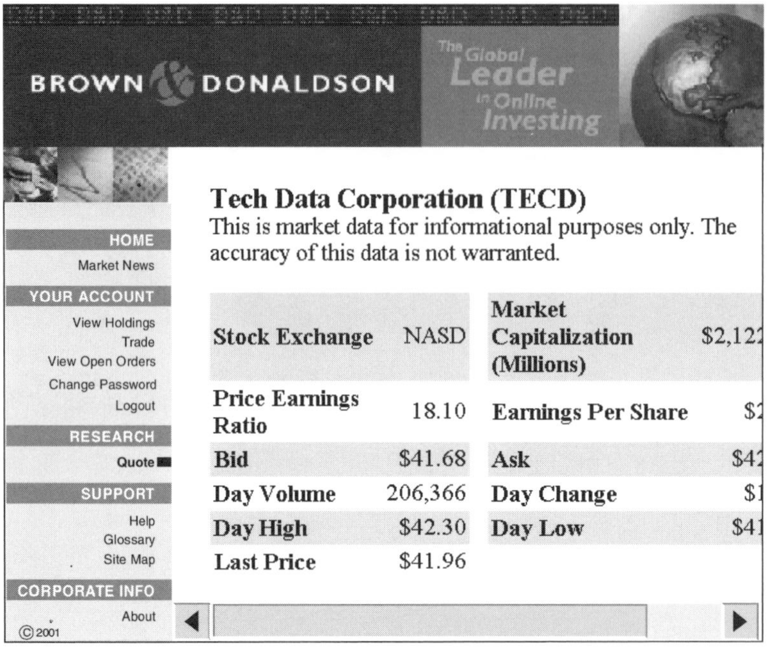

Figure 2-8

B&D's Quote
Page Displayed
Incorrectly Using
a Default Font
Size of 16 Points

Notice that the Price Earnings Ratio and Market Capitalization are now split over several lines. The second sentence of the general information paragraph ("This is market data...") at the top of the page begins at the end of the first line. The right-hand side of the table extends past the banner and the size of the text in the table no longer matches the text in the menu. While none of these "errors" caused any major problems, the presentation of the Web page was degraded simply because the user had a different default font size. A Web page that looks unprofessional detracts visitors from returning. And, in the case of an online brokerage firm, may cause potential clients to wonder whether this firm is competent enough to be trusted with their money.

Figure 2-9 represents an attempt by one of B&D's developers to correct the problems on this Web page by changing the HTML.

Notice that the Price Earnings Ratio and Market Capitalization are no longer split over several lines and the second sentence of the general information paragraph flows better. Unfortunately, the table-to-menu size difference is still noticeable and the right-hand side of the table extends even farther beyond the edge of the banner.

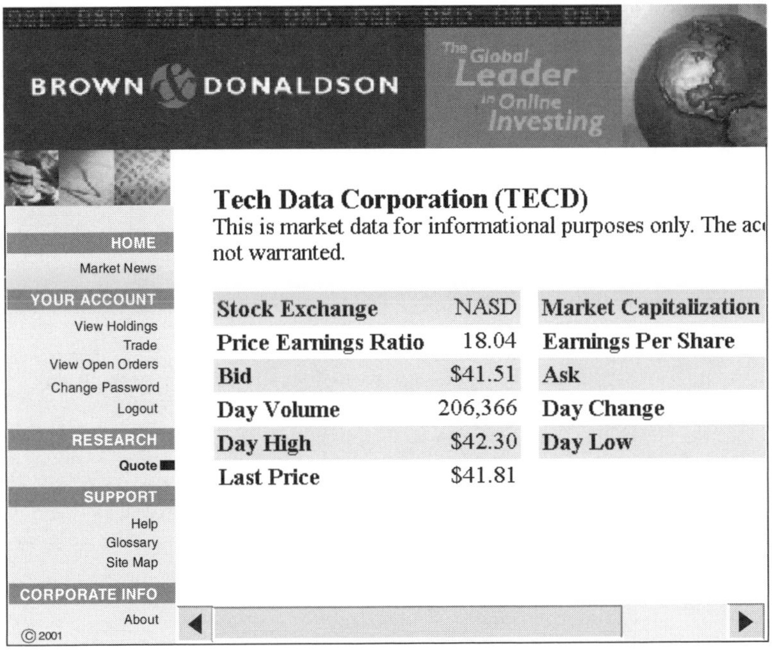

Figure 2-9

Developers Attempt to Correct B&D's Font Problems

Typically, Web browsers must wait until an entire table is received before it can be displayed. Many commercial Web sites use this feature to their advantage by placing the content of a page inside a table, and any paid advertising outside. This ensures that a client sees the advertisement before the content.

When unit testing, you should pay particular attention to tables. They are often the cause of headaches and frustrations due to the complexity of the HTML code used to build them and inconsistencies between various browsers. Some browsers handle empty (null) cells differently. Subsequent cells, for example, may all be shifted to the left. The amount of "white space" or padding between cells also varies from browser to browser. The easiest way to build a table that works is to copy one that has already been thoroughly tested (i.e., a template). If this isn't an option, Table 2-8 lists some basic table validation checks that you could include in your unit testing checklist.

Table 2-8　B&D's Table Checklist

		Table Validation
Pass	Fail	Description
☐	☐	There are no unwanted spaces or carriage returns in the table.
☐	☐	No cell is overpopulated with too much verbiage.
☐	☐	Every cell in the table is populated (i.e., no null values), as some browsers collapse empty cells. Extra scrutiny should be applied if the information is imported from a database dynamically.
☐	☐	The WIDTH and HEIGHT tags were specified for all cells (using screen % instead of absolute pixels wherever possible).
☐	☐	Developers placed the majority of page content inside the table and left paid advertisements (and other information that needs to load first) on the outside.

Templates

A source code template is a generic unit of code that can be used as the basis for creating other unique units. Templates provide Web developers with samples (e.g., entire Web pages, page components such as tables and client-side or server-side scripts, etc.) that can easily be modified to meet specific requirements of other projects. Templates are useful whether your Web site uses a manual (hand crafted by developers) or automatically generated (e.g., Active Server Pages) process to create its pages. Defining a set of templates at the beginning of a

Depending on the size of your organization, you may need to develop a template to help you manage your templates.

Web project will almost certainly reduce the number of bugs found later in unit and system testing.

Table 2-9 lists some basic style guide and template validation checks that you could include in your unit testing checklist.

Table 2-9   B&D's Style Guide and Template Checklist

		Style Guide and Template Adherence
Pass	Fail	Description
☐	☐	The Web page follows (except where documented/approved) the style guidelines documented in the B&D Web site style guide.
☐	☐	The Web page was based on the most appropriate Web page template.

Useful URLs ■■■■■

Table 2-10　Useful Web Sites

Web Site URLs	Description of Services
anybrowser.com, cast.org, htmlworks.com, imagiware.com, matterform.com, netmechanic.com, thewebking.com, watson.addy.com, weblint.com, websitegarage.com, and W3C.org	Online validation services.
"A Real Validator" (arealvalidator.com), Compatibility Viewer (delorie.com), CSE HTML Validator (htmlvalidator.com), Dreamweaver (macromedia.com), HomeSite (allaire.com), Hot Dog Pro (sausage.com), HTML Validator (helphtml.com), LinkBot (watchfire.com), and Tidy (W3C.org)	HTML validation tools.
Amaya (W3C.org) and Opera (opera.com)	Strict HTML-compliant browsers.
Freeappraisal (keynote.com) and Style Checker (NIST.gov/webmetrics)	HTML "style" checkers.
GIF Lube (websitegarage.com) and SmartSaver (ulead.com)	Image analyzers.
CSSCheck (htmlhelp.com), CSS Validator (W3C.org), and StyleT (microsoft.com)	CSS validating services.
GUIGuide.com	Web GUI design standards.
acme.com, download.com, freeware32.com, netscape.com, shareware.com, softseek.com, and tucows.com	Shareware.
sqe.com/bdonline/	Case study Web site and downloadable test plans.

Chapter 3 – Compatibility

Information is abundant and accumulating over the vast expanse of the Internet, but your Web site can easily get lost in the volume of information that's available. Good presentation, however, can help elevate your Web site above the rest in the eyes of your customers. Conversely, poor presentation can persuade your existing and potential customers to remove your Web site from their bookmark lists. Developers and testers must work together to ensure that your Web site is compatible with the clients that view it. There are literally thousands of possible hardware and software combinations that can affect the presentation of your Web site. How can you effectively identify and test every possible scenario? Do you really need to test every possible combination of client hardware and software?

Even though your Web page may be developed in strict compliance with the latest W3C HTML standard, there's no guarantee that it will be displayed exactly the same way when viewed via different browsers. Sometimes, developers may intentionally design their Web pages to display differently in various browsers. For example, developers might add a button to allow the client to download the latest version of Netscape or Internet Explorer, depending on which browser is installed. Or, developers may optimize their Web pages to accommodate the limited screen sizes of Personal Digital Assistants (PDAs).

Developers at B&D discovered that viewing their Web site using MS-IE 5.5 and Netscape 4.7 produced slightly different results. Although both of these browsers were sized to occupy the same amount of screen real estate, the font interpretations and "white space" varied.

Case Study

Review the following *Case Study Test Plans* to see an example of how the topics covered in this chapter can be utilized to test a Web site:

- System
- Post Implementation

Visit: sqe.com/bdonline/

Did you know...

Compliance with the latest W3C HTML standard doesn't guarantee that a Web page will be presented the same way in different browsers.

Notice the minor difference in the text layout and the amount of space at the bottom of each version of the Market News Web page, as shown in Figures 3-1 and 3-2.

■■■■■■■■■■■■■■■■■

Figure 3-1

B&D's Market
News Viewed
Using MS-IE 5.5

Figure 3-3 illustrates how B&D's programmers used a "browser sniffing" technique to detect the capabilities of a visitor's browser. A warning message was posted on the screen indicating that the browser they were using (Netscape 3.0) wouldn't support their style sheets.

Figure 3-4 shows that B&D's Login page displayed correctly when the client used MS-IE 5.5. The Web site correctly detected that this browser was capable of handling style sheets, so it didn't display the warning message.

Figure 3-2

B&D's Market News Viewed Using Netscape 4.7

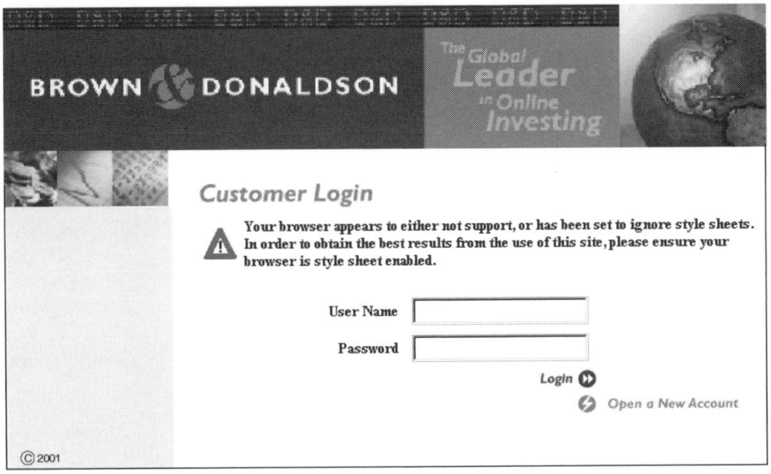

Figure 3-3

B&D's Login Page Uses "Browser Sniffing" to Detect Capabilities

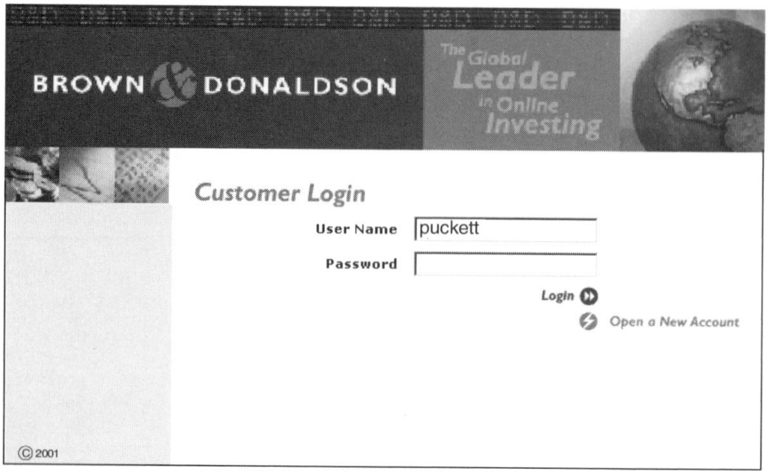

Figure 3-4

B&D's Login
Page Displayed
Correctly Using
MS-IE 5.5

Just for fun, B&D's programmers decided to see what the Login
page would look like through Mosaic 2.0 (a very old browser).
Figure 3-5 shows the disastrous results that they encountered.

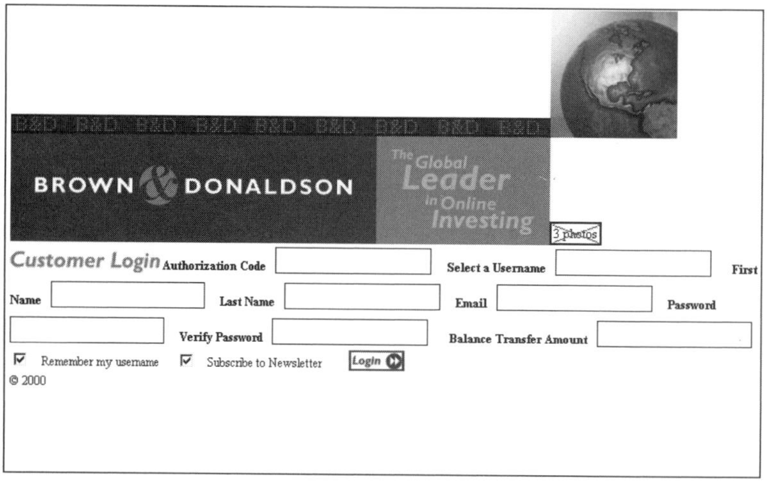

Figure 3-5

B&D's Login
Page Displayed
Incorrectly Using
Mosaic 2.0

Standardizing a Test Environment

Standards make a direct contribution to the quality of your company's Web site. A standardized test environment can help ensure a consistent approach to testing the features and functionality of your Web site and can help yield predictable results. This is especially important when many different individuals are involved in various stages of development and testing. Standards act as the catalyst that pulls together the work of individuals into a focused, concerted effort. Standards help improve efficiency and, consequently, reduce development and testing costs. Unfortunately, the computer industry has its fair share of standards, and selecting which standards to follow can be an extremely time-consuming and confusing process.

If you're going to be responsible for testing your Web site, you should get involved in the Web site's development as early as possible. Getting involved during the requirements phase, for example, allows you to be proactive in helping to select the standard platform(s) that will be used for development, testing, and ultimately production. Typical questions that need to be decided before starting development include determining which (if any) platform-specific features will be permitted (e.g., XHTML, CSS II and/or ActiveX controls). Using some of the more recent or proprietary technologies may make a developer's job easier, but may not meet the Marketing department's goal of reaching as many visitors as possible. Another issue that should be resolved is determining which platforms will be "officially" supported and therefore presumably tested before the Web site goes live. The Marketing department's goal of supporting all potential client-side platforms may not be realistic, given the testing resources that the organization has available.

Which hardware and software combinations should you use when designing a test environment?

Webreview (webreview.com) currently provides a comprehensive list of *features* supported by various browsers and versions:

- Java
- frames
- tables
- plug-ins
- IScript
- CSS
- gif89
- DHTML
- IFrames
- XML

Client Hardware

Computer hardware specifications and requirements are constantly changing. One of the most difficult aspects of buying a computer today is accepting the fact that it will be obsolete the moment that you unpack it. The rate of change in computer technology is breathtaking. The growing capability of chipmakers to put more transistors on a single silicon chip means that more functions and, consequently, more products can be incorporated onto a single chip. The advent of faster microprocessors and the decline in production costs have spawned significant improvements in storage devices, I/O capabilities, and communications speeds. With the price of memory continually declining, organizations are reaping the performance advantages of keeping more application data in main memory rather than on hard disk. Although few applications require an entire 64-bit address space, having more than 32 bits of address space can benefit database servers, Web search engines, Web server caches, and other high-performance computing applications.

Unfortunately, as a result of these changes, there are many possible client hardware combinations that can affect the way that visitors "see" your Web site. For example, a client may attempt to view your Web site using a variety of hardware platforms: IBM PC or PC-compatible, Macintosh, Unix workstation, WebTV, AOLTV, or a handheld device such as a mobile phone or Personal Digital Assistant (PDA). Web sites specifically designed for use with PDAs or hand-held organizers are commonly referred to as "clipped" Web sites. These Web sites typically only use small text snippets called "Web clippings" that can be accurately viewed within the limited viewing available via the PDA's Liquid Crystal Display (LCD).

Did you know…

Approximately every 18 months, a new generation of microprocessor is developed with double the capacity of its predecessor.

This phenomenon is called Moore's law, named after Gordon Moore, one of the founders of Intel Corporation.

For more information on viewing the Internet via a TV, visit:

aoltv.com
webtv.com

The impression that your Web site makes on a visitor is dependent on a number of client-side factors. The microprocessor that your client is using, speed of the processor, amount of RAM that is installed, resolution of the video card/monitor, speed of the Internet connection, and the printer that's attached are just a few of the factors involved. The number of combinations and permutations of hardware configurations can be overwhelming. Table 3-1 lists just some of the options that are available for IBM PC compatible platforms.

■■■■■■■■■■■■■■■■

A detailed explanation of monitor resolutions is provided in the *Usability* chapter. Transmission speeds are explained further in the *Performance* chapter.

Table 3-1 Some Options for IBM PC-Compatible Platforms

Microprocessor	
Manufacturer	AMD, Cyrix, Intel, or Transmeta
Class	286, 386, 486, Pentium, Pentium MMX, Pentium Pro, Pentium II, Pentium III, Pentium IV, or Celeron
Configuration	Single, Dual, or Clustered
Speed	25 MHz to 1 GHz, and faster
Memory	
RAM	4 MB to 1 GB, and more
Virtual Memory	0 MB to 1 GB, and more
Hard Disk Free Space	10 MB to 100 GB, and more
Monitor	
NOTE: Refer to the *Usability* chapter for more information.	
Viewable Size	10" to 22", and larger
Screen Resolution	640 x 480 to 2048 x 1536, and higher
Horizontal Dot Pitch	0.22mm to 0.28mm, and larger
Monochrome/Color	Black & White to 32-Bit Color, and more
Video Card Memory	1 MB to 32 MB, and more
Transmission Speed	
NOTE: Refer to the *Performance* chapter for more information.	
Proxy Server (LAN)	10 Mbps to 1 Gbps
Phone Modem	14.4 Kbps to 56.6 Kbps
Cable Modem	1 Mbps to 30 Mbps
Audio	
Direction	None, Mono, Stereo, or Surround Sound
Quality	Telephone, Radio, or CD
Sound Card Memory	0 MB to 32 MB, and more
Mouse	
Motion	Traditional or Vibrating (mouse vibrates when moving over page links, etc.)

Client Software ■ ■ ■ ■ ■

Software vendors are continually trying to improve their products – sometimes porting their products to new platforms, other times adding new features or simply fixing bugs. Many of these software upgrades and general releases are available in a variety of different formats. A Service Pack (SP), or *point release*, is an official upgrade to the original general release that normally contains fixes to bugs without adding new functionality. Original Equipment Manufacturer (OEM) software is a customized (and often optimized) version of software created by hardware equipment manufacturers such as Compaq (compaq.com), Dell (dell.com), Gateway (gateway.com), Hewlett-Packard (HP.com), IBM (IBM.com), Micron Electronics (micronpc.com), and others to run on their own brand of hardware. Many software vendors also release foreign-language versions of their software. While all of these different flavors provide a client with many choices, it also means that anyone trying to ensure that their Web applications run on all of these potential platforms will have their work cut out for them. Unfortunately all of these flavors may not work exactly the same way as the typical U.S./English version. Table 3-2 lists just some of the client O/S platforms that B&D considered supporting.

■ ■ ■ ■ ■ ■ ■ ■ ■ ■ ■ ■ ■ ■ ■ ■
Did you know...

Client software is often available in several different formats:

♦ general release
♦ service packs
♦ OEM versions
♦ foreign-language versions

Table 3-2 B&D's Possible Client Platforms

Operating System	Version/Flavor
Windows	3.x/DOS, 95 (with/without Active Desktop), 98, ME, or OEM versions
Windows NT	3.x, 4.x, or 2000.x
Mobile O/S	EPOC OS, Palm OS or Windows CE
Windows Emulation	Macintosh or OS/2
Macintosh	6.x, 7.x, 8.x, 9.x, or X.x (10.x)
OS/2	1.x, 2.x, or Warp.x
Unix/XWindows	AIX, HP, SCO, Sun, or Linux (Redhat, VA Linux, Corel)
Niche	Amiga OS, BeOS or Embedded

Web Browsers

Web browsers are available in many different versions, depending on operating system and language requirements. Table 3-3 lists some of the browsers that B&D considered supporting.

Table 3-3 B&D's Possible Browsers

Browser	Version/Flavor
MS-IE	2.x, 3.x, 4.x, or 5.x
Netscape	1.x, 2.x, 3.x, 4.x, or 6.x
Niche	InterNotes (Lotus Notes), Opera, or Oracle
Customized	AOL (MS-IE), MSN (MS-IE), NeoPlanet (MS-IE), or Worldnet/ATT (initially Netscape, then MS-IE)
Legacy	Mosaic
Text-Based Only	Lynx or Mobile Phones
Audio	Home Reader

It's important to understand that each of the major brands of browsers has more than a few different versions. For example, Netscape currently has over 100 general-release (i.e., not including Beta versions) variations of Web browsers. Netscape Navigator version 4.05, as shown in Figure 3-6, has six different versions for the following languages: English, Dutch, French, German, Japanese, and Swedish. Each of these versions is further split into various operating systems. Consequently, one (1) version of Netscape Navigator (4.05) has permutated into thirteen (13) different versions, each with its own set of characteristics.

■■■■■■■■■■■■■■■■■

Browser archives for downloading old and/or niche versions of browsers are available at:

cnet.com
evolt.org

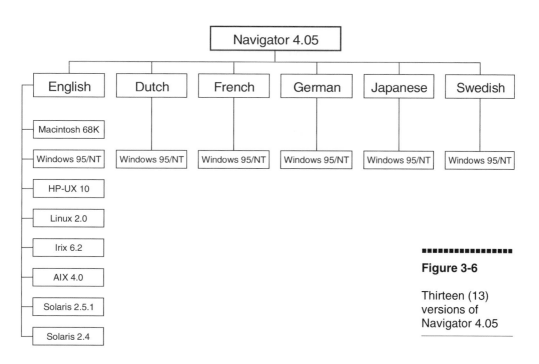

■■■■■■■■■■■■■■■■■

Figure 3-6

Thirteen (13) versions of Navigator 4.05

Similarly, Microsoft's Internet Explorer (IE) has numerous versions of their browser for various languages and operating systems. Microsoft has also licensed MS-IE to numerous software companies to incorporate into their own products. For example, recent versions of AOL use MS-IE as a kernel. Unfortunately, some features that work in native MS-IE will not necessarily work the same way in a licensed version. NeoPlanet currently uses MS-IE as a foundation and allows users to customize the look and feel of their browsers. Consequently, every NeoPlanet user could potentially have a different view of your Web site. The result is many variations permutated from the same product.

If you encounter severe problems when testing specific browsers, you can log the incident for possible correction in future versions, or explicitly state to your customers which browsers and settings are recommended for optimal performance. Which course of action you should select depends on how important that specific browser is to the visitors of your Web site. If only a few visitors use the problematic browser, then you may simply decide not to support it. Either way the decision should be documented.

■■■■■■■■■■■■■■■■■
Did you know...

Netscape and Microsoft's browsers are both descended from Mosaic and utilize common components from Mozilla.

Visit mozilla.org for more information.

Plug-Ins and Helper Applications

In addition to the wide array of software platforms that your visitors may be using, there are many plug-ins and helper applications that your clients may also have installed in order to add specific features or services to their Web browsers. Browsers can automatically recognize plug-ins and integrate their functionality into the main HTML file that is being presented. Helper applications, on the other hand, run separately from the browser and require that a second window be opened. Helper applications were popular when browsers were first introduced. Early versions of Netscape, for example, allowed clients to download, install, and define supplementary programs that played sound clips, displayed motion video, or performed other functions.

Popular plug-ins include Adobe's Acrobat (adobe.com), which is a document presentation and navigation program that lets you view documents exactly as they appear on a printed page, RealNetworks' (real.com) streaming video player, and Macromedia's Shockwave (shockwave.com), which is an interactive animation and sound player. Hundreds of plug-ins are available that perform a variety of functions. With the exception of a few plug-ins that might be installed during the browser's installation, most users will typically wait until they need a particular plug-in before they download it.

Table 3-4 lists some of the most popular plug-ins and helper applications among Internet users today.

Table 3-4   Top 10 Plug-In/Helper Installation Statistics

Plug-In	Percentage of Internet Users Who Have This Plug-In Installed
LiveAudio	75.54%
AVI	67.92%
Flash	64.41%
QuickTime	61.45%
Beatnik	41.45%
RealPlayer G2	36.24%
Shockwave	33.84%
Acrobat	32.42%
Media Player	26.71%

Source: Statmarket.com, January 2000

Plug-ins can be extremely useful if the person visiting your Web page has them installed. Unfortunately, your users may encounter a broken link if the required plug-in isn't installed. Even if your users have the proper plug-in to view particular content installed, the version of the plug-in may not be correct, as many plug-ins are not backward (or forward) compatible. In order to avoid this problem, you could design your Web site to try and detect the presence or absence of the required plug-in before attempting to serve up the content. Perhaps a simpler (and less intrusive) approach is to transfer the burden to your users. To improve the usability of your Web site, consider adding an area that informs your visitors which versions of plug-ins are used and how to proceed if a particular plug-in doesn't appear to work properly. For example, if you have an Adobe Acrobat file on your Web page, you may want to display a message or icon that tells your users how to download and install the required plug-in and which version of Acrobat the file is stored in.

Table 3-5 lists some of the test cases that B&D's team used to validate client-side plug-ins.

Table 3-5   B&D's Plug-In Testing Checklist

Pass	Fail	Description
		Plug-In Validation
☐	☐	The Web site lists the plug-ins (and versions) that are needed to view all of the content on the site.
☐	☐	The Web site (after requesting the client's permission) is able to detect whether or not the required plug-ins (and correct versions) are installed on the client-side.
☐	☐	In the event that the Web site is unable to accurately determine whether or not a plug-in is installed, the Web site contains an area that tells users how to proceed.

B&D's Test Environment ■ ■ ■ ■ ■

Like many other companies, B&D was faced with the problem of designing a standardized test environment for their Web site. Browsers, platforms, processors, operating systems, service packs, and a myriad of other variables added to the confusion. At first glance, B&D found the number of possible client hardware and software products and combinations of products overwhelming. The team found it difficult to decide what should and should not be included in their compatibility testing and correspondingly built into their test environment.

B&D quickly realized that they didn't have the time and resources needed to test every possible hardware and software product. Perhaps more importantly, however, B&D also realized that they couldn't realistically identify and test every possible combination of hardware and software configuration that might be installed anywhere in the world. Consequently, the team adopted the following 4-step strategy to design a standardized test environment.

■■■■■■■■■■■■■■■■■■

Four steps to designing a standardized test environment:

1. Understand the clients' capabilities.
2. Group the products into 3 categories.
3. Reduce the number of combinations.
4. Install the selected combinations of products.

Step 1 - Understand the Client

The first step in designing a standardized test environment is to gain an understanding of your clients' hardware and software capabilities. Only then can you decide which variables need to be considered as part of the equation. There are several different techniques you can take to learn about the hardware and software that your visitors are using.

Ask the Computer

One possible method of gathering information about the visitors to your Web site is to query your clients' computers directly. Developers can write procedures to capture details about a client's screen resolution, operating system, memory, processor, and hard disk space. The information is accurate and extremely valuable to your organization, but the political consequences can be enormous. Privacy becomes an issue whenever you query another computer for information. Client software may alert your Web site's visitors to your query and provoke emotions about your company's code of ethics.

Third Party Market Research

Other, less intrusive, methods of gathering information about your Web site's visitors include reviewing generic Web usage surveys and working with industry research groups. The Gartner Group (gartner.com) provides business technology research, consumer and market intelligence, consulting services, and decision-making tools. Numerous articles provide background information and statistics about the latest trends in technology and the Internet.

The Yankee Group (yankeegroup.com) provides research results in the areas of e-business, enterprise networking, and Internet technology. Articles, audio conferences, and announcements provide valuable clues and statistics on industry trends. Forrester Research (forrester.com) offers comprehensive analysis of the global Internet economy and its impact on society and business. International Data Corporation (IDC.com) provides insight on e-commerce, the Internet, and information technology to help you formulate effective business plans. IDC currently features more than 60,000 documents covering everything from application service providers, e-commerce, and Linux to digital cameras, portals, and the IT skills shortage.

■■■■■■■■■■■■■■■■■
Industry research groups can help you learn more about your Web site's visitors. Visit the following sites:

+ Forrester Research (forrester.com)
+ Gartner Group (gartner.com)
+ International Data Corporation (IDC.com)
+ Yankee Group (yankeegroup.com)

Market Research Study

Market research is a valuable method of collecting information about your clients' capabilities. Before soliciting feedback from their current (and potential) client base, B&D attempted to categorize their expected audience into different customer profiles depending upon their anticipated usage of the Web site.

Survey participants were then selected to ensure that each category was adequately represented. Their research found that one group of users, portfolio managers, would most likely be using the latest and greatest hardware and software available because they needed to research and execute their transactions as quickly as possible. Individual investors, on the other hand, had a wide range of computer skills and might be using anything from a 50 MHz 486 with 8 MB of RAM, a 14" monitor (640 x 480, 16 colors), and a 14.4 Kbps modem to a state-of-the-art system with a cable modem, depending on when they purchased their computer systems.

What's Currently Available?

If the anticipated audience is expected to be fairly up-to-date with the latest technology, then a survey via the Web could be used to determine what hardware and software a potential client has. First, the survey should identify what configurations the large PC manufacturers (e.g., Compaq, Dell, Gateway, etc.) are currently selling. Then, you can select some of the most common configurations that are available from this list.

Web Traffic/Log Analysis Tools

In addition to the basic statistics packages that Web servers provide, several companies offer advanced statistical software for analyzing Web server traffic logs and generating useful reports. Web logs can be analyzed to determine usage statistics such as which versions of browser and operating system visitors are using when accessing your Web site.

While many of these Web traffic analysis tools can be quite useful, there are several key points that you should keep in mind. If you run different tools on the same Web log, you may encounter noticeable differences in the statistics being reported due to the different algorithms that each tool uses to calculate these statistics. Therefore, it's important to make sure that your use of a tool or measure is consistent when comparing results. Since Web logs can grow to several hundred megabytes in size, moving or copying these logs across a LAN or WAN can be troublesome and impact network performance. Conversely, running the analysis tool against the production logs may impact the performance of the Web server.

Yahoo (yahoo.com), Internet.com (serverwatch.internet.com), and the University of Uppsala (uu.se/Software/Analyzers/) provide comprehensive listings of Web log analyzers. Table 3-6 lists some of the vendors of these tools.

■■■■■■■■■■■■■■■■■
Did you know...

Web logs can be used to determine the previous Web site that a viewer was visiting. This can be useful when trying to determine which search engines and/or business partners are generating the most or the least number of "click-throughs."

Table 3-6 Sample Web Traffic Log Analysis Tools

Vendor	Product
Accrue Software (accrue.com)	Insight & Hit List
iLux (ilux.com)	iLux Suite
NetGenesis (netgen.com)	Net Analysis
Sane Solutions (sane.com)	Net Tracker
Web Trends (webtrends.com)	WebTrends

Step 2 - Group the Products

The second step in designing a standardized test environment is to organize the hardware and software configuration information that you collected in the first step into three categories: Gold, Silver, and Bronze, as shown in Figure 3-7.

The Gold Category

The Gold category includes hardware and software products that will be thoroughly tested and, hence, are "guaranteed to work." This might entail repeating presentation test cases for each of the different platforms and/or distributing functional test cases evenly among the various combinations of hardware and software. Any significant bugs or defects found and reported by the testing team would typically be fixed in the next development cycle.

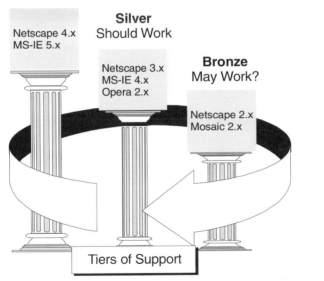

■■■■■■■■■■■■■■■■■

Figure 3-7

3-Tier testing strategy:

♦ Gold
♦ Silver
♦ Bronze

Adding more products to the Gold category will increase the number of test cases that must be executed and, hence, will increase cost or reduce the quality of testing for each product. A reduction in the quality of testing will, consequently, increase the probability that a serious defect might slip through.

The Silver Category

The Silver category includes hardware and software products that undergo less rigorous testing. Since the items listed in this category typically represent a smaller proportion of your Web site's viewing audience, they are assigned a limited number of test cases. These items "should work," but a few defects may slip through your testing as certain combinations of older hardware and software may not be compatible with your Web site. Some of these bugs or defects may be worth fixing in future development cycles, while others may not.

The Bronze Category

The Bronze category includes the hardware and software products that will not be tested. Items listed in this category "may work," but few people (if anyone) will typically care if they don't work. Bugs that are only specific to Bronze category products typically won't be fixed. However, your company's customer support group should still log any incidents that your customers report. This log may serve as a knowledge base of "work arounds" that could be built and maintained.

Assign the Products to Categories

Deciding which category to place each hardware and software product in becomes a balancing act of risk versus resources. There are several approaches to solving this dilemma. The "most used" strategy puts emphasis (i.e., Gold) on testing the hardware and software that is most widely used by prospective visitors.

Another approach is the "lowest common denominator" approach. This strategy assumes that if the oldest (lowest) version of a product is assigned the highest level of testing and is found to work, then it's reasonably safe to assume that more recent versions (or higher specifications) of the same product will also work.

Conversely, the "latest and greatest" strategy assumes that only the most recent version of a product will be tested. This strategy is implemented under the assumption that anyone who experiences a problem with an old version will simply upgrade to the newest version to correct the problems. Unfortunately, this assumption doesn't always hold true.

The recent-history strategy is an extension of the "latest and greatest" approach. Instead of just including the most recent version, all significant versions that have been released within the last two years are included.

The "boundary equivalence" strategy assumes that the oldest and most recent versions of products are both assigned the highest level of testing. If both of these versions work, then all intermediary versions are assumed to work.

If time and resources permit, a formal risk assessment should be performed. Using this approach, an estimate of the probability of finding a defect in a particular product is combined with an estimate of the business cost of missing the defect in order to rank the products into a testing priority.

Whichever approach is used to assigned the various hardware and software products to the different categories, the final selection should be documented. Table 3-7 lists the client-side software products that B&D's team assigned to their Gold category.

■■■■■■■■■■■■■■■■■

There are several methods you can use to weigh risk vs. resources:

- most used
- lowest common denominator
- latest and greatest
- recent history
- boundary equivalence
- risk assessment

Table 3-7 B&D's Gold Client-Side Software Category

Operating System	Browsers	Plug-Ins
Windows ME	MS-IE 5.5	Acrobat 4.0
Windows 98 SE	MS-IE 4.0	Acrobat 3.0
Windows 2000	Netscape 6.0	
Windows NT 4.0	Netscape 4.0	
	AOL 6.0	
	AOL 5.0	
Total = 4	Total = 6	Total = 2

Step 3 - Reduce the Combinations

The third step in designing a standardized test environment is to reduce the number of possible product combinations to a manageable amount. For example, based on the products listed in B&D's Gold Client-Side Software Category (refer to Table 3-7), the testing team would have to execute each test case forty-eight (4 x 6 x 2 = 48) times in order to exhaustively test all of the possible software combinations. Unfortunately, B&D didn't have the resources to conduct such exhaustive combination testing, so they had to come up with another solution. There are several techniques (listed below) that you can use to reduce the number of combinations that need to be tested.

Incompatible Combinations

Not all combinations need to be tested for all test requirements. You may have listed many combinations of hardware and software that are technically infeasible, incompatible with one another, or extremely unlikely to exist. Although these combinations should be documented in your test plan, they may not actually need to be tested. AOL 4 and Windows NT 4, for example, have compatibility issues and consequently are unlikely to be found co-existing on the same client.

Unlikely Combinations

Software combinations that are extremely unlikely to exist in the real world based on their release dates also make good candidates for elimination. Very few Windows 2000 users, for example, are likely to be running MS-IE 4.

Hardware Combinations

B&D found that, with a few exceptions, varying the client-side hardware used for testing had very little effect on whether a test passed or failed. B&D identified and documented the following exceptions to the rule:

♦ The client machine needs to match or exceed the minimum hardware requirements of the client-side software (O/S, browser, and plug-ins). Windows 2000, for example, shouldn't be installed on a 486 PC.

♦ The Internet access method (e.g., modem speed) has a significant effect on performance results. In contrast, adding more memory or upgrading the CPU has a minimal effect on page download performance.

♦ CPU speed and memory have an effect on the performance of client-side executable programs such as Java applets or ActiveX controls and pages that require large amounts of processing to display the correct format (e.g., extremely complex tables). If these executables are particularly video intense, the video card memory can also have a slight effect.

♦ The maximum screen resolution in terms of pixels and number of colors has an effect on presentation results.

♦ The dots per inch (dpi), minimum margin width, and color options of the printer have an effect on the presentation results.

♦ Additional "niche" hardware platforms such as PDAs, WebTV, and mobile phones need to be tested to ensure that the appliance doesn't have any special requirements.

Unfortunately, B&D's testing budget didn't include any money for buying new client-side hardware. Consequently, the hardware platform defaulted to the PCs that the testing team currently had installed as their "standard" configuration: a 667 MHz Pentium III with 128 MB of RAM, and a 17" monitor (1024 x 768, 256 colors). The only permitted expenditure was for several 56.6 Kbps modems and direct outside telephone lines to help simulate real users who typically don't have LANs with T1 Internet access. As an added bonus, one of the testers contributed an old 486 PC from home. With a little help from the network guys, this computer was reconfigured to match the minimum hardware requirements that were specified in the Web site's requirements document. The only color printer available was in the Marketing department, which also used some high-end Macs that could be made available on a limited basis.

Although all of the testing could have been performed using the *minimum* hardware configuration, the time needed to execute all of the test cases would have been longer than necessary. With only a few exceptions, varying the hardware (specifically the Internet access method and/or modem speed) should only affect performance test results, not the functional test results. Therefore, the majority of the testing was conducted using the *standard* hardware configuration. B&D conducted only limited performance testing using the minimum hardware configuration in order to ensure that the Web site met its stated performance requirements using the recommended minimum configuration.

Mathematical Approach

Another more formal approach to handling too many combinations is to use an orthogonal array or "pairwise" algorithm. This technique helps determine what test cases are required in order to test every possible combination of any two variables (e.g., pair of software products). While this technique allows pairing of more than two variables, the drawbacks usually outweigh the benefits as the number of required test cases usually increases faster than the additional number of detected defects found. Testing every "pairwise" combination of B&D's client-side software requires only 24 test cases, as shown in Table 3-8. This is 50% less than the total number of possible software combinations (4 x 6 x 2 = 48).

■■■■■■■■■■■■■■■■■■
For more information on orthogonal arrays, refer to Hedayat et al's book, *Orthogonal Arrays: Theory and Applications.*

Table 3-8   B&D's Client-Side Software Orthogonal Array

Test Case #	Operating System	Browser	Plug-In
1	Windows ME	MS-IE 4.0	Acrobat 4.0
2	Windows 98 SE	Netscape 4.0	Acrobat 3.0
3	Windows 98 SE	Netscape 6.0	Acrobat 3.0
4	Windows 98 SE	AOL 5.0	Acrobat 4.0
5	Windows NT 4.0	MS-IE 5.5	Acrobat 3.0
6	Windows NT 4.0	Netscape 4.0	Acrobat 4.0
7	Windows NT 4.0	Netscape 6.0	Acrobat 3.0
8	Windows NT 4.0	AOL 6.0	Acrobat 3.0
9	Windows 2000	MS-IE 4.0	Acrobat 3.0
10	Windows 2000	MS-IE 5.5	Acrobat 3.0
11	Windows 2000	AOL 6.0	Acrobat 3.0
12	Windows 2000	AOL 5.0	Acrobat 3.0
13	Windows ME	AOL 5.0	Acrobat 3.0

(Continued)

Table 3-8 (*Continued*)

Test Case #	Operating System	Browser	Plug-In
14	Windows ME	Netscape 4.0	Acrobat 3.0
15	Windows 98 SE	AOL 6.0	Acrobat 4.0
16	Windows 2000	Netscape 6.0	Acrobat 3.0
17	Windows ME	MS-IE 5.5	Acrobat 4.0
18	Windows NT4.0	MS-IE 4.0	Acrobat 3.0
19	Windows ME	Netscape 6.0	Acrobat 4.0
20	Windows 98 SE	MS-IE 5.5	Acrobat 3.0
21	Windows 2000	Netscape 4.0	Acrobat 4.0
22	Windows NT 4.0	AOL 5.0	Acrobat 4.0
23	Windows 98 SE	MS-IE 4.0	Acrobat 4.0
24	Windows ME	AOL 6.0	Acrobat 3.0

Orthogonal arrays can be built manually, but such an approach can be very time consuming for anything more than the most simple of arrays. Alternatively, automated test tools can be used to help identify the optimal set of test cases that should be used. Telcordia/Argreenhouse (argreenhouse.com), for example, provides a tool called Aetgweb that creates the optimal set of test cases required to thoroughly test your Web site or application.

Factor analysis and cluster analysis are two other mathematical approaches that attempt to make sense of multivariate data in a systematic manner. Factor analysis searches for hidden variables in order to reduce data that involves many variables down to a small number of dimensions. Cluster analysis searches for hidden groups and classifies cases into related clusters based on the values of several variables. If the classification is successful, the cases within clusters will appear close together when plotted geometrically, and the cases in different clusters will be far apart.

The cases that appear close together should be tested, while the cases that appear far apart may be eliminated.

Step 4 - Configuration Installation

The final step of the standardization process is to install and implement the most likely combinations of hardware and software. By implementing this process, you can derive a manageable list of hardware and software combinations that will help you meet the requirements of the majority of your customers and your budget.

It's important to remember, however, that few Internet users have "clean" software installations. Most of their operating systems have had numerous software packages completely or partially installed and uninstalled, resulting in "dirty" environments. These environments are so numerous that they are beyond comprehensive testing. Therefore, no matter how many "clean" environments are tested, there is no guarantee that a "dirty" environment will work as desired.

Boots and Ghosts

Boot managers allow multiple operating systems to be installed and run on the same computer, thereby reducing the number of physical computers that may need to be purchased. Boot managers allow you to select which operating system you want to use each time you start your system. System Selector (bootmanager.com), for example, allows you to install multiple operating systems on the same computer using a different disk partition for each configuration (an extra large hard drive can come in handy). Alternatively, VMware (vmware.com) provides a means of running multiple operating systems without using

■■■■■■■■■■■■■■■■■

For more information on boot managers, visit:

bootmanager.com
IBM.com
microsoft.com
v-com.com
vmware.com

dual boot/disk partitions. Bundled boot managers include the Windows NT/2000 boot menu and OS/2's boot manager.

Ghosting software allows you to copy the complete contents of one hard drive to another hard drive (local or network). You can copy your hard drive onto a disk image file and that image can then be used as a template, which may be copied to other hard drives. This process is called *cloning* or *ghosting*. For the average home computer user, ghosting software may not be particularly useful. But for a corporation, which may have thousands of servers and computers littered throughout its organization, having a quick way to duplicate a standard system configuration can be extremely useful. Ghosting products such as Norton's (symantec.com) Ghost and StorageSoft's (storagesoft.com) ImageCast allow you to install a "clean" client prior to test execution. This can help to reduce the number of false failures that you may encounter due to corruption of the client's software configuration.

■■■■■■■■■■■■■■■■■■
Did you know…

Ghosting software provides a quick and cost-effective way to duplicate a system.

Installation Checklist

Unfortunately, many software products don't perform clean installs. Instead, they impact other software products that are already installed on the same machine, especially previous versions of the same product. For this reason, it's particularly important to document the order in which the various software products are installed in order to ensure that development, testing, and production environments are all in synch. Wherever possible, you should try to avoid installing multiple versions of the same software product on the same machine. Table 3-9 lists some of the checks included on B&D's installation checklist.

Table 3-9   B&D's Installation Checklist

Test Station Validation		
Pass	Fail	Description
☐	☐	Different versions of the same brand of browser are installed in different instances of an operating system. Since Netscape and MS-IE typically ignore each other, B&D felt that it would be okay to install one copy of each product on the same instance of operating system.
☐	☐	Only general-release software is used. No OEM, SP, or Beta versions are used, with the exception of any required Y2K patches that are necessary in order to make the product work post Y2K.
☐	☐	All of the installations use the installation defaults for directory names, cache sizes, fonts, plug-ins, etc. Windows 95 was installed without the Active desktop option because B&D felt that most users who had experimented with this option had most likely already migrated to Windows 98 or later.

Outsourcing

For a nominal fee, companies like Web Site Garage (websitegarage.com) can provide snapshots of Web pages as seen via a variety of browsers and versions. This can prove to be a cost-effective method of checking the less common hardware platforms such as Apple, OS/2, Linux, and others. If more rigorous testing is required, numerous other third-party testing organizations offer various degrees of compatibility testing services ranging from simple screen presentation checks to running Java applets on different Java Virtual Machines (JVM).

Installability and Serviceability ■ ■ ■ ■ ■

Installability testing is a specific type of compatibility testing that generally only applies to Web applications that will be hosted on another organization's hardware. Installation instructions for a packaged Intranet application, for example, should cover all of the supported platforms. These instructions should specify the exact order in which the components should be installed, the configuration settings that are required or recommended, and ideally the steps needed to cleanly uninstall the product.

Serviceability pertains to the regular maintenance tasks that a client will have to perform in order to ensure that the packaged Web application continues to perform adequately, from both a functional and performance perspective. A product's documentation plays an integral part in its serviceability, and the manuals must adequately describe the necessary service procedures. If a Web application uses a Database Management System (DBMS) to store data, for example, the product documentation should outline when and how often the database should be reorganized. If the product is sold and purchased with the understanding that the client doesn't need to hire a Database Administrator (DBA), then the documentation should adequately describe the reorganization procedure.

Some products take advantage of the Internet to connect to the vendor's Web site to find out about product updates and patches. In some cases, the products will actually update themselves. If your Web application utilizes automatic updates, you should test that it works when installed on any of the supported platforms. You should also test that the automatic updates work properly when other applications have been added and removed (i.e., the environment is a little "dirty"), or when applications are still running (e.g., anti-virus programs) even if the user was instructed to close them. Unfortunately, some users will either ignore or simply not read software installation/removal instructions. Table 3-10 lists B&D's test cases for installing and servicing their Web applications.

Table 3-10　B&D's Installability and Serviceability Checklist

		Packaged Application Validation
Pass	Fail	Description
☐	☐	Product documentation explains the exact order in which the components should be installed and the configuration settings that are required or recommended.
☐	☐	Product documentation explains how to uninstall the product cleanly.
☐	☐	Product documentation adequately describes when and how the data files or database should be reorganized.
☐	☐	Automatic updates install and operate correctly on all of the supported platforms.
☐	☐	Automatic updates install and operate correctly when other applications have been added/removed before and after the update is performed.

Useful URLs ■■■■■

Table 3-11   Useful Web Sites

Web Site URLs	Description of Services
compaq.com, dell.com, gateway.com, HP.com, IBM.com, and micronpc.com	PC manufacturers.
AOL.com, aoltv.com, cnet.com, evolt.org, microsoft.com, mozilla.org, ncsa.uiuc.edu, neoplanet.com, netscape.com, opera.com, palmos.com, sillydog.webhanger.com, spyglass.com, and webtv.com	Browsers.
adobe.com, netscape.com, real.com, and shockwave.com	Plug-ins.
apache.org, beasys.com, microsoft.com, ncsa.uiuc.edu, netscape.com, and W3C.org	Web servers.
accrue.com, ilux.com, netgen.com, sane.com, serverwatch.internet.com, uu.se/Software/Analyzers, webtrends.com, and yahoo.com	Web log analysis.
forrester.com, gartner.com, IDC.com, keynote.com, mycomputer.com, netcraft.com, statmarket, webreview.com, and yankeegroup.com	Research and statistics.
argreenhouse.com, bootmanager.com, IBM.com, microsoft.com, romtecusa.com, storagesoft.com, symantec.com v-com.com, vmware.com, and websitegarage.com	Configuration tools and utilities.
sqe.com/bdonline/	Case study Web site and downloadable test plans.

Chapter 4 – Navigation

Regardless of how innovative your Web site is or how much great information it contains, your message is lost if visitors can't find what they're looking for. Every page in your Web site should provide clear and concise answers to three basic questions, "Where am I?", "Where can I go from here?", and "What will I find along the way?" Although it sounds simple, navigation is one of the most important and often one of the most difficult aspects of designing and testing an effective Web site. Variables such as hierarchy of menus, cultural diversity, and language can affect the way visitors understand and traverse your Web site.

Site navigation is the key to the success (or failure) of virtually every site on the World Wide Web. In order for a Web site to be successful, visitors must be able to find the information they're seeking in the quickest manner possible. When done correctly, navigation testing can reveal many of the functional and performance problems that could potentially frustrate visitors and cause them to leave your Web site. A study by Creative Good (creativegood.com) during the 1998 holiday season on 10 leading Web shopping sites, for example, found that 39% of test shoppers failed in their buying attempts because the Web sites were too difficult to navigate. The same study also found that $1 spent on advertising generated $5 in additional revenue, while $1 spent on "customer experience" improvements yielded more than $60 in additional revenue. How important is navigation to the success of your Web site?

■■■■■■■■■■■■■■■■■■

Case Study

Review the following *Case Study Test Plans* to see an example of how the topics covered in this chapter can be utilized to test a Web site:

- Unit
- System
- Post Implementation

Visit: sqe.com/bdonline/

■■■■■■■■■■■■■■■■■■

Web navigation should answer three basic questions:

- Where am I?
- Where can I go from here?
- What will I find along the way?

Links and URLs ■■■■■

A link is a selectable connection from an object on a particular Web page to another object located on the same or different Web page. Objects can include text, graphics, sound clips, and video clips among other things. The most common form of a link, however, is a highlighted word or picture that can be selected by the user, which results in the immediate delivery and display of another Web page. The Internet address that a link points to is called a Universal Resource Locator (URL).

Internal Links

There are several kinds of links used in Web applications. *Internal* links take the visitor to another page within your own Web site. *Absolute* URLs provide the entire file address for a Web page (e.g., C:/directory/subdirectory/page1.html), while *relative* URLs only point to another page relative to the location of the current page (e.g., subdirectory/page2.html). Generally speaking, internal links should use relative URLs since this will typically make the application more robust and less susceptible to broken links when moved from one environment to another (e.g., from development to system test). Unfortunately, many developers often use absolute rather than relative links. Since most link-checking tools don't care whether a link is absolute or relative, potential problems can easily be missed. You should consider using a simple text-scanning tool to scan your HTML source code files for absolute links that reference specific hard drives (i.e., strings that begin with "C:\" or "X:\" where X is a network drive used by the Web site). This search may return some false positive results that you'll need to sort through before isolating the problem.

■■■■■■■■■■■■■■■■■
Visit the following Web sites to download text-scanning tools:

download.com
freeware32.com
shareware.com
softseek.com
tucows.com

External Links

External links point to Web sites owned and maintained by other organizations. However, it's somewhat risky to point to any page other than another Web site's Home page. Your links may become broken if the developers or Webmasters at the other Web sites change their filenames or the directory structures of their sites without informing your organization. Before using external links that point to non-Home pages, consider the trade-off between the additional maintenance (testing and re-coding) needed to ensure that the link does not become broken and the added benefit gained by the viewer.

Anchors

In general, a link brings a visitor to the top of the desired Web page. An anchor, however, allows a visitor to jump to a specific section of a Web page. The desired section is marked with an anchor tag, and the link specifies not only the URL of the page, but the name of the anchor as well. Anchors are particularly prone to developers "cutting and pasting" duplicate anchor names. This creates links that aren't broken, but don't actually go to the right content. When used incorrectly, anchors can also create usability issues within your Web site. Visitors often expect a link to go to another Web page, not somewhere on the same page. This is particularly problematic when clicking on the anchor doesn't even cause the Web page to scroll. A visitor may interpret this as a broken link.

Broken links are often accepted as a fact of life, but they don't have to be. Broken links negatively affect the image that a Web site is trying to project, but there are preventive measures that can help avoid these problems. Table 4-1 lists several simple guidelines that you can add to your Web standards that will help minimize the probability of experiencing a broken link.

Table 4-1   Guidelines for Avoiding Broken Links

Subject	Description
External Links	These links are typically out of your control. Wherever possible, minimize the number of external links. Ask yourself the question, "Do I really want my visitors to visit this linked site?" Remember that non-Home page links are more likely to become broken than links to a Home page.
Internal Links	Use relative links rather than absolute. Web sites that use relative links tend to be more robust and facilitate renaming directory structures much more readily than Web sites that utilize absolute links.
Dynamic Links	If possible, avoid using run-time variables to build URLs. Testing such code can be extremely time-consuming.
Link Parameters	If possible, avoid links that require a parameter to be passed (e.g., stock quote pages often use a ticker symbol in the URL). When using dynamic links, the number of permutations (including error conditions) is likely to be so large that it may not be feasible to test all possibilities.
Case Sensitivity	Some Web servers are URL case-sensitive. If your Web server is case-sensitive, ensure that your URL naming standard specifies when or if uppercase characters are to be used.

B&D used the test cases listed in Table 4-2 to validate the links in their Web site and, as a result, discovered that their Web site still had an absolute link to C:/windows/temp/frontpagetempdir/image1.gif just days before the application was to be moved into production.

Table 4-2 B&D's Links and URL Testing Checklist

Links and URL Validation		
Pass	Fail	Description
☐	☐	This link is not broken and goes to the most appropriate location.
☐	☐	If this link is an internal link, it uses all lowercase characters.
☐	☐	If this link is an internal link, it uses relative addressing (i.e., it does not use an absolute address).
☐	☐	If this link is an internal link, it does not launch a new browser window unless it's a help page.
☐	☐	If this link is an external link, it does launch a new browser window.
☐	☐	This link adds value to the Web site. Links with little value add to the maintenance load (especially external links) and potentially make a Web page less usable.
☐	☐	The browser's Go/History list is updated correctly after using this link. Some developers manipulate the browser's history and thereby degrade the Web site's usability.
☐	☐	The browser's Forward/Back buttons still work after using this link. Some developers manipulate the browser's history and thereby degrade the Web site's usability.
☐	☐	When using the Back button, previously entered data is not lost.
☐	☐	The link text does not wrap to two lines. This may confuse visitors into thinking that there are two links instead of one.

Redirects ■ ■ ■ ■ ■

Many organizations make their Web sites a little bit more user friendly by displaying a custom error page in the event that a link can't be found. Figure 4-1 shows the "redirect" message that B&D's Webmaster chose to display instead of an unfriendly HTTP 404-error message.

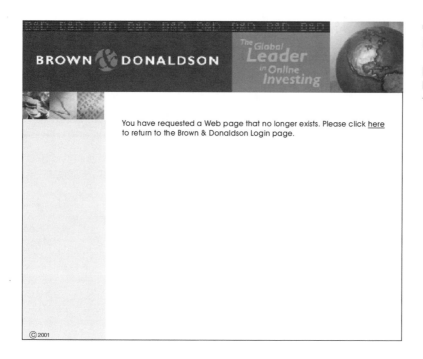

Many Webmasters prefer to use redirects to try to gracefully recover from this type of error. Redirects allow the Web server to serve up a replacement page in the event that a client requests a page that no longer exists. Suppose, for example, that a client bookmarks the "August Special" in August and tries to return to the page in September. Instead of serving up the August page (which has since been removed) or the default or customized 404-error page, a redirect can be used to serve up the "September Special." When setting up a system test environment, check with your Webmaster to find out what redirects (if any) will be implemented in the production environment.

Unfortunately, redirects have some potential drawbacks. One drawback is that redirects require maintenance. The Webmaster, for example, has to intervene again when the "September Special" is replaced by the "October Special." Another drawback is that redirects aren't very good at handling unexpected events. A Webmaster probably wouldn't anticipate installing a redirect for a client that requests the non-existent Web page "companyname.com/fre**d**.html" instead of the correct page (e.g., "companyname.com/free.html"). Some more advanced Web sites handle 404-errors by forwarding the client's request to an internal search engine, which attempts to guess the page that the client was trying to access. The search engine may even provide the client with a list of these guesses to choose from. This approach can potentially work well for handling URL typos and other actions that Webmasters aren't likely to anticipate from the client.

If a link points to a directory instead of a specific Web page, you should ensure that the link ends with a slash (e.g., "companyname.com/directory/" instead of "companyname.com/directory"). The slash indicates to the Web server that the default Web page for the directory is being requested. Leaving the slash off will cause some Web servers to send a redirect to the browser telling it to request the default page, resulting in additional (and hence, slower) communications. In an effort to speed up downloads, some of the more recent browsers automatically add a slash to the end of a URL that doesn't specify a specific Web resource.

B&D used the test cases listed in Table 4-3 to validate the redirects used on their Web site.

Table 4-3 B&D's Redirect Testing Checklist

		Redirect Validation
Pass	Fail	Description
☐	☐	The default 400, 401, 402, 403 and 404-error pages have been developed and properly configured on the production Web server(s).
☐	☐	If this link is being redirected, it goes to the correct final destination and is not re-redirected.
☐	☐	If a link points to a directory (instead of a specific Web page), the link ends with a slash.

Bookmarks and Favorites ■■■■■

A bookmark is a method that visitors can use to mark Web pages that they want to return to later. Electronic bookmarks are similar to paper-based bookmarks in that they both mark a specific page for future reference. A browser will typically use the Web page's title when adding an entry to its list of stored bookmarks. Consequently, page titles should be accurate and "catchy" in order to provide visitors with the most effective means of distinguishing one marked page from another. Table 4-4 lists some example bookmarks used by various financial Web sites.

Table 4-4 Sample Bookmarks - Circa Fall 2000

URL	Bookmark Name
newyorklife.com	New York Life Front Page
hoovers.com/ipo/0,1334,23,00.html	Hoover's Online - Money - IPO Central
merrilllynch.com/woml/inv_rel/womfrb1.htm	The World of Merrill Lynch
ameritrade.com/cgi-bin/login.cgi	Login to Ameritrade

When developing a Web site, developers will often "cut and paste" entire Web pages. Unfortunately, they may forget to update the Web page's title (and hence, any resulting bookmark) with the new purpose and content of the page. You should ensure that your navigational checklist includes a check for accurate bookmarks. Secure Web pages (HTTPS) can also be bookmarked, but should be checked to ensure that any password or login requirements cannot be skipped, simply by requesting a previously bookmarked page.

B&D's team used the test cases listed in Table 4-5 to validate the bookmarks used on their Web site.

■■■■■■■■■■■■■■■
Did you know...

Some Web sites use descriptions that start with the letter "A" in the hope that their bookmark will be used more often, as visitors and browsers often sort their bookmark lists alphabetically.

Table 4-5 B&D's Bookmark Testing Checklist

		Bookmark/Favorite Validation
Pass	Fail	Description
☐	☐	Every Web page has a bookmark that accurately reflects the content of the page.
☐	☐	No bookmark is longer than 32 characters, since browsers typically truncate the display of verbose descriptions.
☐	☐	Each bookmark must start with "B&D – ".

Frames and Framesets

Frames provide Web site developers with the ability to define one or more independently scrollable sections (*frames*) within a single browser window. When two or more frames are contained on the same Web page, they're called a *frameset*. The contents of each frame are taken from different Web pages and presented as a combined set on a single page. This allows visitors to view multiple pages of your Web site simultaneously, without opening more browsers. Figure 4-2 illustrates a typical

Web page that implements a frameset. Frame #1 is used to load advertisements, Frame #2 to display a menu that will be reused across all of the Web site, while Frame #3 is used to display content that will change from page to page.

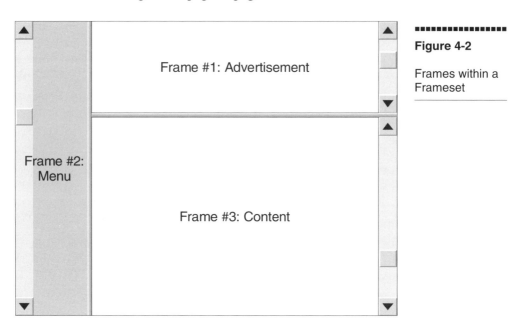

Frame #1: Advertisement

Frame #2: Menu

Frame #3: Content

Figure 4-2

Frames within a Frameset

Frames can also help conserve bandwidth by only having to update a portion of the document (a frame) instead of the entire document (a page). Refer to Figure 4-3. When implemented correctly, developers can significantly reduce the amount of data that needs to be sent for subsequent page requests, potentially reducing the bandwidth needed to refresh the page. Unfortunately, the time required to initially load a frameset is usually greater than the time required to load the same content as a single Web page. Four 20 Kbyte files, for example, may take longer to download than one 80 Kbyte file. Since a Web site that uses frames is often more complex to develop and test than a non-frames site, careful consideration should be given before using a frameset approach on your Web site.

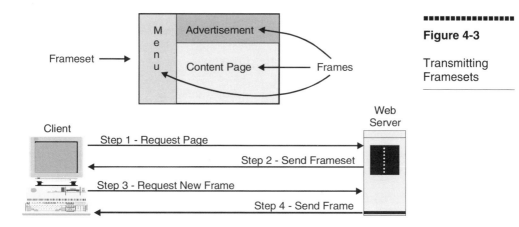

■■■■■■■■■■■■■■■■■
Figure 4-3

Transmitting
Framesets

There are several linking options that developers have available to them when using framesets. Developers may choose to link frames to internal or external Web pages via currently open or new browser windows, as illustrated in Figure 4-4.

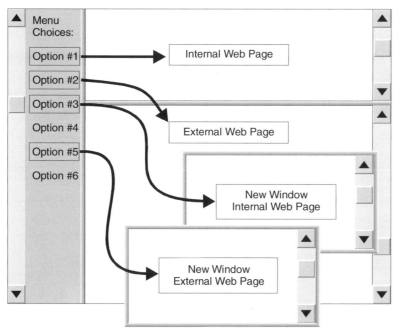

■■■■■■■■■■■■■■■■■
Figure 4-4

Frameset Linking
Options:

♦ Link to internal
  Web page via
  current window
♦ Link to external
  Web page via
  current window
♦ Link to internal
  Web page via
  new window
♦ Link to external
  Web page via
  new window

Framesets that are contained inside other framesets are called *nested framesets*. This technique is useful when a Web page contains a significant amount of related information that must be displayed simultaneously within a single browser window. There are few Web sites that can justify using nested frames, because the amount of screen real estate that's available is usually too small to be useful. Inline or floating frames are another variation of frames, developed by Microsoft, that enable a scrollable frame to be placed anywhere within an HTML document.

All of these frame types can be designed to be a fixed size or resizable. Resizable frames help accommodate the needs of visitors with various screen resolutions and monitor sizes, but can cause havoc in the layout of a frame. In theory, frames provide developers with great flexibility in user interface design. In practice, however, frames can be the source of many potential problems. Table 4-6 lists the test cases that B&D used for validating their framesets.

Table 4-6   B&D's Frameset Testing Checklist

		Using the browsers that most of B&D's clients have
Pass	Fail	Description
☐	☐	Pages using framesets are displayed correctly.
☐	☐	Frames are not resizable.
☐	☐	Pages within the frameset can be bookmarked.
☐	☐	The Back button recalls the URL of the last frame viewed.
☐	☐	The initial frameset is downloaded in an acceptable period of time.
☐	☐	Pages using framesets can be printed correctly or an alternative page is available for printing.
☐	☐	Nested framesets (if used) have sufficient screen real estate assigned to each frame.
☐	☐	All external links launch new browser windows (i.e., third party Web sites are not embedded inside a B&D frameset).
☐	☐	Search engines can find all of the content within the framesets.

Unfortunately, most of the tests listed in Table 4-4 failed. Consequently, B&D decided to abandon their initial frames-based Web site and redesigned their site using a non-frames architecture. While testing the frames version of the Web site, one additional drawback was noted. Frames use a slightly different navigational model that requires visitors to alter their navigation skills and behaviors to varying degrees and, consequently, creates a usability issue.

Site Reorganization ■■■■■

As a Web site grows (i.e., more pages and links are added), the original site structure can become disorganized and subsequently harder to navigate. The problem is that from day to day the site looks pretty much the same. The usability degradation is so gradual that it's often not even noticed by frequent users of the site, including developers and testers.

In an ideal world, a Web site's life cycle might include input from various departments within an organization. Marketing would determine what type of information the Web site should contain. A Library Engineer (or Library Scientist) would design the high-level information capture and retrieval mechanism. Legal, Public Relations, and Senior Management would review the proposed design and ensure that the Web site fits in with any and all corporate policies and budgets. Development would create a detailed design and then build the Web site. The Testing Team would then ensure that all of the stated (and implied) requirements have been met. Customer Support would provide a feedback mechanism to ensure that the Web site is improved appropriately. Unfortunately, this lifecycle (especially the Library Engineer step) is rarely implemented. From a navigational perspective, this is partly why many Web sites don't scale well.

Typically, after a number of months' worth of uncontrolled growth, a Web site will be in need of a major overhaul. The Q/A analyst should be able to decide when a site has reached this critical point, and recommend an overhaul. One technique to help determine the degree of disorganization is to ask a first-time user to try to find a particular piece of information on the Web site under test. The greater the number of clicks needed to locate the required piece of information (page scrolling counts as a single click), the more disorganized the Web site. Tools such as LinkBot from Watchfire (watchfire.com) will visually depict the navigational distance that each Web page resides from its Home (or starting) page. In other words, LinkBot shows you how deep a Web page is buried in the site. Some of the more sophisticated Web log analyzers are able to identify which page a visitor was on when he or she left your Web site. Web pages with unusually high percentages of "quitters" may indicate that something is wrong with the page. Slow performance, poor usability, and bad presentation are all valid reasons for leaving a Web site, and warrant closer inspection or additional testing.

Intranets often deal with large amounts of information created and maintained by multiple departments. The challenge of trying to manage this information so that it's "findable" resembles the challenges faced by large libraries. Correspondingly, solutions to this problem can be found in the science of Information Management. Consider, for example, the Web site for the Institute of Electrical and Electronics Engineers (IEEE.org). The original IEEE Web site grew over a period of six years to a point where it was out of control. The site was cluttered with inappropriate, redundant, and broken links. During 1998 and 1999, the IEEE overhauled their Web site and reduced the number of files by half. The new site is faster, more

■■■■■■■■■■■■■■■■■

Did you know...

The IEEE Internet reference site (IEEE.org) has over 500,000 articles from more than 250,000 authors. Before the launch of the reference site, the articles were only available as a boxed set of 450 CD-ROMs.

user-friendly, and has policies in place to control and better manage future growth.

Navigational efficiency is concerned with ensuring that a user only has to download the minimum number of Web pages necessary in order to accomplish a particular task. Typically, the easiest way to ascertain whether your Web site has an optimal navigational design is to directly compare your Web site with several competitors (or comparable) Web sites and count the number of pages needed to perform the same common task from each site. As an example, consider two Web sites, B&D and a competitor (Bad-Trade.com). Both Web sites perform the same function: they handle online stock trades. However, one Web site may allow the user to navigate its pages more efficiently than the other. B&D's Web site in Figure 4-5 illustrates a more efficient sequence of navigation than Bad-Trade's Web site because the Bad-Trade user must go through two additional steps before reaching the destination page.

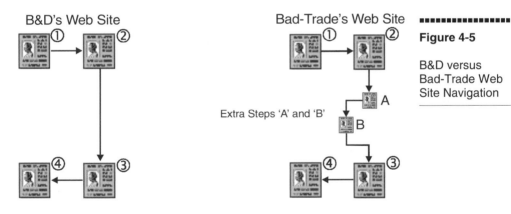

Figure 4-5

B&D versus Bad-Trade Web Site Navigation

Unfortunately, automated tools can't check for navigational efficiency, so manual checks are still needed. From a usability and/or performance perspective, the online investor using Bad-Trade's Web site must navigate six (6) Web pages, compared to B&D's Web site which only needed to display four (4) Web pages to accomplish the same task. Obviously, waiting for six Web pages to download will take significantly longer than waiting for four pages and requires additional hardware, system software licenses, and network bandwidth on the server-side. While it may not be possible to exactly replicate a superior design of another Web site (e.g., for copyright reasons), there's no reason why an industry leader can't be used as a yardstick or benchmark for evaluating the effectiveness of your own Web site.

Table 4-7 lists some of the test cases that B&D executed in order to determine if their Web site needed to be reorganized.

Table 4-7 B&D's Site Organization Testing Checklist

		Does your Web site need to be reorganized?
Pass	Fail	Description
☐	☐	"Core" Web pages can be located within four (4) clicks. B&D's Marketing department has determined that anything more than four clicks may result in losing potential customers.
☐	☐	All Web pages on the Web site can be found by casually browsing the Web site (i.e., no need to resort to a site map or search engine).
☐	☐	Information on the Web site can be found by using the search strategies that a B&D visitor might consider (e.g., stock ticker symbols, company names, and B&D product names).
☐	☐	The Web site does not contain any orphaned files (i.e., files that cannot be reached by following any path from the Home page).
☐	☐	B&D's Web site uses the same or fewer pages than their competitors in order to accomplish the same tasks.

Site Maps　■ ■ ■ ■ ■

Any reasonably sized Web site is typically going to use a site map as a means of improving site navigation. The challenge is to make sure that the site map stays current with the actual page paths available. Figure 4-6 shows the site map for B&D's Web site.

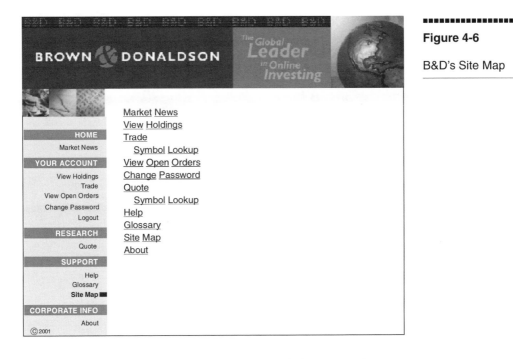

■ ■ ■ ■ ■ ■ ■ ■ ■ ■ ■ ■ ■ ■ ■ ■

Figure 4-6

B&D's Site Map

The site map simply shows the hierarchy of the pages that are available within the Web site. While the structure of the site may seem obvious to developers and testers, it may not be as apparent to visitors who are less familiar with your Web site. Therefore, it's important to include test cases (Table 4-8) to ensure that your Web site's map remains accurate.

Table 4-8 B&D's Web Site Map Testing Checklist

		Web Site Map Validation
Pass	Fail	Description
☐	☐	All "core" Web pages can be found using the site map.
☐	☐	Only "core" Web pages are listed on the site map.
☐	☐	Web pages are listed in an appropriate order/hierarchy.
☐	☐	Links are all functional and go to the correct pages.

Internal Search Engines ■■■■■

Internal search engines can help visitors locate specific information within your Web site. Figure 4-7, for example, shows B&D's internal search engine for finding the correct ticker symbol for a particular stock.

Figure 4-7

B&D's Stock Symbol Search Dialog

Table 4-9 lists the test cases that B&D used to validate that their internal search engine worked correctly under normal loads. Then, the team repeated these tests while the Web site was experiencing stressful workloads. Search engines tend to require more resources than many other transactions and, as such, are often one of the first categories of transactions to deteriorate when a Web site experiences an increase in workload.

Table 4-9   B&D's Internal Search Engine Testing Checklist

		Validate accuracy and performance under normal and stress loads.
Pass	Fail	Description
☐	☐	The first set of results is returned within 5 seconds (excluding Internet transmission times).
☐	☐	The result set is sorted appropriately (e.g., alphabetical or by % likelihood).
☐	☐	The search engine functions correctly when a user enters common words that are likely to generate a huge number of hits such as "the," "a," or "B&D."
☐	☐	The search engine functions correctly when a user enters non-existent words that are unlikely to generate any valid answers such as "sdhjfhsf," or "dhfkd," or null requests.
☐	☐	The search engine ignores the source code used to build a Web page and only indexes the content of the Web page (e.g., requesting information on "JavaScript" will only return documents that reference JavaScript, not all of the Web pages that use JavaScript in their source code).
☐	☐	The search engine does not index sensitive words such as "secret," or "fraud," or competitors' names.
☐	☐	The search engine functions correctly when you enter a search string with the maximum number of characters and a word with the maximum number of characters plus one.
☐	☐	The search engine functions correctly when you enter multiple word requests, with and without the Boolean operators "and," "or," "not," "+," and "-."
☐	☐	The search engine functions correctly when you enter one or more wildcards.
☐	☐	If fuzzy logic is enabled, the search engine offers alternate suggestions for zero hit requests based on searches using a spell-checked version of the initial search string.

Navigational Documentation ■ ■ ■ ■ ■

All too often, the people assigned the responsibility of testing a Web site's navigation are not provided with accurate up-to-date navigational specifications. In many cases, such documentation may be non-existent. If you find yourself in this situation, consider using one or more of following notations to document the core parts of your Web site before starting your navigational testing. Having an accurate navigational "road map" for a Web site will make it easier to perform all categories of testing, not just navigational testing.

Site Navigation Diagram

Navigational tests can be performed before the pages that will make up a Web site have even been coded. By using information gathered during the analysis phase of the project (e.g., use case scenarios, mocked-up page layouts, etc.), it's possible to identify a Web site's navigational requirements. Each use case scenario can be stepped through, identifying which Web page will be needed in order for the user to accomplish each action. This creates a "Storyboard" of pages that illustrate the navigational path that a user would be expected to traverse through the Web site.

Figure 4-8 shows how each navigation action can be expressed as a sequence of Web page links. Solid lines are used to indicate actions initiated by the user, while dotted lines indicate automatic actions. At this stage in a Web site's development, site navigation testing is primarily concerned with ensuring that movement from one page to another is convenient and natural, and that the total number of pages fetched is kept to a minimum.

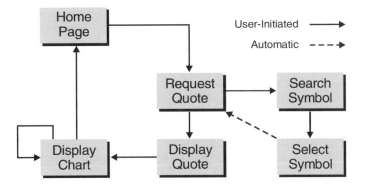

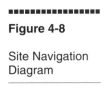

Figure 4-8

Site Navigation
Diagram

Using the Web site navigation diagram and a Web site prototype (storyboard, or the actual code if available), you can explore and evaluate alternative navigation paths. If navigation is clumsy and the task is high-volume and/or time-critical, you should consider requesting that the Web site structure be redesigned. In addition to identifying clumsy or long-winded navigational paths, performing such an exercise may help you discover pages that are not likely to be visited (e.g., functionally orphaned pages). Boxes with no arrows going into them, for example, are candidates for removal. Paths that are too long should be replaced with more direct routes.

A comprehensive Web site navigation map can be built before the Web site has even been coded by stepping through all of the potential use case scenarios for the Web site. This final map is a composite of all of the possible page navigation steps that a visitor might need. Site navigation diagrams work well for Web sites with up to 20 pages. Beyond this point, unless the Web site is extremely hierarchical, the diagram can begin to look like a bowl of spaghetti.

Site Navigation Matrix

For larger, non-hierarchical Web sites, a navigation matrix may prove to be more valuable than a navigation diagram. Consider Figure 4-9, for example. All of the links (i.e., pages) in a Web site are listed across the top of the matrix and along the left side of the matrix. Checkmarks indicate the pages that can be accessed when a visitor navigates *from* the pages listed along the left side of the matrix *to* the pages listed across the top of the matrix. Links within the same page are not considered on the matrix and are indicated by the "no entry" symbols.

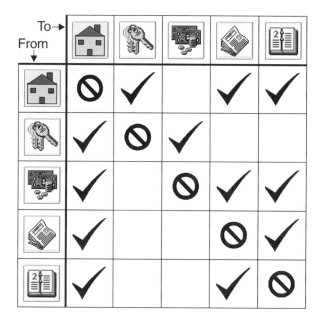

Figure 4-9

Site Navigation Matrix

A site navigation matrix typically works well for Web sites that contain up to 100 pages. Beyond this point, matrices typically become too sparse and time-consuming to accurately maintain.

Site Function Map

A site function map (Figure 4-10) outlines the significant elements and functions that make up a Web page and integrates the main navigational paths used throughout the Web site. The issues (i.e., potential defects) associated with each Web page are also identified and listed on the map.

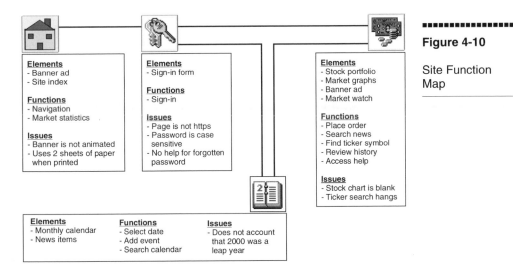

Figure 4-10

Site Function Map

Elements
- Banner ad
- Site index

Functions
- Navigation
- Market statistics

Issues
- Banner is not animated
- Uses 2 sheets of paper when printed

Elements
- Sign-in form

Functions
- Sign-in

Issues
- Page is not https
- Password is case sensitive
- No help for forgotten password

Elements
- Stock portfolio
- Market graphs
- Banner ad
- Market watch

Functions
- Place order
- Search news
- Find ticker symbol
- Review history
- Access help

Issues
- Stock chart is blank
- Ticker search hangs

Elements
- Monthly calendar
- News items

Functions
- Select date
- Add event
- Search calendar

Issues
- Does not account that 2000 was a leap year

A site function map can be used to document your Web site's requirements, but can be extremely time consuming to produce. This format represents the *"crème de la crème"* of layouts. Unfortunately, due to Web Time constraints this format is generally only practical for documenting small, critical portions of a Web site.

Site Navigation Tools ■■■■■

Once a Web site grows to contain more than 100 pages, manually developing and maintaining site navigation documentation typically becomes too time-consuming. Even for Web sites with less than 100 pages, you should consider investing in a tool or service that can check the links of your Web site and also generate supporting navigational documentation. Table 4-10 lists some of the tools and services that B&D evaluated.

Table 4-10   Sample Site Navigation Testing Tools and Services

Vendor	Product
Coast Software (coast.com)	WebMaster
Compuware (compuware.com)	WebCheck
Cyrano (cyrano.com)	WebTester
Ixacta Visual Software (ixacta.com)	Ixsite Web Analyzer
Mercury Interactive (merc-int.com)	Astra SiteManager
Microsoft (microsoft.com)	FrontPage & Site Server
NetMechanic (netmechanic.com)	HTML Toolbox
Rational (rational.com)	Team Test
RSW (rswsoftware.com)	e-Test Suite
Watchfire (watchfire.com)	Linkbot

Microsoft's FrontPage, for example, shows not only all of the outbound links from the selected Web page, but also the inbound links from other Web pages. This can be particularly useful when trying to investigate hard-to-recreate incidents. While not specifically designed for this purpose, many development tools (e.g., FrontPage) and site management tools (e.g., Site Server) provide basic link checkers.

Site mapping tools work best when mapping non-dynamic (i.e., static) Web sites that use different URLs for each of their pages. Web sites that build their pages dynamically, based on the requests received from the visitor, potentially have an unlimited number of pages and are poor candidates for automated tools. Figure 4-11 illustrates some of the different types of links that you may encounter: cyclic, return, frameset, dynamic, and duplicate links.

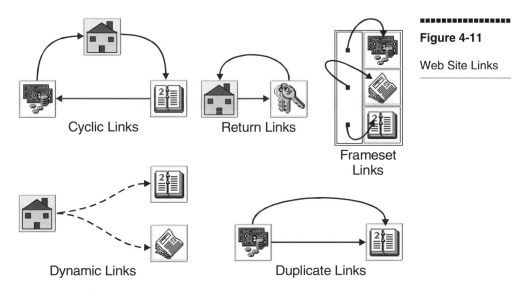

Figure 4-11

Web Site Links

Cyclic Links

Return Links

Frameset Links

Dynamic Links

Duplicate Links

Since many Web sites don't use a hierarchical site structure, but a network site structure, any mapping tool (or manual notation) that you use should be able to deal with the possibility of link recursion. Recursive links occur when Web page 'A' links to page 'B', which links to page 'A', or in a more complicated instance Web page 'A' links to page 'B', which links to page 'C', which links back to page 'A'. A variation of this problem occurs when one page has two links to the same page – some tools may only test the first link.

Many link-checking tools exist to search for broken links. Some of these tools use a modified "binary tree" search to "spider" through the entire Web site. If your tool uses this approach, it may only check the link "one way." Bi-directional links may not be checked, so if page 'A' is linked to page 'B' and page 'B' is linked back to page 'A', the tool may only transverse one of these links. If your tool exhibits this feature, consider using different starting points, not just the Home page. In the extreme case, every page could be used as a starting point for the searches. Some link-checking tools are unable to handle framesets. Instead of regarding each frame as a separate page, they consider the entire frameset to be a single page and don't check all of the frameset's links.

Some link-checking tools are better at handling dynamic Web sites than others. Some tools are able to scan the HTML source code (if available) on the server rather than the dynamically generated HTML code served up to the browser. However, even this approach isn't perfect, because some servers (e.g., Lotus Domino) use binary code as opposed to HTML or some Web pages may use run-time variables as part of a navigational link.

Some sites require their clients to log in before being granted access to the content of a Web site. In order to maintain a session between the Web server and the login client, the Web site may use a number of different techniques including session cookies or user-ids embedded in a URL. If your site requires a user to enter some sort of data in order to access some (or all) of the Web pages on your site, you should confirm that any link-checking tool you are evaluating is compatible with the particular techniques being employed in your Web site.

Automated test tools are not able to check to see if a link actually goes to the right content (e.g., the "Trade" link goes to the "Trading" page and not the "Glossary" page). Consequently, this sort of checking must still be performed manually. In addition to checking the return code (e.g., 404 error) generated by the Web server, some tools check the page size returned by the Web server for suspiciously small files. An extremely small file may be indicative of a customized "page not found" type message. Most link-checking tools don't differentiate between relative and absolute links. However, some tools produce a post-scan report that lists all of the links that were found. This report can be reviewed to determine whether or not any absolute internal links were used. Remember that absolute internal links are generally considered undesirable.

When evaluating a link-checking tool, consider running a series of tests to determine what types of links the tool is able to handle. Table 4-11 lists the checks that B&D ran while evaluating various link-checking tools.

Table 4-11   B&D's Link-Checking Tool Evaluation Checklist

		Tool Checks
Pass	Fail	Description
☐	☐	External links can be checked but (optionally) not scanned any further. No need to check the internal links of another organization's Web site.
☐	☐	When encountering a recursive loop, the tool does not go into a "death-spiral."
☐	☐	The tool does not ignore duplicate links.
☐	☐	The tool is able to handle dynamic links.
☐	☐	The tool is able to handle framesets. Since B&D has currently decided not to implement framesets, this test case will be skipped.
☐	☐	The tool is able to handle cookies (session and/or persistent).
☐	☐	The tool can handle pages that require user input (e.g., forms).
☐	☐	The tool facilitates identifying suspiciously small or large pages.
☐	☐	The tool facilitates identifying absolute links.
☐	☐	The tool facilitates identifying pages that are too deep.

Useful URLs ■■■■■

Table 4-12 Useful Web Sites

Web Site URLs	Description of Services
download.com, freeware32.com, shareware.com, softseek.com, and tucows.com	Text scanning tools.
coast.com, compuware.com, cyrano.com, ixacta.com, merc-int.com, microsoft.com, netmechanic.com, rational.com, rswsoftware.com, and watchfire.com	Site navigation tools and services.
sqe.com/bdonline/	Case study Web site and downloadable test plans.

Chapter 5 – User Interaction

The combination of more sophisticated user demands and rapid improvements in technology is a key force driving the changes in transactional Web sites. Users are better educated, have higher expectations, and have less time and more pressure to accomplish tasks. They know what's possible through Web technology and they expect nothing less than the best. Corporations in the twenty-first century may gradually transform themselves into virtual organizations, as a significant portion of their activities will take place over the Internet. The physical constraints of traditional offices and manufacturing facilities may become insignificant. Automobile manufacturers, for example, may build their new cars using virtual teams of designers, engineers, and other personnel located anywhere in the world and linked together electronically through a high-tech CAD/CAM video conferencing virtual environment. Sales teams will be augmented with computers that can "dazzle" customers with fancy presentations before the sales people step in (online, of course) to close the deal.

The advent of client-side scripting languages and dynamic Web pages provides developers with the tools they need to improve the interactive experience between users and computers. Forms, for example, allow users to submit almost any type of information to a Web server for immediate processing. Customers have the ability to enter and submit credit card information, and initiate and track product shipments. While there are many benefits to providing users with the ability to manage their own transactions, there are also many potential problems. Adding such flexibility makes the data processing on the client and the server more complicated, which consequently

■■■■■■■■■■■■■■■■■

Case Study

Review the following *Case Study Test Plans* to see an example of how the topics covered in this chapter can be utilized to test a Web site:

• Unit
• System

Visit:
sqe.com/bdonline/

necessitates more testing. This chapter focuses on the challenges of testing the Web technologies that are being utilized to implement user interactions (or online functionality).

Forms ■■■■■

Forms are formatted documents that contain blank fields, which users can fill in with data. The data may contain almost anything from contact information to medical or credit history, depending on the purpose of the form. The data is then sent to the Web server for processing and the results are displayed on the client computer, as illustrated in Figure 5-1.

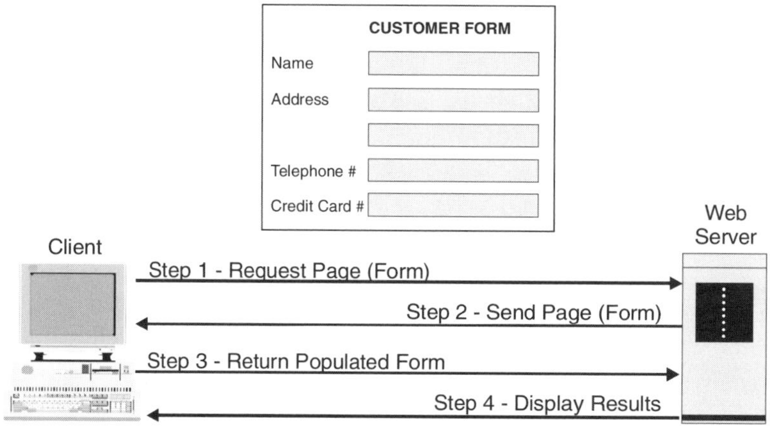

Figure 5-1

Typical Steps in Processing a Form

Forms provide a convenient and effective method of interaction between your Web site and its visitors. Automobile dealerships use forms on their Web sites to allow potential customers to "build" the perfect car. Customers can select everything from paint color to stereo components and calculate the total cost of the vehicle. Forms provide customers with the ability to calculate as many "what if" scenarios as they want before making a purchase decision. All of this flexibility and power is available through the Web site, without the assistance or pressure (and added cost) of a sales person.

Electronic forms are especially common on the World Wide Web because the HTML language has built-in support for displaying form elements such as text fields and check boxes. Unfortunately, forms can cause unexpected and undesirable results if they aren't adequately tested. Using a browser's Back, Forward, Go, History, Reload or Resize buttons, for example, can cause some Web sites that use forms to become confused. Information may be lost entirely or added to the Web site's database multiple times. If a form uses a drop-down data entry field (control), you should check that the options are sorted appropriately and that the field is wide enough to display all of the options. This can be particularly problematic if the options are populated from a database instead of hard-coded by the developer who built the page.

Web application developers typically have little control over how certain keys function on a client. The developers of many browsers, for example, typically define the function of the Tab key. However, Web application developers may be able to specify the *initial* field/control that the browser will place the cursor on when the Web page is first displayed and the order in which the browser should tab through input fields. This is useful when you want to direct the user to enter information in a specific field, or draw the user's attention to a particular location on the page.

There are two possible *methods* (GET or POST) by which information can be transmitted from the form on the Web page back to the server. If the form's data is sent back to the Web server using the HTTP GET command, you should check that the data is not truncated. The GET command appends the data to the URL and is, therefore, subject to a finite length. The HTTP POST command, on the other hand, transmits the data from the form after the URL and header information is sent to the server, and is not subject to the same size limitations as the GET command. When the server sees the word POST, it knows that the data will immediately follow. The POST command is the preferred method of data transfer according to the World Wide Web Consortium (W3C.org).

B&D used the test cases listed in Table 5-1 to validate the forms used on their Web site (some of which also appear in B&D's Navigational Checklists). Your Web site may require additional test cases depending on the nature of the data being captured on your forms.

Table 5-1 B&D's Form Testing Checklist

Pass	Fail	Description
Validating Forms on a Web Site		
☐	☐	All data entry fields have the HTML SIZE attribute set correctly (SIZE is used to specify the width of the field).
☐	☐	All data entry fields have the HTML MAXLENGTH attribute set correctly (MAXLENGTH is used to specify the maximum number of characters a user can enter).
☐	☐	If Radio controls are used, a default is always selected.
☐	☐	All required fields use a visual cue to indicate to the user that the field is mandatory.
☐	☐	If a form uses a drop-down data entry field (control), the options are sorted appropriately and the field is wide enough to display all of the options.
☐	☐	Data is not lost when the user clicks the browser's Back (and subsequently Forward) buttons midway through a series of forms.
☐	☐	Data is not lost when the user clicks the browser's Forward (and subsequently Back) buttons midway through a series of forms.
☐	☐	Data is not lost when the user clicks the Go/History buttons to revisit previous forms.

(Continued)

Table 5-1 (*Continued*)

Validating Forms on a Web Site

Pass	Fail	Description
☐	☐	Data is not lost when the user clicks the Bookmark/Favorite buttons midway through a series of forms.
☐	☐	Data is not lost when the user clicks the browser's Reload button midway through a series of forms.
☐	☐	Data is not lost when the user resizes the browser window.
☐	☐	Duplicate data is not added to the database when a user presses any combination of Forward, Back, Go/History, Bookmark/Favorite, Reload, or Resize buttons midway through a series of forms.
☐	☐	The browser places the cursor on the most appropriate field/control when the form is first viewed.
☐	☐	Using the browser's Tab key allows the client to tab through the input fields on the form in a top-to-bottom, left-to-right order.
☐	☐	If the form's data is sent back to the Web server using the HTTP GET command, the data is not truncated.

Client- vs. Server-Side Validation ■■■■■

Form data can be validated on the client-side or the server-side, depending on your Web site's requirements. Performing basic data validation checks on the client-side (e.g., browser) provides immediate feedback and allows the user to fix the problem with minimal delay.

Unfortunately the client computer might not possess enough information to be able to perform all the checks necessary to validate the data on a form (Figure 5-2). Some checks (e.g., validating a customer's credit card number) can only be performed on the server and can therefore only be checked after the form has been sent back to the server. One significant drawback of client-side validation is that the results may not be reliable. Users can turn off these checks or even modify the code used to perform the validation. By turning a browser's scripting options on and off, it's quite possible to submit invalid data to a Web site that a developer would never have considered possible and, hence, never tested for.

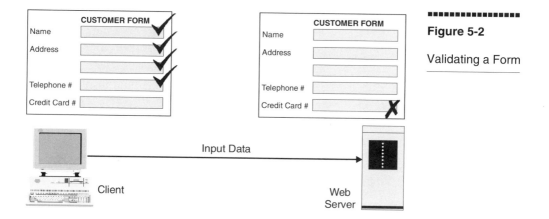

Figure 5-2

Validating a Form

From a functional perspective, the ideal situation might be to replicate all of the client-side validation checks on the server-side. This is potentially the only way to ensure that the input data is actually checked. Unfortunately, performing all these additional checks on the server can introduce new problems. An extended amount of time may be required to inform the user of a data entry error. Depending on the client's configuration, it may take 20 seconds or more to download the rejected form and error message. Another drawback is that additional Web site resources (hardware and system software) are required to run the additional validations. Finally, trying to synchronize changes in both client-side and server-side validations can pose additional configuration management problems, especially when the validations are coded in different languages by different developers.

A pragmatic design approach might involve performing as many validations as possible on the client-side and splitting the server-side validations into three steps. In the first step, all of the simple server-side-only checks are executed. In the second step, client-side re-validations are executed only if all of the checks in the first step pass. Finally, the third step contains all of the expensive (in terms of time or system resources) validations (e.g., contacting a third party to validate a credit card number), which are executed only if all of the checks in the second step pass. From a usability perspective, users typically expect the input data to be validated in a top-down, left-to-right fashion and be informed of all of their errors simultaneously, rather than one error at a time.

B&D used the test cases listed in Table 5-2 to validate the data that users entered into the forms used in the Web site. Due to the sensitive nature of the data transferred between the users and B&D's Web site, B&D decided to validate data on both the client-side and the server-side.

Table 5-2　B&D's Form Validation Checklist

		Validating Data on a Form
Pass	Fail	Description
☐	☐	All data entry fields are checked for invalid data. An appropriate error message is displayed if the data is found to be invalid.
☐	☐	All validations are performed (and error messages displayed) in a top-down, left-to-right fashion.
☐	☐	All required fields are checked on the client-side.
☐	☐	Wherever possible, all field co-dependencies are checked on the client-side. If, for example, the user places a trade that is a "limit" order, the system checks that a value has been entered for the price. Otherwise, this field should be blank.
☐	☐	All basic data formatting checks are performed on the client-side.
☐	☐	All client-side checks are re-checked on the server-side.

Client-Side Scripting ■■■■■

A script is a list of commands that can be executed without user interaction. Some languages were conceived expressly as scripting languages. In the context of the Web, JavaScript, VBScript, and similar script languages were specifically developed to handle forms and other client-side features. Scripting languages are often easier and faster to code than some of the more structured, compiled languages such as C and C++ and are typically easier to port to different platforms. Scripting languages are ideal for developing simple programs that might need to run on different platforms. However, scripts typically take longer to run than an equivalent compiled program. Consequently, scripts are poor candidates for handling large, frequently executed server-side tasks.

JavaScript, originally named LiveScript, was developed by Netscape to be a client-side scripting addition to HTML. When the Java language started to gain popularity, Netscape made the marketing decision to rename LiveScript as "JavaScript." While JavaScript sounds similar to Java (the language) and shares a similar syntax, it's not the same as (or even a subset of) the Java language. Microsoft's equivalent language to Netscape's JavaScript is called JScript, which was first included in MS-IE 3.0. Microsoft also created another scripting language, Visual Basic Script (VBScript), as a subset of Microsoft's Visual Basic for Applications (VBA). Unfortunately, VBScript is currently not supported by Netscape's browsers (unless a plug-in is first installed), which makes it a poor language choice if a Web page is intended to be viewed by both MS-IE and Netscape browsers. Recently, Microsoft and Netscape have agreed to support a common scripting language in their future browsers: the European Computer Manufacturers Association Script

■■■■■■■■■■■■■■■■
Did you know...

In one classic Internet story, a hacker was able to circumvent a Web site's user id/password requirement by simply turning off JavaScript just before the login pop-up was displayed.

(ECMAScript). Unfortunately, LiveScript, JavaScript, JScript, and ECMAScript are all commonly referred to as "JavaScript."

From a testing perspective, client-side scripting presents several challenges. First and foremost, you should ensure that your company's Web site standards state the preferred language and version of scripting language to be used for client-side (and server-side) scripting. The scripting language being used is normally defined near the top of the Web page, as illustrated in Figure 5-3, and can be viewed by using the View Page Source option in a browser. While it's possible to use more than one scripting language on the same Web page, there are obvious advantages to standardizing on one.

■■■■■■■■■■■■■■■■■■
For details on the ECMA-262 ECMAScript language specification, visit:

ecma.ch

```
<SCRIPT LANGUAGE="JavaScript1.2" TYPE="text/JavaScript">
```

■■■■■■■■■■■■■■■■■■
Figure 5-3

Scripting Language Defined

Any Web page that uses JavaScript should be tested from a browser with the JavaScript option turned off to ensure that the page still provides acceptable functionality. Be aware that acceptable functionality may mean displaying a message that tells the user that the Web page cannot be displayed correctly without changing the JavaScript settings or upgrading to a newer browser. A JavaScript that contains incorrectly formatted HTML syntax will often appear on the browser screen as poorly formatted text. This means that the browser has mistakenly interpreted the JavaScript as text instead of code.

When trying to develop test cases, ask the developer of the Web page being tested to provide a list of the Web page controls that utilize a client-side script. This information will help you develop effective test cases and help ensure that all of the client-side scripts used by your Web site are adequately tested.

Dynamic HTML

Dynamic HTML (DHTML) is a marketing term used by Microsoft and Netscape to refer to a Web page that appears to behave dynamically after it's downloaded by the browser. This is typically accomplished using client-side scripts (e.g., JavaScript or VBScript) to manipulate the objects that the browser has already downloaded and/or the Cascading Style Sheet (CSS) used to present these objects. One of the advantages of using CSS is that their properties can be changed after the Web page is initially posted to the screen. Unfortunately, Microsoft and Netscape use different names for the various objects (e.g., form, frame, image, or window) that you might find on a Web page. Netscape, for example, refers to an object's position as *left* and *top*, while Microsoft calls the same properties *pixelleft* and *pixeltop*. In other words, Microsoft and Netscape currently have different Document Object Models (DOM).

Early DOM implementations only allowed limited access to some Web page elements. As the technology evolved, however, more elements were included in the DOM. Unfortunately, Microsoft and Netscape chose to implement these models differently, thereby making it difficult and tedious to develop DHTML documents that work consistently on both sets of browsers.

Having two different DOMs means that a developer either has to develop a Web page knowing that it will only work on one platform, or code the page twice (once for each platform). Developers must create two sets of JavaScript functions in order for the Web page to function correctly in both MS-IE 4.0+ and Netscape 4.0+. Another point to consider is that DHTML is not

Did you know...

Document Object Model (DOM) refers to the attributes that each browser uses to describe the objects on a Web page.

IBM (alphaworks.IBM. com) offers a tool called DirectDom, which allows a developer to generate client-side scripts that manipulate the content of W3C DOM compliant Web pages. IBM refers to these scripts as Weblets.

supported by older versions of browsers. However, there are also many advantages to using DHTML. DHTML files are relatively small in comparison with other dynamic media such as Flash or Shockwave and they don't require the user to download special plug-ins. And, the W3C (W3C.org) is currently implementing a standard for DHTML. Table 5-3 lists the test cases that B&D used to check their DHTML Web pages.

Table 5-3 B&D's DHTML Testing Checklist

		Validating DHTML Web Pages
Pass	Fail	Description
☐	☐	DHTML is appropriate for this Web site because the majority of visitors use MS-IE 4.0+ or Netscape 4.0+.
☐	☐	All of the DHTML code used in the Web site conforms to the W3C DHTML standard.
☐	☐	Pages that contain DHTML code are displayed correctly when viewed through MS-IE 4.0 or higher.
☐	☐	Pages that contain DHTML code are displayed correctly when viewed through Netscape 4.0 or higher.

Client-Side Pop-Ups ■■■■■

Small pop-up windows can be used in a variety of ways on a Web page. Pop-ups can be used to present a dialog box for entering a user id/password or to allow a user to enter search criteria that will be used to populate information on the parent window. Usually these pop-ups are relatively small, so that the majority of the parent window (Web page) is still visible. Simple pop-ups are typically written in JavaScript and transmitted within the HTML of the parent Web page. More sophisticated pop-ups may be downloaded as Java applets or ActiveX controls.

The *Emerging Technologies* chapter provides more details on Java applets and ActiveX controls.

Your Web site standards should specify whether pop-ups are allowed and, if so, which options should be utilized. Tool bars, for example, can provide standard browser functions such as Forward, Back, Reload, and Print. A status bar can be appended to the bottom of the pop-up to provide the user with pertinent information. Scroll bars can be used to move the contents of the page horizontally or vertically. Pop-ups can also be resizable, allowing the user to adjust the size of the window.

One design decision that has to be made when using pop-ups is which Graphical User Interface (GUI) standard should be followed. For example, pop-ups may follow the organization's Web GUI (e.g., Back, Forward, etc.) or the Windows/P.C. GUI (e.g., File, Help) standard. Usability experts generally advise that the GUI be kept consistent. Therefore, you may want to ensure that Web page pop-ups have the same basic look and feel as their parent window (i.e., the browser). Java application pop-ups, on the other hand, might look like a regular Windows/P.C. pop-up in the event that the parent Java application utilizes a classic Windows GUI.

Table 5-4 lists some of B&D's pop-up test cases.

Table 5-4 B&D's Pop-Up Window Testing Checklist

Validating Pop-Ups		
Pass	Fail	Description
☐	☐	The Web site is able to detect a browser that has disabled (or does not support) JavaScript/Java/ActiveX and provides the user with an appropriate message.
☐	☐	The pop-up follows B&D's Web GUI standard (as opposed to B&D's Windows/PC standard).
☐	☐	The pop-up is not too large for the parent window and its initial screen positioning is appropriate.

Streaming Content ■■■■■

The Internet was originally conceived around the "pull" concept (Figure 5-4), whereby a browser must ask for a Web page before a Web server actually sends it. Using the "push" model, on the other hand, the Web server doesn't wait for a browser to request a page or refresh the current page. Instead, the Web server automatically pushes the page to the browser. Consider, for example, an online investor who owns stock in Dell Computer Corporation. The investor may want the B&D Web site to send (i.e., push) an update whenever Dell makes a press release. A day trader, on the other hand, may want the Web site to send (i.e., push) streaming quotes instead of manually having to request a stock price update every few seconds.

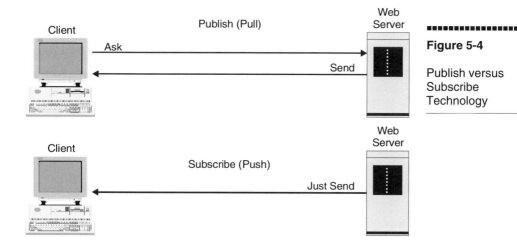

■■■■■■■■■■■■■■■■■

Figure 5-4

Publish versus Subscribe Technology

While "push" technology has some advantages over "pull," it also has two significant drawbacks. In order to take advantage of "push" technology, viewers must be logged on to the Internet. The "push" model typically works in organizations where employees have continuous access to the Internet. However, this model is not as effective for occasional users who dial into an ISP every few days to retrieve their e-mail. Another drawback of "push" technology is its insatiable need for bandwidth. Network administrators and Webmasters generally don't like applications that soak up network bandwidth, and often put blocks on Web sites that use "push" technology. Web sites that push non-business-related information such as baseball scores or real-time stock quotes are often the first to be blocked.

A common implementation of "push" technology is Microsoft's Active Channel technology, which allows developers to deliver or push content directly to items on a user's Active Desktop. Active Desktop items are small Web pages or components, such as Java applets or ActiveX controls, which are displayed directly on the Windows desktop. The content of each Active Channel is described in a Channel Definition Format (CDF) file. The CDF file is an XML-based data format that defines a hierarchy of Web pages included in the channel, how each item will be used or displayed, and when the channel should be updated.

■■■■■■■■■■■■■■■■■
For more information on "push" technology, visit:

entrypoint.com, graham.com, marimba.com, MSN.com and real.com.

If your Web site uses "push" technology, you should consider including a representative client-side network in your system test environment. This can help ensure that your Web application doesn't noticeably increase traffic on the receiving network. In general, performance testing tools generate the test load using the "pull" concept. If your Web site uses "push" technology, you may have to consider an alternate strategy to entice the Web server to generate the desired amount of "push" traffic.

Table 5-5 lists some of B&D's test cases that were used to validate the Web site's streaming quotes feature.

Table 5-5   B&D's Streaming Content Checklist

		Streaming Quotes
Pass	Fail	Description
☐	☐	Quotes are up-to-date and are no more than 1 minute old, 99% of the time.
☐	☐	The streaming quote server and network is able to handle the expected demand for this service.
☐	☐	Clients are able to suspend/restart this service without needing to unsubscribe/re-subscribe.
☐	☐	Clients are able to adjust the frequency of the updates to cater to different client-side bandwidths.

Common Gateway Interface (CGI)   ■ ■ ■ ■ ■

The Common Gateway Interface (CGI) is a standard method by which a Web server can pass information between a user and an application. When a user requests a Web page, for example, the Web server simply sends back the requested page. However, when a user fills out a form on a Web page, the information on the form usually needs to be processed by an application. The Web server typically passes the information from the form to the application via a CGI script, as illustrated in Figure 5-5.

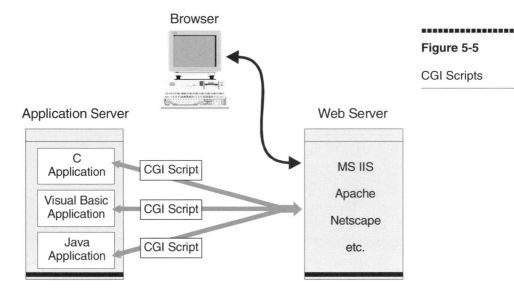

Browser

Application Server

Web Server

C Application

CGI Script

Visual Basic Application

CGI Script

Java Application

CGI Script

MS IIS

Apache

Netscape

etc.

Figure 5-5

CGI Scripts

This method of passing data back and forth between the Web server and the application is called the Common Gateway Interface (CGI). It's important to understand that CGI is a protocol, not a language. A CGI script may be written in a compiled language such as C or a scripting language such as Perl. Other less common server-side scripting languages include Python, Shell, and Awk. Regardless of what language it's written in, a script that uses the CGI protocol allows a Web server to communicate (i.e., pass data) with another application, possibly running on another server.

CGI scripts can receive input from a Web server through a variety of channels including standard input, environmental variables, and command line arguments. Many hardware/system software platforms allow Web servers to "pipe" information to CGI scripts via a standard input device such as a keyboard or mouse. Information can also be made available to CGI scripts through environmental variables. Environmental variables are bits of information that the operating system or server always

Did you know...

A 2000 survey conducted by the Cutter Consortium (cutter.com) found that of 134 companies worldwide:

* 49% had production systems written in Visual Basic
* 40% written in Java
* 34% written in C++
* 27% written in C

keeps track of and makes available for CGI scripts to use. Command-line parameters provide the third method by which information can be passed to CGI scripts. Regardless of the data input method, the CGI script should be robust enough to handle unexpected input. All too often, CGI scripts aren't set up correctly to handle error conditions. A combination of inspections and destructive testing should be used to ensure that each CGI script is robust enough to handle errors correctly.

There are also performance considerations to be aware of when testing CGI scripts. Each time a visitor requests a CGI script to run, a unique copy of the script is loaded into memory unless your server is using a Transaction Processing (TP) monitor such as Microsoft's ISAPI. A TP monitor can be used to manage online access to a database and ensure that transactions that impact multiple tables are fully processed as a single unit. Consequently, Web servers should be checked to ensure that they have enough resources to handle several times the expected number of CGI invocations.

■■■■■■■■■■■■■■■■■
Did you know...

FastCGI (fastcgi.com) is a language-independent, scalable, open extension to CGI that provides higher CGI performance without the limitations of server-specific APIs.

CGI/Database Interaction ■■■■■

There are two basic approaches to the interaction between CGI scripts and a database, as illustrated in Figure 5-6. CGI scripts can access a database directly by embedding SQL code into the script, or an application can be used to make the database calls. The latter approach is typically more robust because applications generally have better facilities for handling unexpected and expected error conditions. When an application makes the database calls, the CGI script passes the data between the application and the Web server.

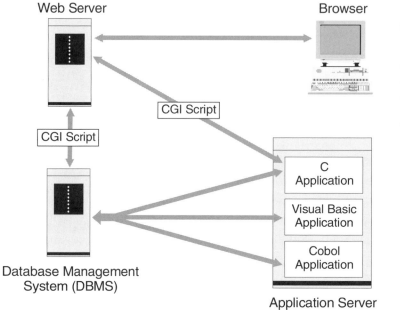

Web Server

Browser

CGI Script

CGI Script

CGI Script

C Application

Visual Basic Application

Cobol Application

Database Management System (DBMS)

Application Server

Figure 5-6

Two Approaches to CGI Script and Database Interaction

If your Web server directly accesses a database via a CGI script, you should consider constructing test cases to ensure that the CGI script is able to handle unexpected results being returned by the database. Table 5-6 lists some of the test cases that B&D used to validate their CGI scripts.

Table 5-6 B&D's CGI Script Testing Checklist

		CGI Script Validation
Pass	Fail	Description
☐	☐	The CGI script is able to parse input parameters containing quotation marks, carriage returns, ampersand symbols, hash symbols, dollar signs, question marks, and other control characters.
☐	☐	The CGI script is robust enough to handle missing and/or out-of-range input parameters.

(Continued)

Table 5-6 (*Continued*)

CGI Script Validation		
Pass	Fail	Description
☐	☐	The CGI script is robust enough to handle null values being returned from the database.
☐	☐	The CGI script is robust enough to handle a "no record found" code being returned by the database.
☐	☐	The CGI script is robust enough to handle a "duplicate record inserted" code being returned by the database.
☐	☐	The CGI script is robust enough to handle multiple records being returned by the database.
☐	☐	The CGI script is robust enough to handle a database timeout code being returned by the database.
☐	☐	The Web server has sufficient resources to handle the expected number of CGI scripts that are likely to be initiated.

Database Middleware Software ■■■■■

Middleware is a layer of utility software that resides between a Web application and the database that stores the information used by the Web site. This small but critical component becomes particularly important when the Web site is hosted by a third party Internet Service Provider (ISP) and shared with other organizations, or when an internal server is shared by multiple departments. It may not be possible to install the particular version of middleware (e.g., database driver) that your Web site was developed and tested with, because it may conflict with other Web sites that are currently being hosted on the same server. If you use a third party to host your Web site, you should find out what their policy is with regard to installing new versions of system software. Your ISP's maintenance/upgrade policies and procedures can become an important issue in the event that you need to install a particular version of a driver.

A common example of middleware is the Open Database Connectivity (ODBC) standard. ODBC was developed for and packaged with Microsoft operating systems in order to provide a simpler method of sharing data between incompatible database management systems, as illustrated in Figure 5-7. In theory, ODBC tools allow application programs to work with different DBMSs without having to be rewritten to take into consideration the nuances of and differences between these systems.

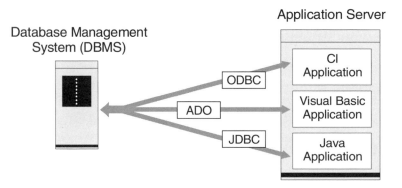

Figure 5-7

Database Middleware Software

Several other middleware standards (interface technologies) are also available. Table 5-7 lists some of the possible database access methods that your Web-based application may be using. Organizations often make decisions regarding the preferred interface technology on a project-by-project basis. Regardless of which technology your organization chooses to use, the standard should be documented in your Web site's requirements and consistently implemented in the development, system testing, and production environments.

Did you know...

Several database vendors have announced plans to provide ways to use XML to interface with their database engines.

Resolving middleware version problems can be extremely time-consuming due, in part, to the middleware interface possibly displaying inaccurate information about which version of driver is actually installed. Each of the following Microsoft products: MS Office, FrontPage, Visual Studio, Access, Visual Basic, SQL Server, and Windows, for example, may install a new (i.e., different) ODBC driver during its installation and thereby overwrite any previous version. This can cause supposedly identically configured servers to have different ODBC drivers (and consequently slightly different behaviors) simply because the various software packages were installed in a different order. To avoid this and other configuration problems, many sites use some form of "ghosting" software to copy a standard software footprint onto each new machine before it enters service.

■■■■■■■■■■■■■■■■■

Ghosting is covered in more detail in the *Compatibility* chapter.

Table 5-7 Database Access Methods

Middleware Software	Description
Open Database Connectivity (ODBC)	A standard database access method developed by Microsoft (microsoft.com) that makes it possible to access any data from any application, regardless of which database management system (DBMS) is handling the data. A middle layer called a database driver sits between the application and the DBMS. The middle layer translates the application's data queries into commands that the DBMS understands.
Java Database Connection (JDBC)	A Java application program interface (API) developed by Sun Microsystems (sun.com) that enables Java programs to execute structured query language (SQL) statements. This allows Java programs to interact with any SQL-compliant database. Consequently, JDBC makes it possible for developers to write a single database application that can run on different platforms and interact with different database management systems.
Active Database Object (ADO), also referred to as ActiveX Data Objects (ADO)	A high-level interface for data objects developed by Microsoft that can be used to access various types of data including Web pages, spreadsheets, and other types of documents.
OEM or Third Party Drivers	Varies depending on the product.

Database and Data File Testing ■■■■■

A Database Management System (DBMS) is a specialized software application used to create, access, control, and manage the information stored in a database. The core component of a DBMS is the database *engine*, which responds to specific commands to create, read, update, and delete records. Common DBMSs used on Web sites include: MS-Access (microsoft.com), DB2 (IBM.com), Informix (informix.com), Ingress (CA.com), Lotus Notes (IBM.com/lotus.com), MS-SQL Server (microsoft.com), Oracle (oracle.com), and Sybase (sybase.com). These DBMSs typically run on either UNIX or Windows NT/2000 platforms. However, Oracle currently offers a special version of Oracle 8i that doesn't require a traditional operating system such as UNIX or Windows NT. Instead, Oracle 8i includes a pseudo operating system called Appliance Server that provides the run-time environment for the program. Many of the DBMS vendors have also produced hybrid Web server/DBMS systems. That is, the DBMS is able to handle basic Web server duties such as processing HTTP requests. By combining the two products into one, more system resources are available for the DBMS to use.

Web sites don't have to use databases to store information. Some Web sites may utilize a basic file server, a Network File System (NFS), or a Storage Area Network (SAN) to store and retrieve information. An NFS is a client-server application that lets a user view, store, and update files on a server as though the files were located on the client computer. Using NFS, the user or system administrator can mount (i.e., designate as accessible) all or part of a file system, which is a portion of the hierarchical tree in any file directory and subdirectory on a computer. The mounted portion of the file system can be accessed with whatever privileges (e.g., read-only or read-write) are assigned to each file. The user's computer needs to have an NFS client and TCP/IP protocol installed in order to send files and updates back and forth. NFS was developed by Sun Microsystems (sun.com) and has become a file server standard. NFS has also been extended to the Internet with WebNFS, a product and proposed standard that is now part of Netscape's browser. WebNFS offers what Sun believes to be a faster way to access Web pages and other Internet files.

A Storage Area Network (SAN) is a high-speed special-purpose network used to transfer data between computer systems and various storage devices. A SAN consists of a communications infrastructure, which provides the hardware and software interconnections needed to organize the storage devices and computer systems for secure and robust data transfer. SANs can support disk mirroring, data backup and restoration, data archive and retrieval, data migration from one storage device to another, and the sharing of data among different servers in a network. SAN technology is available from Veritas (veritas.com), IBM (IBM.com), EMC (EMC.com), and several other companies.

Regardless of whether your Web site uses a DBMS, file server, NFS, SAN, or hybrid to store and retrieve data, you should consider designing and executing self-verifying test scripts to confirm the integrity of the database or file. A self-verifying test script should be able to insert a record, update the same record, query the record (to compare all of the fields and ensure that the update actually occurred), and then delete the record. Table 5-8 lists B&D's data integrity tests cases for a single self-verifying test script.

■■■■■■■■■■■■■■■■■
Did you know...

"Super-caching" refers to the technique of loading an entire database into RAM in order to allow ultra-fast database access.

Unfortunately, this technique is generally only feasible for smaller databases.

Table 5-8 B&D's Database/File Integrity Testing Checklist

Data Integrity Validation		
Pass	Fail	Description
☐	☐	A new record is accurately inserted into the database.
☐	☐	The record can be accurately read from the database.
☐	☐	The record is accurately updated in the database.
☐	☐	The record is completely deleted from the database.

Server-Side Includes (SSI) ■ ■ ■ ■ ■

A Server Side Include (SSI) is a special placeholder in an HTML document that the Web server will replace with data just before the final document is sent to a browser. A SSI placeholder (or command) can vary in complexity from a simple reference to a date or time to the results of a database query executed via a CGI script. Simply viewing the HTML source code from the browser doesn't provide enough information to determine if the HTML is static or built dynamically using SSI. However, you can look for SSI files on the Web server. These files are typically saved with the *.shtml* suffix. You may want to think of a server-side include as an "include" statement in an HTML file that the Web server automatically replaces at run time with the contents of the .shtml file, as illustrated in Figure 5-8.

While SSIs add a great deal of flexibility in developing a Web site, they also complicate the testing process. More time is required to adequately check the HTML syntax because the code is dynamic. Developers, however, can add comments around the embedded SSI statements to help identify the dynamic elements of the HTML. Having the Web server parse through documents can be costly for heavily loaded servers.

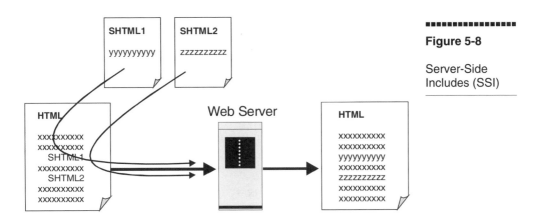

Figure 5-8

Server-Side
Includes (SSI)

Furthermore, enabling SSI on a Web server may also increase your Web site's security exposure, by potentially giving users the ability to execute commands on the Web server. When programs referenced by an "include" statement are executed, they run with the user-id of the Web server. In a properly configured system, the user-id is *nobody* and is assigned no special system privileges. On many systems, however, the server runs as *root*, which has unlimited access to the system. Your Web site could incur significant damage if a hacker installs a virus and invokes it via a server-side include that runs as *root*. Before enabling executable includes, make sure your Web server (or the processes in your child server pool) is running as *nobody*. If you disable the EXEC option entirely, your security risk is reduced but the performance issues still remain.

■■■■■■■■■■■■■■■■

To reduce the security risk to your Web site, you should consider using the "includesnoexec" statement, which disables server-side executable includes.

Different Web servers have different implementations of SSI. This means that there is one more environmental item that needs to be checked in order to ensure that the development, testing, and production systems (especially if a third party ISP is being used) are in sync. Consequently, developers should carefully consider the benefits and drawbacks before activating server-side includes on a Web server. If SSIs are already enabled in your Web site, you should ask your server administrator which environment variables were used – this will help you develop effective test cases.

Extended Server Side Includes (XSSI) provide developers with more functionality (e.g., conditional code such as "If.... Then" statements) than SSI. Using XSSI, it's possible to create pages that display different information depending on criteria such as the browser that a visitor is using or the day of the week. The browser version can be determined from the environment variables created for each visitor on the Web server. While this may allow a developer to use browser-specific HTML extensions, it also increases the amount of effort needed to achieve the same level of test coverage.

The Apache Project (apache.org) is a collaborative software development effort aimed at creating a robust, commercial-grade, feature-packed, and freely available source code implementation of an HTTP (Web) server. Apache JSSI is a Java servlet that supports dynamic servlet output from within HTML documents. It's currently based on the JavaSoft Servlet API 2.0 and can be executed by any Web server that can execute Java servlets. Apache JSSI parses JHTML files, executes the servlets as specified by the <SERVLET> tag, and replaces those tags with the output of the executed servlet. The <SERVLET> tag is the server-side equivalent of a client-side <APPLET> tag. SSI files for Java servlets are called JHTML files in the apache context, while SHTML files are usually used for traditional SSI. The Java Web Server (sun.com) is an exception, which uses SHTML files for Java servlet SSI files and JHTML for compiled Web pages.

Although many of these development options can help enhance the capabilities of your Web site, they can also increase the likelihood that a user will experience problems during a transaction. Table 5-9 lists some of the test cases that B&D's

team used in validating the server-side includes that were implemented on their Web site.

Table 5-9 B&D's SSI Testing Checklist

		Server-Side Includes Validation
Pass	Fail	Description
☐	☐	All SSI and XSSI selection criteria are accurately documented, and each "include" file contains a "start of file" and "end of file" comment.
☐	☐	No JSSI files are used.
☐	☐	The appropriate content is displayed and formatted correctly for each of the possible selection criteria.
☐	☐	No "include" file references another "include" file. While technically possible, this programming style can be difficult to debug and can also impact performance.

Dynamic Server Pages ■■■■■

Microsoft has developed a product called Active Server Pages (ASP), which consists of a single Dynamic Link Library (i.e., ASP.DLL) installed on a Web server running Internet Information Server (IIS) and the Internet Server Application Program Interface (ISAPI). When a user requests a Web page that has a suffix of .asp, IIS parses the server-side scripts contained in the ASP file to generate the entire HTML Web page, as illustrated in Figure 5-9. In essence, ASP is SSI taken to an extreme level. That is, rather than a few lines of code being dynamically swapped in at run-time, entire Web pages are built on the fly.

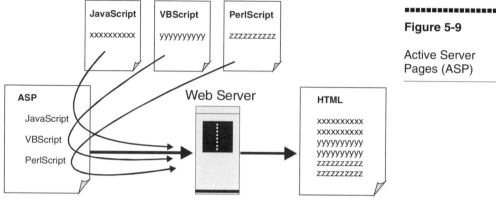

■■■■■■■■■■■■■■■■■

Figure 5-9

Active Server
Pages (ASP)

The Microsoft ASP.DLL file is comprised of six objects: Application, Session, Request, Response, Server, and ObjectContext, that allow Web pages to receive and respond to browser requests and manage application and user-level information. The Application object is mainly useful for storing information that is common to the Web application. However, it can also be used to share information among all of the users of the Web application. The Session object is similar to the Application object in that it maintains a set of variables on the server and provides a way to share data among different Web pages used by the same client. The Request object is used to accept the data that the client passes through the URL or form fields. The Response object is used to send ASP information back to the client. The Server object is primarily used to instantiate other COM components in ASP scripts. The ObjectContext object is used when IIS interacts with Microsoft Transaction Server (MTS) and transactional ASP scripts. While ASP is specifically designed to run with Microsoft's IIS Web Server, other Web servers use similar products. Apache servers, for example, use the Apache Server API and Netscape servers use the Netscape Server API (NSAPI). However, ASP is currently the "mind-share" market leader and has become synonymous with the concept of Dynamic Web code.

■■■■■■■■■■■■■■■■■

Did you know...

Chilisoft
(chilisoft.com)
and Halcyonsoft
(halcyonsoft.com)
sell versions of
ASP that run on
non-Windows
platforms.

A Java Server Page (JSP) is the Java equivalent of an ASP. JSPs combine markup language (e.g., HTML or XML) with Java code to produce dynamic Web pages. The JSP engine automatically compiles each page into a servlet the first time the page is requested. This servlet is automatically executed and the results are returned to the client. Thereafter, the Web server's servlet engine will run the compiled page each time it's requested. It's possible to view the servlet code that is generated by locating it within the directory structure of the servlet engine. Using JRun (livesoftware.com), for example, you can locate and review the source code for your JSP files in servlet form. This can be very helpful when testing your JSP files. Vignette (vignette.com) has a product called StoryServer that works with a Web server to intercept URLs. If it recognizes a URL as a page that needs to be dynamically created, it "points" to a template that has instructions on how to dynamically construct the desired Web page.

■■■■■■■■■■■■■■■■■
Did you know...

Application Programming Interface (API) is a non-Web-specific term used to describe the method(s) prescribed by an operating system or application program. The API allows a developer who is writing the application to make requests of the operating system or another application.

Along with the flexibility, Dynamic Server Pages (DSP) can also present problems for developers and testers. Although it's possible for developers to use multiple server-side scripting languages in a single Web page, it's preferable to use a single language for all scripts within a Web page or the entire Web site. Using multiple languages requires the DSP engine to load and run multiple scripting engines. Consequently, this will reduce the performance and scalability of your Web site. DSP implementations also present another significant problem. If the entire site is being served by a single DSP engine and the engine experiences a problem that is so severe that it causes the engine to crash, then it's possible that the entire DSP-generated portion of the Web site will become unavailable. By comparison, if a CGI script fails, typically only a single instance of the program will be affected and therefore only a single user.

Perhaps the biggest challenge to testing dynamically generated pages is the sheer number of different pages that could be generated. The following are some possible testing strategies for testing large numbers of dynamically built Web pages:

♦ Increase the usage of code inspections and reviews.
♦ Build a test harness, which can feed the DSP engine the various input parameters that cause the DSP engine to create all of the possible Web pages that could be generated. You will typically need to work with the developer of the DSP template or get your hands on the specifications in order to determine the parameters. Depending on the volume of generated pages, you may also need to write an "Oracle" program to generate all of the *correct* answers and compare them against the DSP engine's generated answers.
♦ Implement a "use case" approach to identify the most commonly generated Web pages, then manually test the generation of these pages.
♦ Implement a "risk-based" approach in order to identify the most important pages and navigational paths, then manually test the generation of these pages.
♦ Finally, use a code coverage tool (dependent upon the programming language used) to determine what percentage of the Web site's templates have been exercised using any of the strategies listed above.

B&D used many of the same test cases from their SSI testing checklist (Table 5-9) in addition to the test cases listed in Table 5-10 to validate their dynamic server pages.

Table 5-10 B&D's Dynamic Server Page Checklist

		Dynamic Server Page Validation
Pass	Fail	Description
☐	☐	The dynamically generated Web page is not a candidate for being replaced by one or more static pages.
☐	☐	Developers used a single language for all scripts within each dynamically generated Web page.
☐	☐	No "template" file references another "template" file. While technically possible, this programming style can be difficult to debug and can also impact performance.
☐	☐	All DSP templates have been inspected by at least one senior developer who was not the author of the template.
☐	☐	All high-frequency Web pages have been generated and manually tested.
☐	☐	All high-risk Web pages have been generated and manually tested.

Shopping Carts ■■■■■

Web sites often use the concept of a *shopping cart* to allow visitors to collect several items before purchasing them in a single transaction. Some Web sites have changed the name or image of their shopping cart to fit in with the theme of their Web site. A Web site that sells gardening tools and accessories, for example, might use a wheelbarrow for its icon. A Web site that sells ski equipment might use a sleigh. Unfortunately, usability research has found that the concept of a shopping cart is so well ingrained into online shoppers, that using anything else for storing a shopper's selections degrades usability.

The amount of time that a user is allowed to maintain a shopping cart before checking out varies among different Web sites. Amazon.com, for example, currently keeps visitors' shopping

■■■■■■■■■■■■■■■■■
Did you know...

According to e-buyersguide.com, 60% of online shoppers abandon their carts before purchasing anything.

carts alive for 90 days. Other Web sites may require a visitor to check out before leaving their site. The duration of a shopping cart's life is dependent upon the requirements of your Web site and the development tools that are used. The JavaScript Pro Shopping Cart (javascriptpro.com) is just one example of many tools that are available to develop custom shopping carts for your Web site. If your Web site uses a shopping cart, you should consider designing sufficient test cases to determine what happens if a user subjects your cart to undesirable conditions, such as those listed in Table 5-11.

Table 5-11 B&D's Shopping Cart Testing Checklist

		Shopping Cart Validation
Pass	Fail	Description
☐	☐	If a user adds more than the maximum number of items that the cart can hold, an appropriate message is displayed.
☐	☐	If a user tries to check out an empty cart, an appropriate message is displayed.
☐	☐	If a user removes an item from the cart, the Web application correctly removes the item and displays an appropriate message.
☐	☐	If a user completes a purchase (thereby emptying the cart), but then uses a Back/Go/History button to return to a pre-checkout page, the Web application ignores any attempt to alter the contents of the checked-out cart and displays an appropriate message.
☐	☐	If a user abandons the cart and returns to the Web site at a later date (within a specified period), the Web application recalls the user's selections, resets the elapsed time, and allows the user to continue shopping.
☐	☐	If a user abandons the cart and doesn't return to the Web site within a specified period of time, the Web application releases and recycles system resources.
☐	☐	If a user launches two instances of the same browser and adds items to a cart using both browsers, the Web application correctly updates the contents of the shopping cart(s).

Processing Credit Cards   ■ ■ ■ ■ ■

Every time a credit card purchase is made over the Internet, an electronic process takes place to execute the financial transaction. More precisely, the process to exchange funds between the customer and the merchant must be performed successfully. Each component has a distinct function, but they all work together to transfer the funds from the customer to the merchant. This transfer process is also where a major portion of the cost to support an e-commerce site arises, because fees are charged on a per-transaction basis. Currently credit card transmissions over the Internet are normally encrypted using the Secure Socket Layer (SSL) protocol. This Internet connection option will eventually include built-in support for Secure Electronic Transactions (SET) protocol, which prevents anyone other than the cardholder and the acquiring bank from seeing the credit card number. The general flow of the payment process is outlined below. Refer to Figure 5-10 to see how each of these steps fits into the overall payment process.

■■■■■■■■■■■■■■■■■

For more information on the SET protocol visit:

americanexpress. com, mastercard.com, setco.org, and visa.com

1. When a customer decides to buy something from a merchant site, the merchant's e-commerce application prompts the customer for credit card information, usually along with other supporting information such as a shipping address.
2. The customer enters payment information either into a form secured by the SSL protocol or into a Web browser that is compliant with the SET specification. By using a secured form, the payment information is protected by SSL as it is sent to the merchant.
3. The Web server sends the customer's payment information to an application server, which processes the data on the form.

4. Using the payment software loaded on the application server, the merchant sends the encrypted transaction to the acquiring credit card server for authorization. When the authorization is completed, the funds are held for the purchase.

5. The acquiring credit card server forwards the transaction through the financial network to the issuing financial institution.

6. The issuing bank decides whether to authorize or decline the transaction. Assuming the transaction is authorized, the bank issues an authorization code for a certain amount of money and also advises the merchant of the accuracy of the supporting information (e.g., name, address, etc.). An authorization typically reduces the customer's available credit limit, but doesn't actually place a charge on the customer's bill or move money to the merchant account.

7. If the transaction is authorized, the merchant captures the information from the successful authorization and charges the authorized amount of money to the customer's credit card. For digital products such as software, information access, and immediately accessible online subscriptions, it's common to authorize and capture credit card data at the same time. However, for non-digital products, the capture must take place only after the products are shipped. This may cause a time lag between the authorization and the capture.

8. If the customer cancels the order before it's captured, a void transaction is generated. If the customer returns a product after the transaction has been captured, a credit transaction is generated.

9. The final step is a settlement between the issuing bank and the acquiring credit card server. Captures and credits are usually accumulated into a batch and are settled as a group. When a batch is submitted, the merchant's payment-enabled Web server connects with the acquiring credit card server to finalize the transactions and transfer funds to the merchant account.

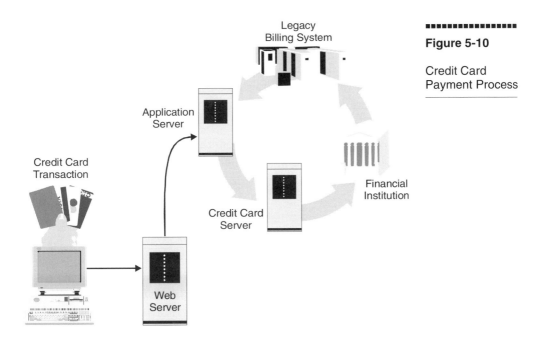

Figure 5-10

Credit Card
Payment Process

Companies such as Authorizenet.com, ClearCommerce.com, CyberCash.com, CyberSource.com, Verifone.com, and others provide the software necessary to process credit cards over the Web. Their packages usually provide a stand-alone application and a Web-based component that can be integrated into most e-commerce Web sites. Depending on the credit card software that your organization chooses to use, your Web site may be enabled with a variety of fraud detection and credit card address verification services. Of course, these services will need to be tested if they are used in your Web site. The major credit/debit card issuers will often provide "dummy" credit card numbers to allow organizations to test their credit card processing systems.

Several companies (e.g., entrypoint.com, microsoft.com, nextcard.com, and verifone.com) are now offering Internet users the ability to store their card information in a client-side application, typically referred to as an e-Wallet. These

Credit card
processing
companies
include:

cardservice.com
cybercash.com
ecash.com
echeck.com
firstdata.com
iBill.com
infodial.com

applications allow users to enter their credit card information once, then purchase numerous products from several different online vendors without having to reenter this information. While e-Wallets are very convenient, they also have obvious security implications. An alternative to storing wallet-type information on the client-side is to store it on the server-side. Verticalone.com and yodell.com are two companies that offer to store this type of information in a central location. Numerous Web sites can then access this information at the central location, thereby allowing "account aggregation."

Scalability is also a concern when launching an e-commerce Web site because it's difficult to predict the number of users that will be visiting your site at any point in time. You can always run multiple Web servers, but credit card transactions can quickly become a bottleneck since they typically require from 5 to 20 seconds to process. The actual time period varies, depending on current Internet traffic and the transaction load on the credit card server that you're using. Consequently, large Web merchants often choose to process their orders offline. That is, the customer places the order online and the merchant processes the credit card at a later time. For the customer, this is a great performance improvement because he or she doesn't have to wait for the results of the transaction. This is beneficial to the merchant because dedicated computers can be used to perform the transactions during off-peak hours. These computers can be separate from the main network, which can improve security and reduce the merchant's per-transaction cost by processing orders in batch mode.

Using the "dummy" credit card numbers provided by a credit card issuer, B&D chose to execute the test cases listed in Table 5-12 to validate their credit card processing system. These are only a few of the tests that may actually be required. Other test cases may be needed, depending on the credit card processing software that your company is using and the specific options that your Web site is utilizing.

Table 5-12 B&D's Credit Card Testing Checklist

Process Validation		
Pass	Fail	Description
☐	☐	If a user enters an invalid credit card number or expiration date, an appropriate message is displayed.
☐	☐	If a user enters invalid contact information, an appropriate message is displayed.
☐	☐	Cancelled or old credit cards are rejected.
☐	☐	Customers with insufficient funds are informed of the situation via an appropriate message.
☐	☐	Credit card numbers (and other confidential information) are stored in an encrypted format.
☐	☐	Credit card information is stored in a separate database/file on a different physical server than other parts of a customer's profile. This reduces the risk and likelihood that a hacker (internal or external) would be able to utilize this information.
☐	☐	Payments are properly received for completed transactions.
☐	☐	Tax collection processing is in place to calculate and collect all appropriate taxes (e.g., Federal, State, County, and other municipalities).
☐	☐	Fraud detection and credit card address verification services are functioning as specified.

Options for Paying Online ■ ■ ■ ■ ■

Credit cards are an integral part of most Internet e-commerce Web sites, as they are currently the leading method of payment for online purchases within the U.S. Web sites that target consumers in other countries, however, typically provide customers with other payment options that often have advantages over credit cards. Directly charging a customer's phone bill, Electronic Funds Transfers (EFT), electronic checks, and digital gold, for example, are all viable methods of processing payments online. These methods are typically handled through a secure server or a payment gateway that encrypts the information, making them safe methods for consumers to purchase products online. When merchants allow customers to use EFT, digital gold, smart cards or digital cash as their payment methods, funds can be verified before the purchase is complete, which reduces the risk of fraud and insufficient funds returns.

There are several companies (e.g., eCharge.com and iBill.com) that provide merchants with the ability to accept payments for purchased products via customers' phone bills. To enable this method of payment, a merchant typically subscribes to a billing service and provides a link to that billing service on the merchant's Web site. Consumers must download software to their computers in order to use the service. The billing service is then connected directly from the customer's computer to a secure server that automatically captures the billing information.

Merchants may also elect to use an Electronic Funds Transfer (EFT) to deduct payments directly from a customer's personal or business bank account (e.g., tradecard.com and checkfree.com). An EFT is a fast, reliable method of payment, as funds are automatically verified and immediately transferred to a merchant's account.

An electronic check (e.g., checkfree.com, ecash.com, echeck.com/epx.com, and iBill.com) generates a form of paper check that follows a payment process similar to that of a standard personal check. E-checks are deposited into a merchant's checking account and, like a standard check, they may be returned for insufficient funds. If funds are not available in a customer's checking account to cover the amount of the e-check, the merchant will need to go through the same collection

---

■■■■■■■■■■■■■■■■■

Did you know...

There are many methods (*other than credit cards*) that consumers can use to pay for online purchases. These are just a few of the options that are available:

- phone billing
- Electronic Funds Transfer (EFT)
- electronic checks
- digital gold
- smart cards
- micropayments
- digital cash
- digital money orders
- barter

steps as are required to recover payment on a standard check. Bank overdraft fees and penalties may be charged to the consumer.

E-gold (e.g., e-gold.com) is an electronic currency that is 100% backed by gold. E-gold is integrated into an account-based payment system that allows consumers to pay specified weights of gold to other e-gold account holders. The ownership of the gold changes, but the total amount of gold in the vault remains the same. Since the value of e-gold is measured by weight of metal, not currency, this method of payment is well suited for international transactions. Other e-metals such as silver and platinum are also available as online payment options.

There are many other options for paying online. Smart cards (e.g., mondex.com and visa.com) allow money to be transferred to a physical card or computer. Micropayments (e.g., millicent.com/compaq.com) provide a method for paying for items that may cost only a fraction of one cent. Digital cash (e.g., digicash.com) provides more anonymity than traditional credit cards. Digital money orders (e.g., westernunion.com and payme.com) and even bartering (e.g., barter.com) are other viable methods for making online payments.

Interfacing to a Legacy System ■■■■■

Web sites/applications often need to interface with legacy systems (i.e., existing systems) in order to process the purchase orders placed by customers visiting a Web site. If the Web site/application interfaces with a legacy system, there are two basic approaches that you can use to develop test cases for validating the interface between your Web site and the legacy system(s): a white-box approach or a black-box approach.

A *white-box* approach typically requires you to apply a reverse engineering process (if documentation is non-existent, outdated, or insufficient) to gain an understanding of the legacy system's operation. The individual components of the system and their inter-relationships need to be identified so a high-level representation of the system's input/output processes can be documented. Being able to "see into" the application allows you to specifically design test cases that can execute every instructional path and/or every line of code. Effective test cases can be generated based on the relationships between each of the components of the legacy system and the Web site. Unfortunately, a white-box approach is time consuming and usually requires intimate knowledge of the legacy system's operation and a clear understanding of the Web site's code.

There are many tools available to help you perform white-box testing. Code coverage estimators, for example, determine which lines of code have been executed during a test run. However, many code coverage tools require an intimate knowledge of the code under review. Some tools are even designed to "plug into" developers' tools. Before investing in a code coverage tool, you should determine which personnel within your organization have knowledge of the source code and will be assigned to use the tool.

A *black-box* approach, on the other hand, involves examining the overall functionality of the legacy system in relation to the Web site. Detailed knowledge of the code used to develop the legacy system is not required for black-box testing. Indeed, if the legacy system was purchased from a third party, it may not be possible to view the source code, in which case white-box testing is not an option. Unfortunately, black-box testing can be potentially less effective than white-box testing because it only considers the program's interface, but ignores internal components.

Table 5-13 lists some possible test cases that may be used to validate the interface between your Web site and legacy systems.

Table 5-13 B&D's Legacy System Testing Checklist

Pass	Fail	Description
		Interface Validation
☐	☐	The security of the legacy system is not compromised by its link to the outside world via the Web server(s). That is, the Web servers are granted the minimum required security levels.
☐	☐	The legacy systems are able to handle the increased workload caused by the addition of the Web site. This should be confirmed during a combination of peak Web site activity and peak legacy system activity, which may follow a different business cycle such as end-of-month and/or quarterly processing.
☐	☐	Messages between the legacy systems and the Web site are not corrupted or lost (i.e., adequate buffers exist).
☐	☐	Taking the legacy system off-line does not hang the Web site/application.
☐	☐	Taking the Web site off-line does not hang the legacy system.

Cookies ■■■■■

A cookie is a unique piece of data that a Web server sends to a browser. This block of data can contain almost anything. It can be a unique user-id generated by the server, the current date and time, the IP address of where the browser is logged onto the Internet, or any other chunk of data that might be useful to the Web server. When a client PC requests a Web page X, the Web server sends the requested page to the client along with a cookie, as illustrated in Figure 5-11. If the client requests another page, Y, from the same Web site, the cookie is sent back to the Web server along with the request for page Y. After the browser receives a cookie, it will send the same cookie back to the Web server that originally sent it whenever the browser requests another Web page from that domain.

Client PC   Web Server

Step 1 - Request Page X

Step 2 - Sends Page X and a Cookie

Step 3 - Requests Page Y with a Cookie

Step 4 - Sends Page Y and an Updated Cookie

Figure 5-11

Exchanging Cookies

Typically, the purpose of a cookie is to identify visitors when they return to a Web site. Cookies benefit Web site developers by allowing them to track individual requests. This allows the Web server to prepare customized Web pages based on a visitor's past experiences at that site, track a visitor's past and present activities, or perform a variety of other functions. This is useful when developers want the browser to remember specific information across several Web pages. Consider, for example, browsing through a virtual shopping mall. A customer will typically add items to a shopping cart while searching for other items. A list of the items that the customer has collected can be kept in the browser's cookie file so that all of the items can be purchased simultaneously when the customer has finished shopping. Most browsers support several different types of cookies, as listed in Table 5-14.

Did you know...

The name *cookies* was originally derived from the Unix term *magic cookies*, which referred to objects that could be attached to a user or program and change depending on the areas entered by the user or program.

Table 5-14 Types of Cookies

Type of Cookie	Description
Session	Session cookies reside in the browser's memory and "live" as long as that instance of browser remains open. Each open browser instance will have its own session cookie for a Web site. If developers don't explicitly set the *expires* parameter, it defaults to end-of-session. The length of a session can vary depending on browsers and Web servers, but it's generally the length of time that the browser is open (even if the user is no longer at that particular Web site).
Persistent (by page name)	Persistent cookies continue to "live" after the browser (and operating system) have been closed. A Web server may send a new cookie each time a visitor requests a different page. These cookies can create an extremely frustrating experience for visitors who have their browsers set to warn them before accepting any cookies, which in part explains why they are comparatively rare.
Persistent (by domain name)	Persistent cookies with or without an expiration date can reside on a client's hard drive for a long period of time.

A Web browser continually performs maintenance on its cookies. Every time you open your browser, your cookies are read from disk. Every time you close your browser, your cookies are re-saved to disk. When a cookie expires, it's discarded from memory and no longer saved on the client's hard drive. If the client's computer runs short on memory, a session cookie may be swapped out to the hard drive (i.e., virtual memory). If the browser terminates abnormally (e.g., the browser crashes), it would most likely not clean up its virtual memory and the session cookie would be left visible to anyone viewing the hard drive.

Browsers typically provide users with the option to accept all cookies, disable cookies (persistent and/or session), or only accept cookies that get sent back to the original server. The

■■■■■■■■■■■■■■■■■
Did you know...

MS IE stores each cookie as a separate file in a folder called *cookies*. While Netscape stores all of its cookies in a single file called *cookie.txt* latter option is usually the most secure. If cookies are only sent back to the original server, then the Web server can't "see" if a browser contains cookies that were set by other Web sites. From the client-side, you should be suspicious of cookies that are sent to a different Web server than the one they were originally downloaded from. Contrary to popular belief, however, a cookie is not an executable program. It can't format your hard drive or steal private information from you. A cookie can only return the same information that was initially downloaded from a Web server. If high security is an issue, however, the contents of a cookie can be encrypted so that nobody other than the generating site can understand it. Parity checks can be used on a cookie to ensure that it's not tampered with while resident on the client or in transit from the client. You should check your Web site's requirements (explicit or implied) to determine whether or not your cookie should be encrypted.

■■■■■■■■■■■■■■■■■■

For more information on cookies, visit:

cookiecentral.com
microsoft.com
netscape.com

Web sites that are designed to use cookies (session or persistent) can still be made to work with browsers that either don't support cookies or have cookies "turned off." There are several other possible strategies that could be used instead of a cookie. You can store the equivalent information in the URL, embed it in a non-visual portion of HTML/JavaScript, or even include it as HTML text, where the text has been set to be the same color as the background and/or as a tiny font.

If the download speed of your Web pages varies significantly depending on whether or not the viewer has cookies turned on/off, then ensure that an adequate mix of cookie and no-cookie client browsers are included in the performance test for your Web site.

A cookie is composed of several parameters, as illustrated in Figure 5-12. This cookie was automatically generated by Netscape 4.7 while a client was visiting the B&D Web site.

```
.bd-trade.com FALSE /bdonline FALSE 1002641937 login networkski
```

Figure 5-12

Example Netscape 4.7 Cookie

By comparison, Figure 5-13 is the cookie that was created when visiting the same Web site with MS-IE 5.5. The exact format of the cookie will vary from Web site to Web site and with each version of browser.

```
login networkski bd-trade.com/bdonline/ 0 3048924960 29346345
3061065240 25373935 *
```

Figure 5-13

Example MS-IE 5.5 Cookie

You can easily change these parameters by editing the cookie file using any text editor (e.g., WordPad). Having the ability to change these parameters can be extremely useful when testing cookies. When rolling out a new version of a Web site that uses cookies, you should check that the new version is able to read all previous cookie formats, not just the last one. Your Web site should replace old cookie formats with the new version without requiring the user to re-enter the information stored in the old version.

Table 5-15 shows the checklist that B&D followed while validating cookies used by their Web site. A legitimate user of your Web site wouldn't normally perform many of these actions. However, a malicious user (or even a competitor) may use any one of these techniques to try to disrupt your Web site. This makes it essential to thoroughly test each of these possibilities.

Table 5-15   B&D's Cookie Testing Checklist

		Cookie Validation
Pass	Fail	Description
		When cookies are:
☐	☐	<u>disabled before</u> accessing the site, <u>either</u> one of two things happens: ◆ The site works correctly (albeit more slowly). ◆ The site issues a warning message telling the visitor that the site can only be accessed with cookies turned on.
☐	☐	<u>disabled midway</u> through a transaction, the site is able to detect the situation and handle it gracefully.
☐	☐	<u>deleted midway</u> through a transaction, the site is able to detect the situation and handle it gracefully.
		When the cookie is edited and some parameters are:
☐	☐	<u>added</u>, the site detects the situation and handles it gracefully.
☐	☐	<u>deleted</u>, the site detects the situation and handles it gracefully.
☐	☐	<u>swapped</u>, the site detects the situation and handles it gracefully.
☐	☐	<u>set to null</u>, the site detects the situation and handles it gracefully.
☐	☐	<u>some parameters are edited</u> and set to invalid values, the site detects the situation and handles it gracefully.
		Other validation tests include the following:
☐	☐	When the client PC's memory and/or disk cache is <u>cleared midway</u> through a transaction, the site is able to detect the situation and handle it gracefully. Session cookies are stored in memory and typically don't get saved to the hard disk. Persistent cookies may need to be deleted manually.
☐	☐	When control characters or special operating system commands are added to a cookie, the site detects the situation and handles it gracefully.
☐	☐	When multiple entries for the Web site are added to Netscape's *cookies.txt* file, the site detects the situation and handles it gracefully.
☐	☐	When the user identification field in the cookie is changed midway through a transaction, the site detects the situation and handles it gracefully. Consider replacing the regular user-id account with values such as *Admin*, *Test*, *Superuser*, or *Guest*.

Before beginning a new test, make sure to clear your computers' memory and disk cache and delete any permanent cookies from your Web site that are stored on your disk drive(s). After successfully completing the cookie checklist in Table 5-15, repeat each of the test cases from the same client using two identical browsers (same brand, same version) to access your Web site. This will help you determine if the Web site is able to handle two browsers running simultaneously and using the same persistent cookie to store/retrieve information. Then, try using two or more different browsers (same brand, different versions) to access your site. You may generate some different results.

Maintaining a Session ■■■■■

There are several different methods that can be used to maintain a session (Figure 5-14) across multiple Web pages. Web applications can use cookies to revalidate users (i.e., maintain a session) or store specific information about users.

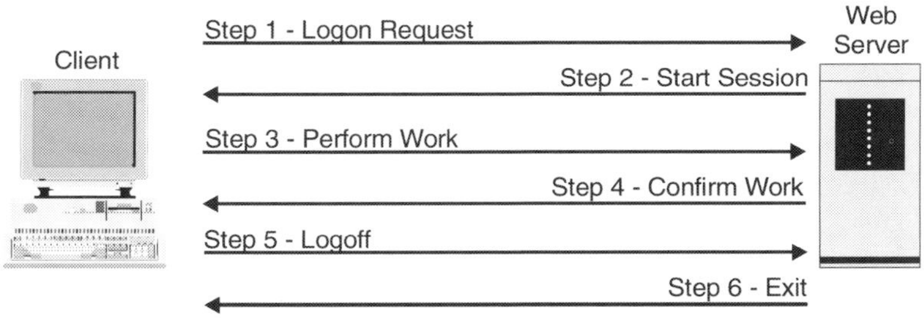

■■■■■■■■■■■■■■■■■

Figure 5-14

Maintaining a Session Between a Client and the Web Server

Some Web applications embed user information into a URL in order to maintain a session. AT&T, for example, used the modified URL in Figure 5-15 to maintain a session for a user. Unfortunately, this approach has serious security implications.

The URL will be carried over to the next Web site that the user visits and can be seen by the new Web site.

https://www.catalog.att.com/eatt/ssl-cgi/process_order.cgi? pass_vid=E.0888753.000932474069&pass_pid=E.0888445 .00093247409

■■■■■■■■■■■■■■■■■

Figure 5-15

Modified URL

Other alternatives include hiding or embedding the information in the HTML code or using a Java applet or ActiveX control. If you're unable to obtain the design specification that explains where the session-id is stored within the transmitted HTTP/HTML code, you can use a text comparison tool to compare the HTTP/HTML script produced by two different users requesting the same Web page. The session-id should appear as a "difference" between the two scripts. Generally, it's better to store only a session-id on the client computer and the session's data on the Web server rather than storing everything on the client. Table 5-16 lists some possible test cases that may be used to validate that your Web site is capable of maintaining a session without interruption.

Table 5-16 B&D's Session Testing Checklist

		Maintaining a Session
Pass	Fail	Description
☐	☐	The Web application is capable of maintaining a single session through multiple browsers running on the same client.
☐	☐	The Web application is capable of simultaneously accessing the same account through multiple clients.
☐	☐	Adequate database locking strategies have been documented in the specification and have been properly implemented.
☐	☐	The Web application time/date stamps transactions using the clock on the Web server, not the clock on the client.

(Continued)

Table 5-16 (*Continued*)

Pass	Fail	Description
Maintaining a Session		
☐	☐	The Web application is able to handle a user disabling cookies (session and/or persistent) midway through a session.
☐	☐	The Web application is able to handle a user clearing the cache (disk or memory) midway through a session.
☐	☐	The Web application is able to handle a user disabling JavaScript and/or VBScript midway through a session.
☐	☐	The Web application is able to handle a user disabling Java applets and/or ActiveX controls midway through a session.
☐	☐	The Web application is able to handle a user deleting the Query portion of the Web site's URL midway through a session.
☐	☐	The load balancer (if used) is able to maintain a session.

Some testing tools are unable to handle embedded session-ids or timestamps. If your Web site embeds transactional data in the HTTP/HTML script, you should verify that any testing tool that you're considering purchasing supports this feature.

Concurrent Users ■■■■■

Each user that maintains a session on a Web site utilizes resources on that site, as illustrated in Figure 5-16. Consequently, the Web site needs to determine a mechanism to free these resources, or the Web server may eventually run out of memory, the database may lock up, or the application server may run out of disk space.

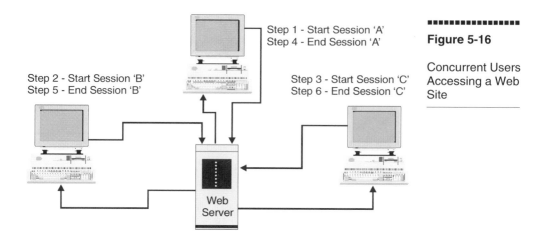

■■■■■■■■■■■■■■■■■

Figure 5-16

Concurrent Users
Accessing a Web
Site

Step 1 - Start Session 'A'
Step 4 - End Session 'A'

Step 2 - Start Session 'B'
Step 5 - End Session 'B'

Step 3 - Start Session 'C'
Step 6 - End Session 'C'

Web
Server

Many developers choose to use session/transaction timeouts to manage their Web site's resources. If a transaction is not completed or refreshed within a certain period of time, the transaction is rolled back and system resources are released.

Test cases should be designed to determine how long each session or transaction can remain dormant before it should be cancelled. If the delay is too long, the Web site may not be able to support the desired number of concurrent users. If the delay is too short, users may become frustrated with having to re-submit transactions too often.

When conducting a large-scale performance test, one strategy that some testers have used is to reduce the wait or "think" time between Web requests in a test script. The theory behind this test script tinkering is that by reducing the time that a client spends "thinking" between Web pages by a factor of 10 (e.g., from 10 seconds to 1 second), the workload of the Web server will increase by a factor of 10. Unfortunately, this strategy has a major flaw – "thinking" or dormant users still consume resources. A Web site that may be able to handle 1,000 users requesting a Web page every second may not be able to handle

■■■■■■■■■■■■■■■■■

Did you know...

One concert-ticketing Web site was notorious for timing people out too quickly. Users had to re-submit their requests, which increased the number of requests that the Web site had to handle. In turn, this caused the Web site to run even slower, which in turn caused more transactions to time-out.

10,000 users requesting a Web page every 10 seconds (even though the number of page requests remains the same).

Test cases should also be designed to confirm that all system resources are properly freed when a user completes a session or a transaction (e.g., when they select the "Log-Off" button). Table 5-17 lists some the test cases that B&D used to validate that system resources were properly freed.

Table 5-17   B&D's Concurrent Users Testing Checklist

		Managing Concurrent Users
Pass	Fail	Description
☐	☐	Server memory is freed when a user completes a session or a transaction.
☐	☐	Network connections are properly closed when a user completes a session or a transaction.
☐	☐	Disk space is freed when a user completes a session or a transaction.
☐	☐	Software licenses are freed and made available to other users when a user completes a session or transaction.

State-Transition Diagrams ■■■■■

The objective of a state-transition diagram is to provide a time-sequenced view of a transaction and identify the problems, errors, and exceptions that the system should handle. State-transition diagrams have been around for many years and have proven to be very effective tools for identifying possible flaws in a "conversational session," especially when the transaction has a high business risk (e.g., money or lives). State-transition diagrams also provide a useful tool for validating the overall transaction design and error handling abilities of your Web site. These diagrams introduce an overall view of the sequence of

The notation that this book uses for state-transition diagrams is based on the notation specified by the Unified Modeling Language (UML).

For more information, visit:

rational.com

event processing, which forces a thorough review of the transaction and can often detect errors that may otherwise be missed or prove costly to correct.

Mapping Normal Events

In many ways, designing an Internet transaction is similar to designing a pseudo-conversation transaction in a host-terminal environment such as CICS on an IBM mainframe. A state-transition diagram should be created for each transaction that requires more than one user interaction. The diagram should show the sequence of events and transitions that occur during the life of the transaction. Normal (expected) events should be connected using solid lines with arrows that indicate the chronological sequence of these events. However, it may not be necessary to create a state-transition diagram for every transaction that occurs within your Web site. Instead, concentrate on the transactions that occur in high volume or present a high business risk. The normal paths in each transaction should be considered first, while special cases or exceptional situations should be included later.

Common Patterns in Diagrams

Figure 5-17 shows some patterns that are commonly found in state-transition diagrams. Diagram 'A' has a very simple life. It is created, exists for a period of time, and is then terminated. This diagram may describe a user's request for news pertaining to a particular stock.

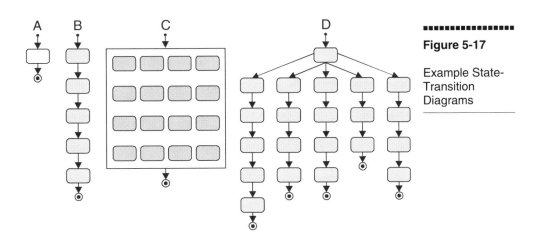

Figure 5-17

Example State-
Transition
Diagrams

Diagram 'B' has a straightforward life, driven by a static sequence of user interactions. This diagram may represent a market survey captured over a series of forms. Diagram 'C' has a very unpredictable life. This diagram may represent a chart of information that has been downloaded to a Java applet and then redisplayed in a number of different formats. Unfortunately, this type of diagram is the most common implementation on the Web and can be the most difficult to test. Diagram 'D' looks suspiciously like it might be better represented by five separate transactions. After logging into an account, for example, the client can initiate five different tasks before eventually logging off.

Mapping Error Conditions

Once the normal sequence of transitions (events) has been mapped out, error conditions, exceptions, and validation failures should be added to the state-transition diagram. If the state diagram for a transaction is too complicated to draw, then it's probably too complicated to code. Consequently, you should expect to find a higher density of defects than normal.

There are several questions that you should ask yourself when building upon the normal series of events. What would happen if the starting point were changed? What happens during an early termination of the transaction? Can the transaction revert to an earlier point in the path? What about error conditions? For example, what should the Web server do if it never receives a trade confirmation? Random or unexpected events like these should be connected using dotted lines with arrows that indicate the chronological sequence of these events.

Consider the "Back Button" event in Figure 5-18, for example. This event assumes that the client's browser will send an HTTP request to the server after the client presses the Back button. However, if the browser reloads the Web page from cache, the Web server may never be contacted and wouldn't know that the client moved. This event would actually be a non-event to the server. Even with this simple transaction, there are so many possible events that the diagram is likely to look like a bowl of spaghetti (state transitions) with a few meatballs (states). If you don't understand what should happen under unexpected circumstances, you will experience difficulty drawing the state-transition diagrams for your Web site. Similarly, it's unlikely that a developer has considered all of the possible events that could happen to a transaction (hence the need to test).

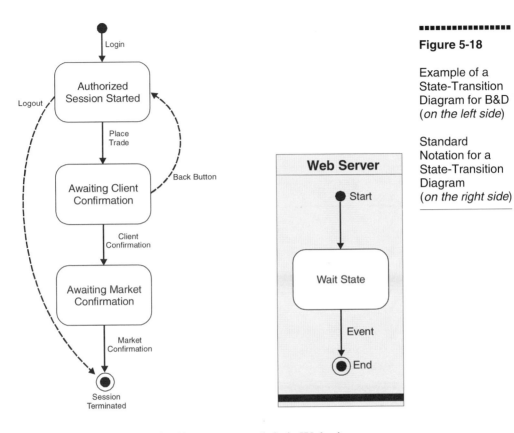

Figure 5-18

Example of a
State-Transition
Diagram for B&D
(*on the left side*)

Standard
Notation for a
State-Transition
Diagram
(*on the right side*)

B&D, for example, originally constructed their Web site so users could get to the Request Sell Order page only from the Secure Login page. However, one tester was able to circumvent this design by first logging on with a valid user id/password. Upon reaching the Sell page, she saved the page on her hard drive, logged off, and re-opened the saved page. She was then able to access restricted pages without going through the normal login process.

Using Your Diagrams

State-transition diagrams can be used for both static testing and execution testing of user transactions. Table 5-18 lists some possible test cases for validating your state-transition diagrams.

Table 5-18 B&D's State-Transition Diagram Testing Checklist

		Static Validation
Pass	Fail	Description
☐	☐	All possible wait states and normal events have been included in the state-transition diagram.
☐	☐	All possible unexpected events have been included in the state-transition diagram (e.g., the client utilizes bookmarked or cached pages that would normally occur later in the transaction, premature termination such as when the server waits for a trade confirmation that never arrives, etc.)
☐	☐	If non-occurrence of a particular event is significant in the completion of another event, the state-transition diagram indicates the proper error routine. If, for example, a trade is not executed on the stock market, final confirmation should not be sent.
☐	☐	No other transactions affect the interaction between any two consecutive wait states shown on the diagram. If, for example, the NYSE suspends trading of a stock midway through a sell order, is the sell order still processed?
☐	☐	There are no redundant wait states or wait states that don't have an exit.
☐	☐	All of the wait states can be reached (i.e., every wait state has at least one entry event).
☐	☐	Transactions do not contain sub-transactions that would be better represented on their own diagrams.

Although the list of possible errors and test cases may seem endless, it can be reduced. You should concentrate on the errors that carry a high business risk. When first developing state-transition diagrams, many developers and testers make the mistake of creating a wait state for every step in a transaction within the Web site. When validating a state diagram, you should ask yourself, "What makes this wait state different from all the others?" This will help you eliminate redundant and otherwise unnecessary events. When designing execution test cases (as opposed to static test cases), you should use standard code coverage techniques to determine what percentage of wait states and events have been covered. Ideally, every wait state and event should be covered by at least one test case.

Scriptors   ■ ■ ■ ■ ■

A scriptor is a tool used to capture a sequence of events that occur in a computer exactly as these events previously occurred. Scriptors are extremely useful in testing a Web application's user interactions as they allow you to retrace and replay the exact steps that a user may follow in order to achieve a particular result.

Test scriptors can be grouped into three basic categories, as illustrated in Figure 5-19: 1) capture with playback, 2) variable capture with playback, and 3) variable capture with variable playback. Test scriptors in the capture-with-playback category are capable of capturing a user's interactions and then playing them back exactly as the user had originally entered them. Test scriptors in the variable-capture-with-playback group are capable of capturing a user's interactions and allowing a developer or tester to modify the stored test input script before playing it back.

Test scriptors in the variable-capture-with-variable-playback category can capture a user's interactions and allow the tester to modify the stored test input script before playing it back. Additionally, they allow the expected output script to be modified prior to running a comparison.

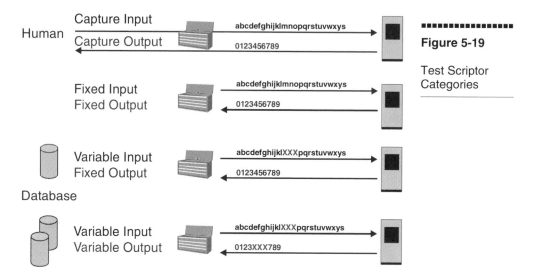

Figure 5-19

Test Scriptor
Categories

Typically, the more flexible the scriptor, the more complicated (and costly) the tool is going to be to use. Different scripting tools use different techniques to capture a Web page. Before selecting a scripting tool, check that the tool can handle a large number of minor page content changes (e.g., moving or resizing a graphic), since most Web sites live in such environments. The more sophisticated tools track page objects using Microsoft and Netscape document object models (DOM) and are subsequently more tolerant of minor presentation changes. Many organizations purchase test scriptors to help automate their functional regression testing, once their Web sites have become relatively stable and don't require new scripts to be written for each release.

Did you know...

Creating scripts that use variable data is also sometimes referred to as using a *data-driven approach*.

Browser-Dependent Scriptors ■ ■ ■ ■ ■

Some legacy client/server testing tools that have been repackaged for the Web can capture their input via calls directly to the operating system. Consequently, these tools require the same browser to be present when performing the playback. Unfortunately, this can be problematic if the browser has been upgraded or some of the default settings have changed since the baseline was captured. Tools that are dependent on a browser are sometimes referred to as *thick clients*, while those that are able to submit and receive HTTP commands on their own are sometimes referred to as *thin clients*.

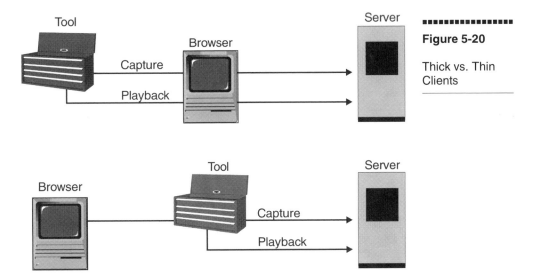

Figure 5-20

Thick vs. Thin Clients

When selecting a capture/playback tool, you should check if the tool is browser-independent. In other words, does the tool need a browser in order to play back the captured script? Since many tool vendors often lag behind the latest release of Web browser or Web server, you should ask your tool vendors when they started supporting the latest version of browser X. The release date of browser X can easily be researched to determine how up-to-date your vendors have been in the past and, consequently, how up-to-date you can expect them to be in the future. A vendor that continually releases product patches and updates may actually represent an aggressive attempt to keep pace with the latest Web technology. When evaluating functional testing tools, you should ask your vendor which languages can be used to develop the test scripts. Some vendors require that test scripts be written in a proprietary language (often based on Pascal or C), while others use industry standard languages such as JavaScript.

Scripting Tools ■■■■■

Table 5-19 lists various testing tools that can be used to build test scripts to playback against Web sites. When selecting a tool, you should consider the tool's ability to support or handle features such as persistent cookies, session cookies, session-ids stored in a URL, proxy servers, user authentication, variable input data for forms, and calls to CGI scripts and Web server APIs.

Table 5-19 Sample Scripting Tools

Vendor	Product(s)
Compuware (compuware.com)	TestPartner
Cyrano (cyrano.com)	WebTester
Online Computer Library Center (oclc.org)	WebART
Mercury Interactive (merc-int.com)	WinRunner, Xrunner, and Astra QuickTest
Rational (rational.com)	TeamTest and Test Studio
Empirix/RSW (rswsoftware.com)	e-Test Suite
Segue (segue.com)	SilkTest
Software Research (soft.com)	eValid

Useful URLs ■■■■■

Table 5-20 Useful Web Sites

Web Site URLs	Description of Services
ECMA.ch, IBM.com, microsoft.com, netscape.com, and W3C.org	HTML and scripting language syntax.
entrypoint.com, graham.com, marimba.com, MSN.com, and real.com	Push technology. .
CA.com, EMC.com, fastcgi.com, IBM.com, informix.com, lotus.com, microsoft.com, oracle.com, sun.com, sybase.com, and veritas.com	File and database access.
apache.org, microsoft.com, netscape.com, and vignette.com	Dynamic server pages.
cookiecentral.com, microsoft.com, and netscape.com	Cookies.
americanexpress.com, authorizenet.com, barter.com, cardservice.com, checkfree.com, clearcommerce.com, cybercash.com, cybersource.com, digicash.com, ecash.com, echarge.com, echeck.com, entrypoint.com, firstdata.com, iBill.com, infodial.com, mastercard.com, millicent.com, mondex.com, nextcard.com, payme.com, setco.org, tradecard.com, verifone.com, visa.com, and westernunion.com	Payment processing.
baan.com, oracle.com, and sap.com/sap-ag.de	ERP systems.
rational.com	UML notation.

(Continued)

Table 5-20 (*Continued*)

Web Site URLs	Description of Services
compuware.com, cyrano.com, oclc.org, merc-int.com, rational.com, rswsoftware.com, segue.com, and soft.com	Test scriptor tool vendors.
sqe.com/bdonline/	Case study Web site and downloadable test plans.

Chapter 6 – Usability and Accessibility

Usability is a measure of whether potential users of your Web site are able to find what they need with reasonable effort and within a reasonable period of time. Usability also encompasses how easy it is for new or infrequent users to learn to use your Web site. Data collected from usability and ease-of-learning tests go hand in hand. Ease-of-learning goals can easily be quantified and measured in order to help you determine a level of usability. For example, you can measure how long it takes a visitor to navigate to a specific page in your Web site over several attempts. Analysis of this data can give you concrete evidence of the usability of your Web site. In general, you need to strike a balance between ease of use and ease of learning how to navigate your Web site in order to optimize usability.

The U.S. Bureau of Census (census.gov) defines an individual with a disability as a person having difficulty performing one or more functional daily activities or one or more socially defined roles or tasks. In the context of a Web site, accessibility is a measure of how easy it is to access, read, and understand the content of a Web site. But accessibility goes far beyond a person's ability to simply "read" and understand a Web page. Organizations must be aware of the needs of people with disabilities in order to create a truly usable Web site. In 1994, the World Health Organization (who.int) estimated 38 million people worldwide were blind, while another 110 million suffered from low-vision impairments. The census report *Americans with Disabilities: 1991/1992*, published in January 1994, recorded a total of 48.9 million people with disabilities in the U.S. alone. Of these people, 24.1 million were severely disabled and 24.8 million had some minor form of disability. These statistics are

■■■■■■■■■■■■■■■■

Case Study

Review the following *Case Study Test Plans* to see an example of how the topics covered in this chapter can be utilized to test a Web site:

- Unit
- System

Visit:
sqe.com/bdonline/

■■■■■■■■■■■■■■■■

How would you log on to the Internet if you couldn't see your computer monitor?

For many people with disabilities, the Internet is their best hope for full and equal access to information.

---

too important to ignore. Usability and accessibility work hand-in-hand. You can't claim that your Web site is usable without ensuring it's accessible to everyone.

In a stricter definition, accessibility is a set of properties that allow hardware, software, and services to be used by people with a wide range of capabilities. These capabilities may refer to a person's individual abilities or the hardware and software configuration of the client's computer. Visitors with slow modems who choose to turn off graphics, for example, may experience similar issues as people with vision impairments. When you consider the similarities, accommodating your Web site for people with disabilities may inadvertently help you solve access issues for visitors with limited hardware and software configurations. Solutions for adding text captions for the hearing impaired may also aid in the development of text indexes for searching video and audio clips.

■■■■■■■■■■■■■■

Check out the World Population Clock (popclock) at:

census.gov

The Cost of Usability Problems

In the old mainframe days, usability often took a back seat to functionality and ease of programming. In those days, there wasn't much that a user could do if he or she didn't like the interface for a particular program. Typically, several weeks of training (e.g., the SABRE airline reservation system) were required before a user was up to speed using a particular application. Then, Graphical User Interfaces (GUIs) arrived in the form of shrink-wrapped PC packages and in-house client-server applications. Once users were exposed to GUIs, they formed a higher level of expectation for all other computer applications. Unfortunately, if the in-house developed GUI was not very intuitive or required a large number of windows to

■■■■■■■■■■■■■■

The Graphical User Interface (GUI) changed the "face" of software forever.

accomplish a single task, there was little that the user could do about it, until now…

The Internet has brought about a whole new kind of user. This user typically has very little loyalty to a Web site. He or she won't even stay long enough to use the Web site if it isn't immediately clear how the site should be used without any training whatsoever! The biggest mistake that any e-commerce Web site can make is to try to mold its customers into doing business the way the company wants to do business. Too many Web sites have adopted the "our way or else" approach. Organizations need to understand how to do business the way their customers want, or their customers will go elsewhere. Unlike traditional in-house end-users, Internet users aren't "captured" and are therefore free to choose to view or use another company's Web site. This significantly increases the impact that a poorly designed GUI has on its Web site.

Consider the following example. B&D decided to launch a true e-business application, but it could only be reached by mutual fund managers who were required to dial directly into the B&D Web server (i.e., an extranet). B&D believed that initially setting up their Web site as an extranet would facilitate testing both the design and the code. Once the site was working well, they hoped it would form the basis for transforming B&D into a successful online brokerage firm.

B&D found some of their Web site's usability problems early. They discovered that all of the developers had 20" monitors and were using a 1280 x 1024 pixel resolution, while the mutual fund managers (extranet users) typically only had 17" monitors running at 1024 x 768. Not only did these users have to scroll up and down, but also left and right, to view the entire Web page. Some of these users had also changed their browser's color settings to override the Web page's default colors. Consequently, they didn't receive some of the visual cues to help

■■■■■■■■■■■■■■■■■
Did you know...

When eBay's auction Web site went down in June 1999, they initially lost many of their customers to competitors.

When the Web site was up and running again, many of those "lost" customers returned. Why?

Returning customers frequently stated that eBay's Web site was the easiest to use.

them make their stock trading decisions. The extranet didn't provide any mechanism for users to provide feedback. Users couldn't e-mail the Webmaster with questions or comments about Web site options or functionality. The site map was out of date and didn't match the actual layout of the Web site. The bookmarks, in some cases, were outdated, misleading, or blank. Users experienced information overload with too much information and too many dancing icons on a single page. There was no internal search engine to help users quickly find what they needed. Perhaps worst of all, monetary transactions were correctly initiated but sometimes left uncompleted. The user had to reload the page to complete these transactions.

Some companies may argue that usability and accessibility testing is too expensive. These organizations may attempt to reduce testing schedules in order to rush their Web sites to the Internet to obtain "instant orders." Unfortunately, this could have disastrous results.

According to Jared Spool's (uie.com) study of fifteen large commercial Web sites, users could only find information 42% of the time even though they were taken to the correct Home page before they were given their tasks.

A study from Zona Research (zonaresearch.com) found that 62% of Web shoppers had abandoned their attempts to find and purchase items online. Approximately 20% of these Web shoppers had quit more than three times during a two-month period.

■■■■■■■■■■■■■■■■■

More information on Web usability and usability guidelines can be found at:

GUIGuide.com
usableweb.com
uie.com
uiereports.com
useit.com

and in Jakob Nielson's book *Designing Usability.*

■■■■■■■■■■■■■■■■■

When developing a Web site, the old cliché "*Ignorance is far more expensive than education*" applies.

Unfortunately, few organizations ever calculate the cost of ignoring poor usability.

Most notably, though, Forrester Research (forrester.com) audited twenty major Web sites and found that only 51% complied with simple Web usability principles such as, "Is the Web site organized by user goals?" and "Does a search display retrievals in order of relevance?" In other words, the average Web site violated half of these simple design principles. According to Forrester, an organization may lose approximately 50% of the potential sales from its Web site if people can't find what they're looking for.

When you consider the cost of lost business, the cost of repairing usability and accessibility problems isn't as large by comparison. Table 6-1 lists the costs associated with repairing various Web site usability problems.

Table 6-1 Costs of Web Site Usability Problems

Problem	Solution	Cost to Repair
Quick Fixes: 3 to 6 weeks, $8,500 to $17,000		
Site navigation is unreliable	Run quality checks and repair bad links	$1,900 to $3,700
Button text is illegible	Fix text or replace buttons	$1,200 to $2,000
Body text is illegible	Enlarge type	$3,000 to $7,500
Words are inconsistent	Replace inconsistent commands and prompts	$1,200 to $1,900
Text is jargon	Replace jargon	$1,200 to $1,900
Rehabilitation: 10 to 26 weeks, $35,000 to $90,000		
Performs inconsistently	Shrink or cut animation and irrelevant graphics	$2,000 to $6,000
Content not at 2nd or 3rd levels	Combine menus to reduce the number of levels	$14,000 to $37,000
Inconsistent controls	Replace inconsistent buttons and toolbars	$5,500 to $10,000
Navigation elements are hidden	Visually identify all clickable elements	$5,000 to $12,000
Irrelevant content	Eliminate off-target features	$8,500 to $25,000
Tear Down: 24 to 39 weeks, $780,000 to $1.56 million		
Not organized by user goals	Re-architect site structure and content	$130,000 to $200,000
Information incomplete	Audit content catalog and build new content	$350,000 to $935,000
Site does not offer transactions, interactivity, personalization, or search	Add transactions, dealer locators, interactivity, customer profiles, recommendations, and search	$300,000 to $425,000

Source: Forrester Research, Inc., Cambridge, Mass., Why Most Web Sites Fail, September 1998

Web Usability Testing   ■ ■ ■ ■ ■

There are two types of Web usability testing: site-level (system) testing and page-level (unit) testing. Site-level usability testing is concerned with information architecture, navigation, page templates, site layout, consistent graphics, linking strategy, and search capabilities. Page-level usability testing pertains to specific issues and problems that occur on individual Web pages. Page-level problems, for example, may be present when a user can't understand the links, graphics, icons, forms, or error messages in the same way that the developers had intended.

Usability and style are very personal things. What works well for one person might not work at all for another person. So, how can you objectively test how usable your Web site is to another person? There are five basic steps you can follow when testing the usability of your Web site: 1) define clear goals and objectives, 2) set up your test environment, 3) select suitable participants for your usability test, 4) conduct the test, and 5) review the test results and report your findings. While there are many different techniques for conducting a usability test, this process explains some of the most common techniques that can be applied to both site-level and page-level tests.

■■■■■■■■■■■■■■■■
Five steps to testing the usability of your Web site:

1. Define clear goals and objectives.
2. Set up your test environment.
3. Select suitable participants.
4. Conduct the test.
5. Report your findings.

Step 1 - Define Your Goals

First and foremost, you should define a clear set of goals and objectives that you want to accomplish. What do you want to determine from your Web site/application usability test? Usability testing is typically most effective when it attempts to determine how much time a user needs to complete a task (or series of tasks) or how much difficulty the user has in completing the tasks. Usability testing can help you determine how users perform specific tasks, how they engage specific interface elements such as icons and menus, how they work with help systems and wizards, and how satisfied they feel about each of these things.

Step 2 - Set Up the Test

Usability testing can't make up for poor analysis and design, but it's possible to objectively measure your Web site's degree of usability. One common technique is to identify the most frequent tasks that users try to perform. If your initial analysis included a use case study, then the most frequent tasks should have already been identified. A usability test can be set up to determine the length of time (or number of Web pages/links) that it would take a new user to navigate to the desired Web page. You should pay particular attention to the links that are selected incorrectly and the Web pages that have a high rate of abandonment.

■■■■■■■■■■■■■■■■■

There are many types of usability tests. Some of these include:

- controlled laboratory
- field observation
- focus groups
- questionnaires
- surveys

There are many types of usability tests to choose from. Some of your choices include controlled laboratories, field observation, focus groups, questionnaires, and surveys. Surveys and questionnaires can help determine how users perform specific tasks, how they engage specific interface elements such as icons and menus, how they work with Java applets/scripts, and how satisfied they feel about their overall experience with your Web site or application. Related to these methods are focus groups, in which moderators orally question groups of users and record their responses. Another type of testing is field observation, where testers watch the participants use the Web site/application in their home or work environments.

The most sophisticated (and perhaps, the most expensive) method of Web site usability testing occurs in a usability lab. Controlled tests of specific user tasks can take place with full observation, recording, and reporting facilities. Unfortunately, the obvious disadvantage of this method is the cost of equipment and personnel. However, if the purpose of conducting Web usability tests is to help ensure user satisfaction and sustain (or increase) profits, then the benefits will likely exceed this cost disadvantage.

Step 3 - Select the Participants

One popular, inexpensive, and obvious choice for participants in a controlled usability test is fellow employees. Company employees can be asked to play the role of test participants and be assigned to work through specific tasks or processes within your Web site or application. This arrangement can be informal when participants are allowed to time their own efforts and record their own results. Alternatively, this arrangement can be quite formal when observers are assigned to keep time and record the results. Unfortunately, while convenient, employees who are already familiar with the organization's "jargon" may not accurately reflect the background of a typical user.

In all types of usability testing, you must keep in mind that the Web site or application, not the participant, is being tested. Participants must be told in advance that they are not the subjects of the tests; they only facilitate obtaining the usability results. Because the purpose of usability testing is to determine where the Web site/application's design fails, some tests will almost certainly lead the participant toward failure. It's easy for the participant to feel stupid.

■■■■■■■■■■■■■■■■■

Remember that you're testing the Web site or Web application, *not* the participants.

Don't allow your test to make your participants feel "stupid," as this may skew your test results (*and cause hurt feelings*).

Step 4 - Conduct the Test

The type of usability test that you selected in Step 2 (above) will determine how you conduct your test. Surveys and questionnaires should be administered in a controlled environment, if possible, in order to yield the most accurate results. If the environment can't be controlled (e.g., users fill out the surveys at home), you should ensure that the participant records his or her results during the test or very soon after the test. This will reduce the risk of obtaining skewed results due to fatigue, boredom, or loss of memory.

Step 5 - Report Your Findings

The results of surveys, questionnaires, and focus groups should be carefully analyzed *before* implementing any design changes to your Web site. You should ensure that these test results are accurate and haven't been skewed by the participants' personal biases or unreliable memories. Field observation results should be analyzed to ensure that users weren't distracted by "unusual" real-world events. Normal distractions should be included in the results because they accurately represent the real world where your Web site will be used. Your final test results should be forwarded to management, which is responsible for deciding whether the results warrant design changes to your Web site and, if so, to what extent.

B&D discovered that their particular usability test with five participants uncovered 80% of their site-level problems and approximately 50% of their page-level problems. However, the actual number of test participants that are required and the results

■■■■■■■■■■■■■■■■■
Make sure your results aren't skewed *before* you report your findings to management.

Results may be skewed by many factors including:

- boredom
- distractions
- fatigue
- loss of memory
- personal biases

that you will achieve depend on the size of your Web site and the amount of time and money allocated for the project.

Tables 6-2 and 6-3 list some of B&D's site-level and page-level usability guidelines. These guidelines were used to form a basis for B&D's usability testing.

■■■■■■■■■■■■■■■■■
Repeating usability tests on a regular basis will show how a Web site's usability varies over time.

Table 6-2   B&D's Usability Testing Checklist

		Site-Level Usability Validation
Pass	Fail	Description
☐	☐	There are no framesets in the Web site. Framesets can be difficult to navigate, take too long to download, and cause print problems.
☐	☐	Content is structured in terms of simple hierarchies.
☐	☐	The user's mental model is consistent across the entire Web site. Web page controls, behavior, and aesthetics remain consistent.
☐	☐	The amount of time (based on number of pages) needed to complete a multi-page task is perceived as reasonable by the user.

Table 6-3   B&D's Usability Testing Checklist

		Page-Level Usability Validation
Pass	Fail	Description
☐	☐	Graphics and other bandwidth-intensive elements are kept to a minimum.
☐	☐	Key functions such as search and help buttons are easy to find.
☐	☐	There are no competing/duplicate actions or options that might confuse the user or cause him or her to make an error.
☐	☐	The content is current. Previously published content is available via an archive.
☐	☐	Related information on the same page has been grouped, thereby minimizing eye movement.
☐	☐	Critical information has not been placed on the lower portion of the Web page. If the position of this information requires the user to scroll down, most visitors are unlikely to ever read it.

(Continued)

Table 6-3 (*Continued*)

Pass	Fail	Description
□	□	Content makes up 50% to 80% of the screen real estate.
□	□	Vertical scrolling has been kept to a minimum, especially on navigational pages.
□	□	When viewed via the clients' anticipated hardware/software, the page fits without the need for a horizontal scroll bar.
□	□	When printed via the clients' anticipated hardware/software, the page prints without being truncated.
□	□	B&D's name and logo is clearly visible on the page.
□	□	Browser (e.g., HTML, JavaScript, etc.) features that have been available for less than 1 year have not been used. A significant number of users use browsers that are at least 1 year old.
□	□	No pop-ups that open new browser windows are launched.
□	□	All links and graphics have a TITLE or ALT tag defined. Decorative images (e.g., white space or formatting borders) should have a blank ALT tag defined.
□	□	URLs are all lowercase.
□	□	There are no areas of large bright colors.
□	□	No more than 4 colors (ignoring graphics) have been used on the page.
□	□	The page background color is not dark.
□	□	All controls have been outlined in black for clarity, unless they are exceptionally small (i.e., less than 16x16 pixels).
□	□	Browsers' default link colors have not been overridden or altered.
□	□	Page object sizes have been specified as % of available screen rather than a fixed pixel size
□	□	Text has not been placed inside graphics files. This approach typically takes longer to download, can be more work to translate for multilingual Web sites, and may have quality issues with low-resolution displays such as WebTV.

Page-Level Usability Validation

(*Continued*)

Table 6-3 (*Continued*)

Pass	Fail	**Page-Level Usability Validation**
		Description
☐	☐	If using CSS, the Web page's presentation is still acceptable when CSS is turned off or not available.
☐	☐	Three (3) alternative fonts (in the same order) have been specified for all text.
☐	☐	Font sizes have been specified as relative sizes (e.g., heading 1) rather than as absolute sizes (e.g., 8 pt).

Source: Adapted in part from Jakob Nielson's *Designing Web Usability*, New Riders Publishing, 2000

Readability

Readability and legibility are critical elements in effective and efficient communication. Readability affects a user's ability to review text and graphics and comprehend their combined meaning. Good Web page design depends on the visual contrast between one font and another, and the contrast between blocks of text and the "white space" that surrounds them. Well-designed Web sites present information in small manageable units, rather than long contiguous blocks. This makes the information in the Web site easier to comprehend and maneuver through. Within each of these units, fonts, font sizes, font styles (e.g., bold, italic, etc.), color combinations, and background textures can all affect the readability of your Web page. If all of the text on your Web page is bold, then you've lost the point that you wanted to emphasize. If your Web page is crammed with too much text without sufficient white space, your visitors may reject the information and go elsewhere.

People read words by recognizing the overall shapes of words, not by parsing each letter individually and then assembling a

With so many variables, how can you effectively test the readability of your Web site?

recognizable word. This allows people with good memories to read faster, and with greater comprehension, than people who have poor memories. Readable Web pages avoid using all-uppercase text because it's much harder to read and comprehend. Uppercase letters don't allow the reader to form discernable shapes around words and, consequently, reading speed and comprehension decrease significantly.

Letter spacing can also influence readability. Studies have shown that proportional-width fonts can be read faster than fixed-width fonts. Proportional (or variable-width) fonts use varying amounts of space between each character. A capital "W," for example, uses more horizontal line space than a lower-case "i." On the other hand, fixed-width (or constant-width or monospace) fonts allot the same amount of horizontal space for each character. Figure 6-1 illustrates the visual differences between proportional and fixed-width fonts.

■■■■■■■■■■■■■■■■
Did you know...

Courier is the most commonly available fixed-width font.

■■■■■■■■■■■■■■■■
Figure 6-1

Proportional versus Fixed-Width Fonts

| Times New Roman is an example of a proportional-width font. |
| Courier is an example of a fixed-width font. |

Measuring Readability

The readability of a Web page can be scientifically measured using various techniques. There are many different formulas available to help you assign a value to readability.

Gunning FOG Readability Index

The *Gunning FOG Readability Index* is one of the easiest to use and possibly the most popular readability index. The steps for using the Gunning FOG Index are as follows:

1. Randomly select one 100-word passage from your Web site.
2. Determine the average number of words per sentence.
3. Determine the percentage of difficult words (i.e., words with three or more syllables).
4. Add the two results together and multiply by 0.4.
5. The result is the minimum U.S. school grade level at which the writing is easily read and understood.

For people unfamiliar with the U.S. school system, a child's grade level depends on his or her birthday and learning abilities. A 6-year-old child, for example, would typically be found in the first grade, while a 16-year-old child would normally be in the eleventh grade.

You should use caution when testing your Web site using a readability formula. A low style of writing may result from a slavish use of readability indexes. In other words, a monotonous succession of short sentences and simple words can make your Web site dull, which won't hold a visitor's attention.

The Fry Graph

Another popular formula for measuring readability is based on a chart called the *Fry Graph*. The steps for using the Fry Graph are as follows:

1. Randomly select three 100-word passages from your Web site.
2. Plot the average number of syllables versus the average number of sentences per 100 words on the following graph.
3. Use the Fry Graph to determine the estimated reading age (in years) of the material.
4. Selecting more passages from your Web site should improve the accuracy of your results.

Points located below the curve in Figure 6-2 typically imply that sentence lengths are longer than average. Points above the curve represent text that contains an unusually difficult vocabulary, such as science textbooks.

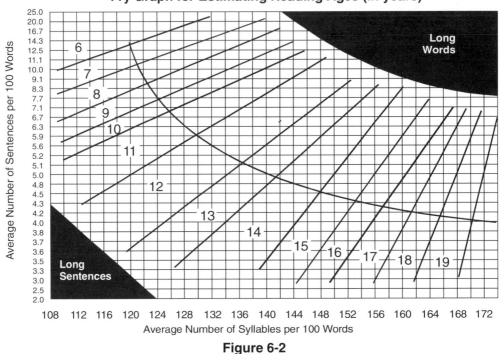

Figure 6-2

Other formulas for measuring readability include Dale-Chall, Flesch Reading Ease, Flesch-Kincaid Grade Level, McLaughlin SMOG, FORCAST, Powers-Somner-Kearl, and Spache. Many of these techniques focus on simple counts such as the number of words per sentence (more is harder to read) and the number of syllables per 100 words (more is harder to read). In order to calibrate some fixed points on the readability scale, the reading ages for various types of literature were determined using the average of four tests (Fry, Gunning, Flesch-Kincaid, and

Forcast). You can use the results listed in Table 6-4 as a point of reference when calculating the readability of your Web site.

Table 6-4 Readability Scores for Various Types of Literature

Reading Age (in years)	Description of Literature
25	Initial Public Offering (IPO) Legal Contracts
17½	Financial Newspaper
15	*The World of Physics*, by Avison
13	*A Tale of Two Cities*, by Dickens
11½	*To Kill a Mockingbird*, by Lee
11	*Lord of the Flies*, by Golding
5	Disney Book

Source: Timetabler.com

Recent versions of word processors include built-in readability tools. MS-Word 97 and 2000, for example, use the Flesch Reading Ease and Flesch-Kincaid Grade Level scoring formulas. You can use the word processor to calculate the readability of your Web page by opening the HTML file directly, or copying and pasting the text from your browser's window. The MS-Word Flesch Reading Ease score rates text on a 100-point scale; the higher the score, the easier it is to understand the document. For standard documents, many authors aim for a score between 60 and 70. The MS-Word Flesch-Kincaid Grade Level score rates text on a U.S. grade school level, so a score of 8.0 means that an eighth-grader (average 13-year-old) can understand the document. For standard documents, many authors aim for a reading age between 12 and 13.

B&D decided that it would like to have its Web site initially geared towards the professional investor. Therefore, B&D felt that their Web site should have an average readability score similar to many Financial Newspapers (i.e., a reading age of approximately 18). Table 6-5 lists some of the test cases in B&D's readability checklist.

Table 6-5 B&D's Readability Checklist

		Readability Validation
Pass	Fail	Description
☐	☐	A random selection of passages all scored at least 16 when measured using the Fry algorithm.
☐	☐	A random selection of passages all scored less than 25 when measured using the Fry algorithm.

Multiple Languages ■ ■ ■ ■ ■

Competing in the global economy means making your Web site/application usable for visitors from around the world. Table 6-6 lists the countries with populations of 50 million or more, which comprised nearly 75% of the world's population in 1998. Of these countries, only three (United States, Nigeria, and United Kingdom) use English as the official or majority language. While there are many other countries that have adopted English as their primary language, these countries represent a relatively small percentage of the world's total population.

Acceptance of the Internet around the world has not evolved equally. As businesses continue to globalize, the need to localize Web sites becomes more compelling. If your Web site can be viewed only in English, you're accommodating the needs of only a small percentage of the world's Internet population. If your anticipated Web site audience is worldwide, you should give serious consideration to either developing multiple Web sites (one per country/language) or allowing a single Web site to be viewed in different languages.

■■■■■■■■■■■■■■■■■
Did you know…

Even within the U.S., a large proportion of the population speaks Spanish as their first language.

■■■■■■■■■■■■■■■■■

There are many Web sites that provide statistics on the world's Internet usage:

cmg.co.uk
consumeronsite.com
cyberatlas.com
domainstats.com
emarketer.com
glreach.com
nsol.com
nua.ie
un.int

Table 6-6 Selected Countries and Languages Around the World

Country	Official/Majority Language	1998 Population	Percentage of 1998 World Population
China	Chinese	1,255,698,000	21.28%
India	Hindi	982,223,000	16.64%
United States (US)	English	274,028,000	4.64%
Indonesia	Indonesian	206,338,000	3.50%
Brazil	Portuguese	165,851,000	2.81%
Pakistan	Punjabi	148,166,000	2.51%
Russian Federation	Russian	147,434,000	2.50%
Japan	Japanese	126,281,000	2.14%
Bangladesh	Bangali	124,774,000	2.11%
Nigeria	English	106,409,000	1.80%
Mexico	Spanish	95,831,000	1.62%
Germany	German	82,133,000	1.39%
Vietnam	Vietnamese	77,562,000	1.31%
Philippines	Filipino	72,944,000	1.24%
Egypt	Arabic	65,978,000	1.12%
Iran (Islamic Repub.)	Persian	65,758,000	1.11%
Turkey	Turkish	64,479,000	1.09%
Thailand	Thai	60,300,000	1.02%
Ethiopia	Amharic	59,649,000	1.01%
France	French	58,683,000	0.99%
United Kingdom (UK)	English	58,649,000	0.99%
Italy	Italian	57,369,000	0.97%
Ukraine	Ukrainian	50,861,000	0.86%
1998 Total Population of Selected Countries		4,407,398,000	74.65%
1998 Total Population of the World		5,901,054,000	100%

Source: United Nations, Population Division, Department of Economic and Social Affairs

If a second language is added, you may be able to check your document's syntax using an automated tool such as a spellchecker in a word processor. Unfortunately, a tool is unlikely to be able to check the semantics of your document. Unless you have some bilingual staff on hand, you may have to make arrangements with a third party to have your foreign language documents adequately proofed. This will obviously require some pre-planning.

In the event that your organization doesn't have anyone available to translate your Web site into the foreign language, you may want to consider hiring a paid translation service to do the work and then use another third party to "test" the translation created by the first third party translation service. Another option is to convert the translated Web site back into English, using one of the free Web-based services that are available. If the English translation closely matches your original Web site, then it's reasonably safe to assume that your paid translation service did an acceptable job.

■■■■■■■■■■■■■■■■■
Did you know...

Yahoo (yahoo.com) and Dogpile (dogpile.com) list numerous companies that offer fee-based translation services:

berlitz.com
bowneglobal.com
lhsl.com
uniscape.com

Many Web sites offer online translations of individual Web pages:

altavista.com
lhsl.com
systransoft.com
transparent.com

Language Interpretations

There are many issues to consider when developing and testing a Web site for multi-language support. One important factor to consider is the use of potentially offensive terminology. Many words and phrases that are commonly accepted by people living in a specific country, state, province, or region may be considered rude or ignorant in other areas. Consider, for example, the common practice of U.S. citizens referring to themselves as "Americans." People who live within the United States commonly make this reference and accept it. People who live in North and South America outside of the U.S., however, consider this statement rude and an example of Americans'

■■■■■■■■■■■■■■■■■
The Microsoft Office 2000 Command Translator (microsoft.com) includes more than 4,300 commands with translations into 29 languages.

geographic ignorance. Arab Web sites typically don't display photos or images of women because many Arabs view women involved in business as inappropriate. As another example, because of its negative cultural connotations, Asian Web sites rarely use large amounts of the color black (e.g., black backgrounds). You should make sure to include specific test cases to help ensure that your Web site doesn't contain these kinds of potential problems.

Client-Side Language Attributes

Language attributes can be used to indicate which language a particular piece of text is written in. Alternatively, visitors can utilize the language option in their browsers to indicate their language preferences, thereby helping the Web server select which version of a particular Web page to send to the user. For example, a Web server that hosts copies of the United Nations Charter in several languages could automatically send the Chinese version to a viewer who had indicated Chinese as the preferred language. A visitor can choose one of the built-in language codes in his or her browser or manually specify the language code with an optional regional code. Any two-letter ISO 639 (ISO.ch) language abbreviation can be used as a language code, while any two-letter ISO 3166 country code can be used as a optional regional code. For example, a user could enter "FR-CA" to specify French/Canadian.

The LANG attribute can be added within any tag to specify the language of the contained element. This attribute can also be added within the HTML tag to specify a language for the entire Web page.

■■■■■■■■■■■■■■■■■
Did you know...

There are over 130 different language codes and over 250 different country codes.

Currently MSN Messenger Service (msn.com) and Real (real.com) use the browser's two-letter character preference to automatically determine which version (language) of software to download.

Server-Side Language Attributes

Another important consideration when developing and testing your Web site for multiple languages is which version of HTML you should select as your standard. Different versions support different character sets. HTML 2.0 and 3.2 are based on 8-bit character sets, which limit the number of different characters (or glyphs) to 256 per set. HTML 4.0 implements a standard called *Unicode*, which uses a 16-bit character set. This allows over 65,000 glyphs, which is enough room for just about every glyph from the various writing systems used around the world including Greek, Chinese, and Japanese. As Unicode continues to gain popularity and support, it will likely replace ASCII as the preferred standard for character coding. Bitstream (bitstream.com), a leading developer of font technology, has created a TrueType font called *Cyberbit* that contains a large percentage of the Unicode character sets. That is, it includes all of the typographic characters for most of the world's major languages.

■■■■■■■■■■■■■■■■
For more information on *Unicode*, visit:

unicode.org

B&D wanted to extend its Web site to the European audience. One of the possible solutions that they considered was to create a separate "portal" for each of the major languages. Each portal was to provide B&D's standard online brokerage services in their clients' native languages. One strategy that many multi-lingual Web sites use to reduce the amount of presentation testing is to use German as the primary testing language. German tends to be the most verbose European language. Consequently, German is the most difficult language to present (i.e., format) within the same Web page as other European languages. B&D used the German language and the test cases listed in Table 6-7 to help uncover text formatting problems.

Table 6-7 B&D's Language Testing Checklist

Language Validation

Pass	Fail	Description
☐	☐	No presentation problems occur when the page is displayed in German.
☐	☐	No local slang words or sayings are used (e.g., bear market), since they typically don't make sense in many foreign languages.
☐	☐	No offensive (when translated) terms are used.
☐	☐	Character sets for foreign languages are displayed correctly.
☐	☐	Foreign currencies are displayed correctly and converted if necessary.
☐	☐	Date and time formats are displayed correctly for the target countries (e.g., 20/01/00 for European versus 01/20/00 for U.S.).
☐	☐	Address formats are displayed correctly for the target countries.
☐	☐	Foreign tax rates, import duties, and rules are applied correctly.
☐	☐	A second third party was used to "unit" test the translations created by the first third party translation service.
☐	☐	Translated words have been placed in the correct order on each Web page. Unlike European languages that read from left to right, some languages read from top to bottom (e.g., Japanese, Chinese) and others read from right to left (e.g., Arabic, Hebrew).
☐	☐	Each Web page can be viewed using a browser without any special modifications (e.g., the user doesn't have to install any non-standard fonts).
☐	☐	Alphabetic and/or numerical lists are sorted correctly for each language.
☐	☐	Supporting documentation has been translated (e.g., help systems, error messages, user manuals, audio and video clips).
☐	☐	The colors and symbols used on this Web site have a consistent meaning across all of the required languages (e.g., red implies danger or stop in North America, but happiness in China).
☐	☐	Databases are set up to allow non-standard alphabets (e.g., double-byte characters).

Color Combinations

Using more colors on a Web page than a client's monitor can support may result in two different page colors being displayed using the exact same color. This can be a problem if the two colors are used as a visual cue (e.g., cueing a user when to buy or sell a stock) or the color of the text on a control button is the same color as the button itself. While 256 colors may seem like a lot, graphic files use colors to bleed one color into the next in order to create an aesthetically pleasing image. A graphic that appears to contain only 2 colors to the human eye, for example, may actually contain 16 or more colors. Unfortunately, the larger the number of colors used in a graphic, the larger the corresponding file and the longer it will take to download.

When selecting the color palette for your Web site, make sure that the colors are "browser safe" and are used in a fashion such that color-blind viewers will be able to see them (e.g., don't use green text on red buttons). British Telecom Labs (labs.bt.com) and VisiBone (visibone.com) provide background information on the use of Web/browser-safe colors, information about color-blindness, and tools (some are currently free of charge) for determining appropriate hexadecimal HTML and decimal RGB/CMYK color codes.

It's possible for a Web site to interrogate the client's operating system, determine the number of colors and screen resolution that a client is currently using, and then customize the Web page to fit the client's environment. This approach is generally considered undesirable due to the obvious privacy issues. Table 6-8 shows B&D's color testing checklist.

Can your Web site be viewed accurately via a client using the following color combinations?

- black & white (e.g., Personal Digital Assistant or PDA)
- grayscale
- 16 colors
- 256 colors
- 64k (16-bit)
- millions (32-bit)

StatMarket (statmarket.com) provides research on the screen resolutions and number of colors used by the current Internet population.

Table 6-8   B&D's Color Testing Checklist

Color Validation		
Pass	Fail	Description
☐	☐	The colors used on this Web site are friendly to color-blind viewers.
☐	☐	The colors used on this Web site are accurately displayed when using the minimum expected number of colors on a client.
☐	☐	All colors used on this Web site are browser-safe.

Screen Size and Pixel Resolution

If your developers used a higher screen resolution than was defined in your Web site standards, there's a high probability that some of your Web pages may be displayed too large at lower screen resolutions. Consequently, the browser may use undesirable horizontal and/or vertical scroll bars that will occupy additional pixels. Different browsers/versions will use different amounts of "white space" pixels between page objects. If your developers are using every last pixel, you may want to test the appearance of each Web page using several different browsers/versions to ensure that the page is rendered correctly.

In addition to desktop and laptop computers, there are many other devices that are being used to display Web pages. Portable Digital Assistants (PDA), for example, currently belong to either of two categories: Palm O/S devices or Windows CE devices. Palm O/S devices typically have a screen resolution of 160 x 160 pixels, whereas Windows CE devices are currently capable of a resolution of 240 x 320 pixels. While Wireless Application Protocol (WAP) mobile phones are currently only capable of displaying 96 x 65 pixels on each screen today, their screen

■■■■■■■■■■■■■■■■

Can your Web site be viewed accurately via a client using the following screen sizes?
- 2" (PDA)
- 10-14" (laptop)
- 14-22" (desktop)
- 22"+ (workstation)

Using the following resolutions?
- 96 x 65
- 160 x 160
- 240 x 320
- 640 x 480
- 800 x 600
- 1024 x 768
- 1280 x 1024
- 1600 x 1280
- 1800 x 1440
- 1920 x 1440
- 2048 x 1536
- and higher…

resolutions can be expected to increase significantly over the next few years.

With so many different kinds of Internet-capable devices available, you need to have a clear understanding of which of these devices your clients are likely to use to access your Web site. Table 6-9 provides a sample checklist for validating the screen size and pixel resolution capabilities of your Web site.

Table 6-9   B&D's Client-Side Display Testing Checklist

		Screen Size and Pixel Resolution Validation
Pass	Fail	Description
☐	☐	The Web site has been designed to fit the requirements of the lowest likely screen size and pixel resolution used by a client. If the clients' capabilities vary significantly, then multiple Web sites (or sub-sites) have been developed to accommodate each client.
☐	☐	The appearance of each Web page has been tested using several different browsers/versions to ensure that the page is displayed as intended (e.g., no horizontal scroll bars).

Personalization

Visitors often have very different needs, and many Web sites have gone to great lengths to accommodate these specialized requirements. Many Web sites can automatically tailor their content based on customer profiles. These Web sites use Customer Relationship Management (CRM) systems to predict the type of information that a visitor might be interested in seeing. Companies like Angara (angara.com), for example, provide services that employ demographic and geographic information stored in anonymous cookie-based profiles to help Web sites classify unidentified visitors into defined market segments. This allows participating Web sites to deliver content that is most interesting to their visitors. Visitors identified as Vermont residents, for example, may see advertisements for skis and lift tickets, while residents of Miami might see advertisements for sunglasses. The personalized advertising possibilities are almost unlimited.

Some Web sites (e.g., my.yahoo.com) allow visitors to customize their own content. A visitor, for example, can configure a Web site to display the latest stock quotes and local weather reports each morning. Another visitor may prefer to read the latest business headlines and horoscopes. Web sites that allow visitors to choose their own content have a clear marketing advantage over those that don't provide this type of service.

■■■■■■■■■■■■■■

Blue Martini
Software
(bluemartini.com),
Broadvision
(broadvision.com),
and E.piphany
(epiphany.com) all
provide information
on how Web sites
can be personalized
for each visitor.

You should find out what criteria (if any) are being used to determine the personalized content that is served up by your Web site. Once you have a clear understanding of the criteria that your Web site is using, you should design your test cases to ensure that a sufficient number of these various possibilities are tested. Table 6-10 lists some of the test cases that B&D used to validate the personalization capabilities of their Web site.

Table 6-10   B&D's Personalization Testing Checklist

		Personalization Validation
Pass	Fail	Description
☐	☐	The criteria used to determine the personalized content of the Web site have been identified and documented.
☐	☐	The user is able to personalize the specific type of market news that is displayed (e.g., only articles pertaining to Dell, Microsoft, and Lucent).
☐	☐	The user is able to personalize how his or her Watchlist (list of equities that he or she would like to follow closely) is displayed.

Accessibility ■ ■ ■ ■ ■

An aspect of Web testing that is often overlooked is checking how accessible your site is to people with disabilities. Those of us with 20/20 vision and perfect hearing sometimes find it difficult to understand the obstacles and challenges that people with disabilities have to face every day. Table 6-11 lists just some of the disabilities that affect Web site accessibility.

There are many tools and services available to help you test the accessibility of your Web site. The Center for Applied Special Technology (cast.org) provides a free utility called *Bobby* that will check a Web site using criteria based on the W3C guidelines to determine if the site is "accessible." Bobby can currently also be used to analyze Web pages for compatibility with various browsers. By default, Bobby checks Web sites for compatibility with HTML 4.0. Currently, Bobby can also be configured to test against many other standards including HTML 2.0, HTML 3.2, AOL 2.5 through 3.0, MS IE 2.0 through 5.0, Netscape 1.1 through 4.5, Lynx 2.5 through 2.7, WebTV 1.1 through 2.2, Opera 3.5, and Mosaic 2.1. Once a Web site receives a Bobby Approved rating, it's entitled to use the "Bobby Approved" icon.

Text-to-speech tools such as Home Reader from IBM (IBM.com) and JAWS from Henter-Joyce (HJ.com) allow visually impaired Internet users to access the content of the Web. Organizations such as the National Braille Press (braille.com) and the American Foundation for the Blind (AFB.org) provide more resources for blind Internet users.

■■■■■■■■■■■■■■■■■

"*The power of the Web is in its universality. Access by everyone regardless of disability is an essential aspect.*"

– Tim Berners-Lee, *Inventor of the World Wide Web.*

■■■■■■■■■■■■■■■■■

Did you know…

One lawsuit filed against AOL in 1999 by the American Foundation for the Blind (AFB.org) alleged that AOL did not abide by the Americans with Disabilities Act because its Web services were unusable by blind people.

Table 6-11   Disabilities That Affect Web Accessibility

Disability	Description
Blindness.	Users may experience difficulty: • obtaining any information via visual representation. • using input tools other than a keyboard (e.g., mouse). • understanding spatial metaphors for navigation. • discerning synthesized speech from other sounds.
Low vision.	Users may experience difficulty: • perceiving color, contrast, and depth differences. • understanding size-coded information. • discriminating between various fonts. • locating and/or tracking pointers, cursors, and hot spots. • entering information into online forms.
Hearing impairments.	Users may experience difficulty: • hearing certain frequency ranges. • localizing sounds. • picking up sounds against background noise.
Deafness.	Users may experience difficulty: • sensing auditory information. • producing recognizable speech. • using English as a second language (sign language is first).
Mobility impairments.	Users may experience difficulty: • pressing multiple keys simultaneously. • reaching for the keyboard or mouse. • performing actions that require precise movements.
Attention, memory, reading, & cognitive impairments.	Users may experience difficulty: • reading without sounding the words out loud. • performing actions in specific time frames. • learning and understanding online help. • understanding graphical objects without text labels.

Source: International Business Machines (IBM.com)

In an effort to improve awareness, the World Wide Web Consortium (W3C.org) launched the Web Accessibility Initiative (WAI), which provides guidelines and checklists to assist you in determining if your Web site is "accessible." Table 6-12 summarizes the guidelines that B&D decided to implement.

Table 6-12 B&D's Accessibility Testing Checklist

		Accessibility Validation
Pass	Fail	Description
☐	☐	ALT tags are included with all images and TITLE tags are included with all links.
☐	☐	Color should not be used as the sole means of conveying information.
☐	☐	Web pages that make use of style sheets should still be readable in browsers that do not support (or have turned off) this functionality.
☐	☐	Techniques that cause screen flicker are not used.
☐	☐	If image maps are used, an alternate list of corresponding links is provided.
☐	☐	If applets or scripts are used, the Web page is still usable if this functionality is turned off or not supported by the browser.
☐	☐	If audio files are used, transcripts are also provided. In addition to viewers with hearing difficulties, some viewers may not have speakers installed (common in a business environment) or may not want them turned on.
☐	☐	If video files are used, sub-titles are also available.
☐	☐	The Web page is understandable when heard through an audio-only browser.
☐	☐	The Web page is understandable when viewed through a text-only browser.
☐	☐	Multiple key combinations can also be entered sequentially or are mapped to a single key.

Disclosures and External Audits

Concerned with consumers' online privacy, both U.S. Federal and State legislators are currently considering introducing regulations that govern what information Web sites can collect from online visitors and how this information can be collected. To prove that they mean business, the U.S. Federal Trade Commission (ftc.gov) has recently taken action against a number of Web sites that did not live up to the privacy statements posted on their sites. Europe, on the other hand, already has much more stringent personal privacy rules than the United States. U.S. companies that intend to do business or are currently doing business in Europe may want to review their privacy policies and ensure that they comply with European regulations.

From a testing perspective, you should ensure that the processes in place within your organization don't conflict with any privacy statements made by the Web site. If there is a conflict, it should be reported to management for a decision on what (if anything) needs to be done to resolve the issues.

The public accounting profession has developed and is promoting a set of principles and criteria for Business-to-Consumer (B2C) e-commerce known as the WebTrust™ Principles and Criteria. Web Trust (CPAWebtrust.com) also has a corresponding seal of assurance that is often referred to as CPA WebTrust™ or CA WebTrust™. Public accounting firms and practitioners who have a WebTrust business license issued by the American Institute of Certified Public Accountants (AICPA.org), Canadian Institute of Chartered Accountants (CICA.ca), or other authorized national institute can provide assurance services to evaluate and test Web sites for conformance to these principles and criteria.

■■■■■■■■■■■■■■■■

The Direct Marketing Association (the-DMA.org) and MSN Link Exchange (linkexchange.com) both provide tools to help an organization develop a Privacy Policy/Statement.

■■■■■■■■■■■■■■■■

Among others, the following accounting firms have a WebTrust business license:

Arthur Andersen (arthurandersen.com)

Deloitte & Touche (deloitte.com)

Ernst & Young (ey.com)

KPMG International (kpmg.com)

PriceWaterhouse (pwcglobal.com)

The WebTrust seal of assurance is a symbolic representation of a practitioner's unqualified report. It also indicates to customers that they need to click to see the practitioner's report. This seal can be displayed on the entity's Web site together with links to the practitioner's report and other relevant information.

Specially trained CPAs are assigned to examine a company's Web site and evaluate whether or not it meets the prescribed WebTrust principles and criteria. If it does, a report indicating the Web site's compliance is issued and the site is granted the rights to submit an application for the WebTrust seal. Consumers can click on the seal to access the examination report as well as the WebTrust principles and criteria. The site is regularly revisited by the examining CPAs to ensure compliance.

The following Web sites provide more information about the WebTrust program:

AICPA.org/webtrust
CICA.ca
CPAWebtrust.com
verisign.com/webtrust

WebTrust is based on the following three broad principles:

- ◆ Business Practices Disclosure: The Web site owner discloses business practices for e-commerce transactions and executes those transactions in accordance with its disclosed business practices.
- ◆ Transaction Integrity: The Web site owner maintains effective controls to ensure that customers' orders are fulfilled and billed as agreed.
- ◆ Information Protection: The Web site owner maintains effective controls to ensure that private customer information is protected from uses not related to its business.

In addition to WebTrust, several other external audit programs are available. PriceWaterhouseCoopers, for example, launched their own variation of WebTrust, which is called BetterWeb (pwcbetterweb.com). The Better Business Bureau has taken its existing business model and ported it to the Web to create a BBB seal. Another popular external audit program, similar to WebTrust, is called TRUSTe™. By displaying the TRUSTe

Additional information about the TRUSTe and BBB programs is available at:

BBBonline.org
truste.org

mark, a Web site has agreed to notify its visitors of what information the site gathers and tracks about them, what it does with the information, and who it shares the information with.

Unfortunately, if you're wondering which external audit program is the best, there's no clear answer. In August 1999, *The Industry Standard* magazine (thestandard.com) reported that 588 companies had received the TRUSTe seal, 47 companies had received the Better Business Bureau (BBB) seal, and 20 companies had received the WebTrust seal.

Many e-commerce Web sites are subjected to some kind of external audit. These audits provide customers with a certain level of "peace of mind" when doing business with these Web sites. Table 6-13 lists B&D's privacy checklist.

■■■■■■■■■■■■■■■■
Did you know...

CNET Networks (cnet.com) currently uses the BBB online rating system to provide its viewers with a better idea of the quality of service that various online retailers offer for specific products.

Table 6-13 B&D's Privacy Checklist

Pass	Fail	Description
		Privacy Validation
☐	☐	The Web site has a legally valid privacy statement posted.
☐	☐	B&D meets or surpasses all of the claims it makes on its Web site.
☐	☐	The B&D Web site is approved by at least one external audit.
☐	☐	The third party's seal of approval is accurately displayed alongside B&D's privacy statement.

Useful URLs ■ ■ ■ ■ ■

Table 6-14 Useful Web Sites

Web Site URLs	Description of Services
bitstream.com, guiguide.com, ISO.ch, usableweb.com, uie.com, uiereports.com, unicode.org, useit.com, and W3C.org	Usability guidelines and standards.
cmg.co.uk, consumeronsite.com, cyberatlas.com, domainstats.com, emarketer.com, forrester.com, glreach.com, nsol.com, nua.ie, statmart.com, un.int, and zonaresearch.com	Usage statistics.
altavista.com, berlitz.com, bowneglobal.com, lhsl.com, systransoft.com, transparent.com, and uniscape.com	Translation services.
labs.bt.com and visibone.com	Browser-safe colors.
angara.com, bluemartini.com, broadvision.com, epiphany.com, and my.yahoo.com	Personalization software.
AFB.org, braille.com, braille.org, cast.org, CBIB.ca, trace.wisc.edu, and W3C.org	Accessibility guidelines.
HJ.com and IBM.com	Text-to-speech software.
AICPA.org, arthurandersen.com, CICA.ca, cpawebtrust.com, deloitte.com, DMA.org, ey.com, ftc.gov, kpmg.com, linkexchange.com, pwcbetterweb.com, pwcglobal.com, truste.org/truste.com/etrust.com, and verisign.com	Online privacy.
sqe.com/bdonline/	Case study Web site and downloadable test plans.

Chapter 7 – Performance

Although Internet bandwidth and Web server capacity have improved in recent years, Web site performance problems continue to challenge developers and testers. The combination of complex Web-based applications and the dynamic characteristics of Internet traffic can cause significant degradation in Web site performance. Performance problems can occur at many points along the route between your Web site and its visitors. These problems may be caused by a variety of events, many of which are predictable. Perhaps your Web site historically experiences a significant increase in traffic during the holidays. Maybe the opening bell of the New York Stock Exchange signals the beginning of a short burst of heavy traffic to your online trading Web site. Perhaps the April 15th tax deadline sends thousands of visitors to your site for last-minute tax advice. Or, maybe your Web site has surpassed the maximum capacity of your server (explained in *Chapter 8, Scalability*). The list of predictable events that can affect the performance of your Web site may be quite lengthy, but counter-measures can be taken to avoid these problems.

Performance problems caused by unpredictable events, on the other hand, are more difficult to identify and resolve. What happens, for example, if your Web site is affected by a late-breaking news report? Consider what would happen to online brokerage firms, for example, if the Federal Reserve announced a surprise interest rate hike that sent U.S. stock markets tumbling. On one occasion during a period of stock market instability, thousands of B&D's online customers tried to log onto B&D's Web site immediately after hearing a particularly gloomy news report. Many clients wanted to liquidate their

■■■■■■■■■■■■■■■■
Case Study

Review the following *Case Study Test Plans* to see an example of how the topics covered in this chapter can be utilized to test a Web site:

♦ System

Visit:
sqe.com/bdonline/

■■■■■■■■■■■■■■■■
Did you know...

Zona Research (zonaresearch.com) estimated that, in 1999, lost revenue due to unacceptable load times at all commerce Web sites exceeded $362 million per month.

The most affected sector was securities trading, followed by travel and book publishing.

---

positions as quickly as possible, so they placed market orders to sell. Other investors (called *bottom fishers*) logged onto the Web site just to watch stock prices fall in real time. These clients would try to predict where the bottoms might be and place orders to buy at those prices. Unfortunately, many of B&D's clients experienced catastrophic results. Some clients received the message, "Server not available." Others were unable to log onto the Web site and were given the message, "Login incorrect. Please try again." Perhaps worst of all, some customers who placed orders to sell, were subsequently dropped from the server without confirmation or status of their orders, and were unable to log back in again.

There are many consequences of under-performing Web sites. Slow pages can render expensive marketing campaigns less effective, and "dropped" transactions can result in lost revenue, regulatory agency fines, and even law suites. This chapter and the next focus on the Web technologies that affect a Web site's performance and capacity, and the strategies for testing them. Rather than create one large chapter to explain Performance testing, we have divided the subject matter into two chapters: Performance and Scalability. The first chapter (Performance) covers the basic issues that affect all Web sites, big or small. The next chapter (Scalability) examines the challenges and solutions to testing larger Web sites.

■■■■■■■■■■■■■■■■■
Did you know...

When Schwab's Web site (schwab.com) went down for 90 minutes on February 24, 1999, their PR department counted over 300 news broadcasts about the outage.

When Should You Start? ■■■■■

When should you start performance testing? At the beginning of the development cycle? At the end? In the middle? The longer you wait to begin performance testing, the more costly the problem may become, as illustrated in Figure 7-1. From a strictly financial point of view, performance testing should begin as early as possible during the development cycle. However, this doesn't necessarily imply that beginning performance testing early will guarantee that you won't have any performance problems, just that it will cost less to resolve them.

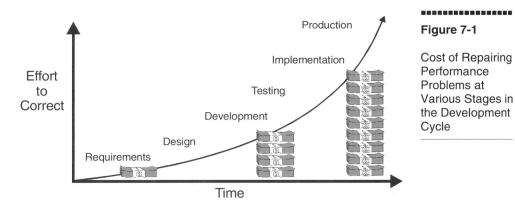

Figure 7-1

Cost of Repairing
Performance
Problems at
Various Stages in
the Development
Cycle

The Newport Group (newportgroup.com) conducted a recent survey of 117 companies with annual revenues of at least $200 million. The survey found that of those companies whose Web-based applications scaled as expected, 94% started performance testing prior to deployment. Approximately 90% of the companies that didn't do performance testing before deployment experienced scalability problems. The detailed results of the survey are provided in Tables 7-1 and 7-2.

The survey suggests that the odds of experiencing performance problems will significantly increase if performance testing is not done before deploying your Web site.

Table 7-1   Web Applications Did Scale as Expected

% of Companies	Description
94%	Did do performance testing before deployment.
6%	Did NOT do performance testing before deployment.

Table 7-2 Web Applications Did NOT Scale as Expected

% of Companies	Description
32%	Did do performance testing in the development stage.
68%	Did NOT do performance testing before deployment.

The best time to begin performance testing your Web site is highly dependent upon your specific organization, its development process, and the type of Web-based application that you're developing. For instance, it may be possible to start load testing your Web site infrastructure before the applications that will run on it have even been written. Industry benchmarking applications such as Webstone (mindcraft.com) and WebBench (zdnet.com) can be used to compare different hardware and system software configurations.

Performance Testing Objectives ■ ■ ■ ■ ■

Before developing performance test cases for your Web site, you should identify your performance pass/fail criteria to assess what performance testing objectives have been set. All too often, testing is started without first having a clear understanding of what should be tested. In other words, you need to know what requirements have to be met in order to determine what needs to be measured or tested and what constitutes a pass or fail. This will also help you make educated decisions when evaluating and purchasing Web performance testing tools and services. You won't know what features you'll need in a test tool unless you clearly understand the objectives that you need to achieve. Table 7-3 lists some of B&D's performance objectives.

Table 7-3   B&D's Performance Testing Objectives

Objective	Description
1	Tune the various Web site components to support the maximum load possible using the current hardware.
2	Ensure that 95% of non-encrypted page requests are downloadable within 10 seconds (15 seconds for encrypted) when accessed by a typical client.
3	Determine the average response time that will be experienced by a typical U.S.-based client.
4	Determine the maximum number of concurrent users, session initiations per hour, and/or transactions per second that the current Web site infrastructure can handle while still providing an acceptable level of performance.
5	Determine the maximum number of concurrent users, session initiations per hour, and/or transactions per second that the current Web site infrastructure can handle before causing a system failure.
6	Determine the amount of network bandwidth needed to support the Web site when it processes the maximum number of transactions per second that it can handle.
7	Determine how the Web site handles loads greater than its maximum capacity.
8	Identify the slowest (5%) and fastest (5%) Web pages to download.

Response-Time Requirements ■■■■■

Visitors who have to wait more than 10 seconds for "something to happen" are likely to become impatient and start re-clicking buttons. Unlike brochureware Web sites, resubmitting or canceling orders on transactional Web sites can create significant problems. Databases may become corrupt, resulting in lost orders, wrong order quantities, or other erroneous information. While it may have been a "nice to have" requirement for a brochureware site, a maximum 10-second turnaround time is essential for most transactional Web sites. Table 7-4 lists the basic "rules of thumb" that B&D used for its response time requirements.

Table 7-4   Acceptable Response Times

Time (in seconds)	Description of Action
Less than 0.1s	This is the limit for having the user feel that the system is reacting instantaneously. That is, no special feedback regarding the time delay is necessary other than displaying the results. Example actions include button clicks or client-side dropdown menus.
Less than 1.0s	This is the limit for the user's flow of thought to stay uninterrupted, even though the user will notice a slight delay. Normally, no special feedback is necessary for delays between 0.1 and 1.0 seconds. The user may, however, lose the feeling of operating directly on the data. Example actions include the initiation of page navigation or Java applet execution.
Less than 10s	This is the maximum amount of time that can lapse while keeping the user's attention focused on the dialogue. Example actions include completion of page navigation.

Source: Adapted from Jakob Nielson's, *Designing Web Usability*, New Riders Publishing, 2000

For longer delays, users will typically want to perform other tasks while waiting for the computer to finish. In these situations, the server should provide the user with feedback regarding when it expects to be done processing the data. Feedback is especially important when the response time is likely to vary from user to user, so they know what to expect and when to expect it. Unfortunately, most Web browsers fail to provide useful progress bars and they don't communicate what percentage of the entire page has been downloaded. From a usability perspective, it's important to ensure that different Web pages download in approximately the same amount of time, thereby giving the user a consistent feel to the Web site. Although a Webmaster wouldn't want to slow down a page because it downloads too fast, a super-fast Web page could be redesigned to take some of the workload from slower Web pages. By allowing a super-fast Web page to download graphics that it doesn't need, other slower Web pages can quickly access these graphics through a browser's cache.

Response time requirements vary from Web site to Web site. Some organizations use the response time requirements listed in Table 7-4 as a guide for developing their performance objectives. Other organizations may place limits on the physical size of their Web pages, which, in turn, affects response time. For example, an organization may require all of its Web pages to be less than 50 Kbytes, based on the assumption that it will typically require approximately 6 seconds to download over a 28.8 Kbps modem. The overall objectives remain the same regardless of which approach you use to define your requirements. Table 7-5 lists the average response times for some popular Web sites.

Table 7-5   Response Times for Popular Web Sites (at 56.6 Kbps)

Web site	Response Time (in seconds)	Availability (% of uptime)
amazon.com	23.88	97.2
barnesandnoble.com	16.78	96.8
cdnow.com	18.67	87.2
ebay.com	17.28	96.1
etoys.com	18.67	93.2
gateway.com	18.37	96.2
landsend.com	17.60	97.9
macys.com	35.41	92.6
wal-mart.com	22.28	97.7
wine.com	24.52	89.4
Average	**21.36**	**94.4**

Source: USA Today December 9, 1999 in cooperation with Keynote Systems.

Categories of Performance Tests

As we discussed earlier in this chapter, performance problems are based on events that fall into two categories: predictable and unpredictable. Thus, performance tests should be designed around both kinds of events. But what is performance testing? With so many variables, how can we actually measure the performance of a Web site? In its broadest sense, performance testing allows you to observe and evaluate a Web site's responses under all possible load conditions for all possible periods of time. Web site performance testing typically falls into the following categories: smoke, load, stress, and spike/bounce tests. The results of these measurements can then be analyzed and related back to the performance objectives of the Web site. If incidents are found, the information can be forwarded to the appropriate people so decisions can be made regarding possible remedies.

Performance tests can be grouped into the following categories:

- smoke
- load
- stress
- spike/bounce

Smoke Testing

Smoke tests are used to evaluate whether or not a software release is really ready for testing. Smoke tests can be as simple as performing a few manual functional tests with a 28.8 Kbps modem and a stopwatch, or they can be as complex as running a fully automated load that reports on the approximate performance of the entire Web site. These smoke tests can then be used as entry criteria for more rigorous testing by the performance testing team.

In addition to running a smoke test before executing any large-scale performance test, you should ensure that any shared resources needed by the test environment (e.g., network bandwidth) are available and that running the performance test

Did you know...

The term *smoke test* originated in the hardware testing industry, where some products that were being tested would literally start to smoke.

will not impact other users (e.g., developers) without their prior consent. Smoke testing is also referred to as "sanity" testing or "drive-by" testing. Just like shopping for a house, you might drive by a neighborhood to determine whether it's worth spending the time to actually get out of the car to view a particular house.

Load Testing

Load testing is used to model the anticipated real-world performance of a Web site over a short period of time. The results of a load test can help you determine whether your specific combination of hardware and software (e.g., Web server, application server, database, network bandwidth, etc.) will allow your Web site to meet its performance requirements. Load testing allows you to determine the average response times of typical users under normal conditions. When implemented early in the development cycle, load testing may be used to help determine the feasibility of a particular architecture before your organization buys expensive hardware and heavily invests in software development. B&D's load testing checklist is shown in Table 7-6.

Table 7-6 B&D's Load Testing Checklist

Average Response Time Under Normal Conditions		
Pass	Fail	Description
☐	☐	95% of Web pages download in less than 10 seconds when using a 28.8 Kbps modem from any location within the continental U.S.
☐	☐	During market hours, quotes are never more than 20 minutes old.
☐	☐	Market orders are completed within 2 minutes of the user's request.
☐	☐	Confirmations of completed transactions are sent to users within 30 seconds.

Stress Testing

Stress testing is used to determine if your specific combination of hardware and software (e.g., Web server, application server, database, network bandwidth, etc.) has the capacity to handle an excessively large number of transactions during peak operating hours. Additionally, stress testing is used to determine what will happen when the maximum capacity is actually reached.

■■■■■■■■■■■■■■■■■
Do you know what happens to your Web site after it reaches its maximum capacity?

Suppose, for example, your Web site only has enough resources to support 100 concurrent users. What will happen when the 101st user tries to access your Web site? Upon receiving a request from the 101st user, which of the following actions should your Web site take: shut down the server, send a "server not available" message to the 101st user, or place the 101st user in a holding queue until resources are available? Strange as it may seem, many servers shut down and reboot themselves if their resources are stretched too thinly. What happens to the 101st user shouldn't be a surprise to you. Since Web site performance should ideally degrade slowly and predictably, you should have a clear understanding of exactly how your Web site will react when your server is extended beyond its capacity.

Particular attention should be paid to the functional integrity of the Web site while it's being stressed in order to ensure that the functionality that worked correctly during periods of low load still works correctly while the site is being stressed. If, for example, a user of B&D's Web site wants to know the dividend yield on a particular stock, will the Web site still calculate the yield accurately while the site is under stress?

Data integrity is one of the most important aspects of any transactional Web site. What would happen if, due to excessive workloads, the Web site incorrectly calculates 1 in every 1,000 requests for a stock's yield (e.g., 7% instead of 0.7%)? Depending on the circumstances surrounding the situation, the impact could be minimal or it could be catastrophic. The point is that you shouldn't leave the integrity of your data to chance. Stress testing can help avoid a potentially disastrous situation. This is especially important if your Web site utilizes load balancers and/or data replication servers in order to improve performance. Your test cases should include the possibility of conflicts, and you should clearly understand what actions your Web site will take to resolve them.

Stress tests typically include transactions that require extensive computations or significant manipulation of data. Test cases should include activities that will add, change, and delete records from the database in order to place excessive stress on your Web site's input/output processes and services. Peak operating hours may be any period of time when an excessive number of users are attempting to access your Web site concurrently. B&D, for example, typically experiences peak operating hours from 9:30 to 10:15 a.m. and from 3:30 to 4:00 p.m. Eastern Standard Time. These are the periods immediately after the opening bell of the New York Stock Exchange and immediately before the closing bell, when investors flood B&D's Web site with orders.

B&D had two main goals for stress testing their system: 1) to find when and where the system would break and 2) to analyze what would happen when it does break. B&D's team used the list of stress testing objectives and test cases shown in Tables 7-7 and 7-8 while conducting their stress tests. However, some of these test cases may not be desirable or appropriate for your particular Web site. Stress test cases are highly dependent on the specific nature of your application and the responses that are acceptable to you.

Table 7-7 B&D's Stress Testing Checklist I

Maximum Value	Description
Determining Stress Points	
☐	Determine the maximum number of transactions per second that the Web site can be expected to support.
☐	Determine the maximum number of session initiations per hour that the Web site can be expected to support.
☐	Determine the maximum number of concurrent users that the Web site can be expected to support.

Table 7-8 B&D's Stress Testing Checklist II

Pass	Fail	Description
		System Approaches Maximum Capacity
		At 80% Capacity
☐	☐	Until the system returns to normal operating conditions, new clients who try to log on will be given a message to try again later
☐	☐	Inactive clients will be given a warning message that they may be dropped from the system and not permitted to log on again until conditions return to normal.
☐	☐	Non-critical services (e.g., stock graphs) will be shut down in the order of least to most important.
☐	☐	Pager or e-mail notification of potential gridlock is sent to technical support personnel.
		At 90% Capacity
☐	☐	Inactive clients will be logged off.
☐	☐	Backup Web sites will be activated.
☐	☐	Pager or e-mail notification of potential gridlock are re-sent to technical support personnel.

(Continued)

Table 7-8 (*Continued*)

Pass	Fail	System Approaches Maximum Capacity Description
		At 100+% Capacity
☐	☐	The system does not allow any new transactions to be initiated.
☐	☐	The system does not reboot itself.
☐	☐	The system does not shut down security services.
☐	☐	The system does not suspend transaction logging.
☐	☐	The system does not gridlock.
☐	☐	Hardware components do not fuse (e.g., melt down).
☐	☐	Page or e-mail notification of impending gridlock are sent to technical support.
		At Any Capacity
☐	☐	The system maintains its functional integrity.

Spike/Bounce Testing

Spike testing of Web sites is analogous to predicting hurricanes. Weather forecasters are always wondering, "When will the storm hit? Where will it hit? How strong will it be?" Well, we already know the answer to one of these questions. The "storm" will hit your Web site, although some sites are more susceptible to these "storms" than others. This is due to the combination of predictable and unpredictable events throughout the world. Holidays, late-breaking news stories, special events, and product or service announcements can all cause spikes. The only question remaining is, when will the spike hit and how strong will it be?

One possible variation of spike testing is to follow the spike with a low and then with another spike. "Bouncing" the load up and down will allow you to determine how well the Web site can

■■■■■■■■■■■■■■■■■
Did you know...

Spike testing is sometimes referred to as *overload* testing, *soak* testing, and *surge* testing.

Bounce testing is also called *elasticity* testing.

handle the change in load and whether it's able to claim and release resources as needed.

Spikes are characterized by random arrivals of client requests that significantly exceed normal averages. A Web site may experience exceptional load growth over a very short period of time. While a Web site may be able to handle the load in a gradual ramp-up, the sudden nature of a spike can cause serious problems. A state lottery Web site, for example, may expect a surge in users immediately after a drawing. Some Web sites experience such rapid growth that they can't handle the surge. If you can anticipate some spikes, you may want to design your test cases around these scenarios.

B&D developed the test cases listed in Table 7-9 to test the performance of their Web site during spikes. They also identified specific periods of time when spikes were most likely to occur: immediately after the opening bell of the New York Stock Exchange, or shortly before the closing bell.

Table 7-9 B&D's Spike Testing Checklist

Performance During Spikes		
Pass	Fail	Description
☐	☐	No users who were logged in to the Web site prior to the spike are dropped.
☐	☐	Transactions that were started before the spike are still in progress and successfully completed after the spike.
☐	☐	New users are able to log in to the Web site during and after the spike.
☐	☐	Security services remain active during the spike.

User Profiles

W̲hile the total number of hits, page views, or unique visitors per day are useful measures to have for marketing purposes, they don't provide much information on your Web site's performance. From a testing perspective, the number of transactions per second, the megabytes of network traffic per second, the number of users that are simultaneously able to access the Web site (i.e., concurrent users), and the number of session initiations per hour (i.e., new people arriving) are better gauges of how much load is being applied to your Web site.

User Profiles may also be referred to as *operational profiles* or *Web site usage signatures*.

Once you've determined an estimate for the number of transactions per second, network traffic, and users that the Web site can be expected to attract, the next step is to build "user profiles" for these visitors. User profiles can help you gain an understanding of what these users are doing on the Web site and what characteristics they possess that might affect the performance of the Web site. The more accurate these user profiles can be made, the closer the performance tests will be to modeling the real-world conditions that your Web site will ultimately have to survive.

The following sections provide an overview of the various parameters that you should consider when building user profiles that will be used to performance test a Web site.

User Activities

Many transactions occur more frequently than others, and should therefore comprise a larger proportion of the test data and scripts used for performance testing. In order to simulate the real workload that your Web site is likely to experience, it's important that you use test data and test scripts that realistically represent the types of transactions that your Web site is expected to handle. If your organization typically only sells one product for every 50 visitors, for example, it would be unrealistic to weigh a "browse" and a "buy" script evenly. A better approach would be to use a 50:1 weight ratio in which there are 50 browsers for every 1 buyer.

The mix of transaction types may change depending on the time of day. One large U.S. e-tailer, for example, discovered that the number of visitors to its Web site peaked in the early evening, but purchase transactions peaked during lunch hours.

Think Times

The time that it takes for a client (or virtual client) to respond to a Web site has a significant impact on the number of clients that the site can support. People, like computers, have a wide range of different processing levels and abilities. Different users require various amounts of time to think about the information that they have received. Some users race from one Web page to another, barely pausing long enough to comprehend what they've seen between pages. Others need some time to contemplate what they've just read before moving on to the next page. The length of this pause is called *think time*. Think time is generally considered to be the time taken from when a client receives the last data packet for the Web page currently being viewed to the moment that the client requests a new page. Table 7-10 lists some of the types of users that you may expect to visit your Web site and their corresponding think times.

Table 7-10   Think Times for Various Types of Visitors

Type of Visitor	Description of Think Time
Aggressive	Only thinks about the most recent Web page for a few seconds.
Casual	Typically needs 30 seconds to several minutes before requesting a new Web page.
Out to Lunch	Hasn't moved on to another Web site, but has become preoccupied with another task. Expects to be able to return to the Web site minutes or even hours later and continue wherever he or she left off.

In theory, a Web site that can support a maximum of 100 "10-second aggressive" clients should be able to support 300 "30-second casual" clients because both types of clients result in 600 transactions per minute.   Unfortunately, this theory only holds true for the most rudimentary of Web sites.   The more interactive Web sites require resources for both active and dormant clients. Therefore, 300 casual clients are likely to require more resources than 100 aggressive clients.   The content on a Web page can also influence the amount of time that a client spends viewing or thinking about that page.   A two-page news article, for example, would typically be viewed longer than a "click here to enter" home page.

When recording or writing test scripts for performance testing, you should consider how much time each of the various types of clients might spend thinking about each page.   From this data, you can create a reasonable distribution of timings and, possibly, a randomizing algorithm.   Web logs can be a good source for estimating think times for Web pages that have already been hosted in production.

Some performance tests may require that certain clients attempt specific steps within their test scripts at the exact same moment in time.   To help you accomplish this, some test tools allow you to specify synchronization points in your test scripts. Synchronization points help ensure that even if different clients require varying amounts of time to arrive at a critical point in the test script, they will all initiate their designated requests at the same point in time.

Site Arrival Rates

Unfortunately, even if the number of users remains constant, network requests don't arrive evenly spaced but, instead, they arrive in bunches. When designing a performance test, you should make sure that your page requests arrive in a random order rather than at regular intervals. Network engineers and testers are familiar with this consideration and often use "Queueing Theory" techniques to help apply an appropriate degree of randomness to their network traffic patterns. Gunter Bolch et al.'s book, *Queueing Networks and Markov Chains: Modeling and Performance Evaluation With Computer Science Applications*, provides an explanation of how Markov chains can be used to design the load for performance testing a Web site. Session initiations per hour can be an effective method of specifying the workload that a Web site is expected to handle.

Under exceptional circumstances, input data that is precisely spaced out (e.g., generated by a load testing tool) may cause the Web site to behave in an unusual way. If the interval of the input data is the same as (or a multiple of) the natural resonance of the Web site under test, the Web site may perform for this specific interval period exceptionally well (or poorly). This effect is sometimes referred to as a "strobe effect" or "metronome effect."

If an error occurs using a random load, it's often useful to be able to reproduce this problem on-demand. This is possible if the randomizing algorithm uses a "seed" to generate the first and subsequent random values.

Site Abandonment

Simple test scripts/tools assume that a client will wait until a Web page has been completely downloaded before requesting a subsequent page. Unfortunately, in real life, some users may be able to select their next page before the previous page has been completely downloaded. These users may already know where they want to go as soon as the navigation bar appears. Alternatively, some users will simply go to another Web site if they have to wait too long for a requested page to appear. To mimic these conditions, your test scripts may need to terminate some (or all) of the script's page requests prematurely.

The percentage of users that abandon a Web site will vary from site to site, depending on how vital the content is to the user. A user may only be able to get his or her bank balance from a particular bank's Web site, for example, but the same user could get a stock quote from numerous competitors. One thing is certain, the longer a user has to wait, the more likely it is that he or she will abandon the Web site. In order to model the real world, test scripts should include a randomized event that will terminate a test script's execution for a particular client if the client is forced to wait too long for the page to download. The longer the delay, the more likely that the client will be terminated.

Usage Patterns

Unlike typical mainframe or client-server applications, Web sites often experience large swings in usage depending on the type of visitors that come to the site. Retail customers, for example, typically use a Web site in the evenings (7:00 p.m. EST to 11:00 p.m. PST). Business customers typically use a Web site during regular working hours (9:00 a.m. EST to 4:00 p.m. PST). The functionality of a Web site can also have a significant impact on usage patterns. Stock quotes, for example, are typically requested during market trading hours (9:30 a.m. EST to 4:00 p.m. EST).

When attempting to model the real world, you should conduct some research to determine when peak usage ramp-up and ramp-down occurs, peak usage duration and whether any other user profile parameters vary by the time of day, day of the week, or another time increment. Once your research is done, you should schedule your tests to run over the Internet at appropriate times.

■■■■■■■■■■■■■■■■■

The following Web sites provide statistics on Internet traffic and usage around the world:

Internettraffic report.com
mids.org
statmarket.com

Client Platforms

Different client-side products (e.g., browsers and operating systems) will cause slightly different HTTP traffic to be sent to the Web server. More importantly, if the Web site has been designed to serve up different content based on the client-side software that is used (a technique commonly referred to as browser sniffing), then the Web site will have to perform different operations with correspondingly different workloads.

Some browsers allow users to change certain client-side network settings that affect the way the browser communicates and the

■■■■■■■■■■■■■■■■■

B&D found that 10% of their visitors used a Mac, but less than 1% of their active traders were Mac users.

corresponding workload that a browser puts on a Web server. Although few users ever change their default settings, different browsers/versions have different defaults. Consequently, a more accurate test load would vary these default values.

The Connections (or Threads) setting is used by the browser to determine the maximum number of network connections it can use to connect to a Web server. Netscape 3.0, for example, has a default value of 4. The text on a Web page and each image associated with the Web page are typically stored as separate files. To bring each of these files to the client, the browser must open a separate connection to a Web server. The browser can then bring in a Web page's text and multiple image files simultaneously by opening more than one connection to a server. By specifying a larger number of connections, the user is actually specifying more simultaneous connections. However, this can slow down the speed of each individual connection and place a greater strain on the Web server. Figure 7-2 illustrates how different browsers can be configured to utilize a different numbers of connections.

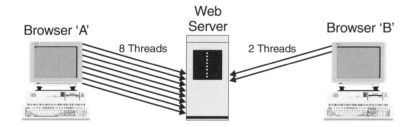
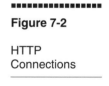

Figure 7-2

HTTP
Connections

In theory, browser 'A,' which is configured with 8 threads, can download the Web page four times faster than browser 'B,' which is configured with 2 threads. Unfortunately, by specifying too many simultaneous connections, a client can actually slow down the speed of each individual connection and place a greater strain on the Web server by maintaining too many connections for too long a period of time.

The HTTP version 1.1 network protocol includes an option called "Keep Alive," which when enabled or available (i.e., some older browsers and Web servers do not support this feature) allows the browser and Web server to reuse HTTP connections. Rather than having to renegotiate a separate HTTP connection for each file on the Web page, multiple files (e.g., graphic files) within the same TCP transmission (e.g., Web page) can be sent one after the other via the same connection. This improvement can make a significant difference to client download times and to the workload experienced by the Web server.

The network buffer size is the number of kilobytes of memory that a user wishes to allocate for network data transmissions. The network buffer size determines the amount of data that can be received in a network data transmission. For example, Netscape 3.0's default value is 1 Kbyte. Larger buffers mean more data and less work for the Web server, but they may also saturate the client.

Client Preferences

While most browsers allow users to change various client-side preferences, few users actually change their default settings. However, different products/versions of a browser may have different default settings. For example, the French version of a browser will typically have the default language set to French.

◼◼◼◼◼◼◼◼◼◼◼◼◼◼◼
Language preferences are covered in more detail in the *Usability* chapter.

If encryption is going to be used to send and receive secure Web pages, the strength (or key size) of the encryption used to transfer the data is dependent upon a negotiation that takes place between the Web server and the browser. The stronger the encryption (the larger the key), the harder it is for an eavesdropper to decipher. Unfortunately, the stronger encryption schemes utilize more network bandwidth and increase the processing requirements of the CPUs that perform the encrypting and deciphering (typically the Web server). Consequently, users with low settings (e.g., 40-bit keys) will put less of a strain on a Web server than users with high settings (e.g., 128-bit keys).

A Web site visitor can speed up the delivery of a Web page, consume a smaller portion of the Web site's bandwidth, and establish fewer Web server connections by simply indicating that he or she doesn't want graphics or applets to be downloaded. If present in significant numbers, these easy-to-satisfy clients can have a noticeable effect upon the performance of the Web site.

While the user typically has the option of turning scripting languages on/off, the effect on the Web site is likely to be negligible unless developers of the site have built alternate Web pages for those visitors who don't want to (or can't) run client-side scripts. The same holds true for language preferences. Unless the developers have opted to provide different content based on a client's language preference setting, the impact on performance measurements will be minimal.

Clients who turn off cookies may place a smaller demand on the Web site, because cookies consume network bandwidth. Alternatively, turning off cookies may actually require the Web site to use less efficient methods in order to maintain a session and, consequently, place a greater strain on the Web site. Before deciding whether or not the cookie parameter should be included in a user profile, you may want to evaluate the impact (if any) that using cookies will have on the Web site's performance.

The size of a browser's cache (memory and/or disk) is typically large enough to store all of the HTML and graphic files utilized by a single test script. Therefore, this client preference typically doesn't affect the load being placed on a Web server, unless the Web site contains exceptionally large files such as bitmaps and/or the test scripts are extremely long.

In summary, client preferences typically include turning on/off scripting languages, applets or ActiveX controls, graphics, and cookies. A client also has the option of selecting a language, the strength of encryption supported (if any), and the size of the browser's memory and disk caches.

Web logs can be analyzed to determine some of the preference settings of the Web site's audience. For example, B&D found that 5% of their clients had disabled cookies, while 90% had the capability to use 128-bit data encryption (a requirement for trading via the Web site).

Client Internet Access Speeds

Bandwidth is analogous to a water pipe or a garden hose. The greater the size of the pipe, the larger the volume of water that can pass through it at any given time. Smaller pipes can only allow smaller amounts of water to pass through them. To apply this concept to the Internet, think of bandwidth as a communications pipe. The larger the communications pipe, the more information can be transmitted through it at a specific instant in time.

The transmission speed or bandwidth that visitors of your Web site are using may have a significant impact on the Web site's overall design, implementation, and testing. In the early days of the Web (circa mid-1990s), 14.4 Kbps was the most common communications speed available. Hence, 14.4 Kbps became the lowest common denominator for Internet access. When 28.8 Kbps modems were introduced, however, they offered a

■■■■■■■■■■■■■■■■■
Did you know...

Before the Web gained popularity, many slower modems were commonly in use:

- ◆ 300 bps
- ◆ 1200 bps
- ◆ 9600 bps

significant performance improvement over 14.4 Kbps modems and quickly surpassed 14.4 Kbps modems in popularity. When 56.6 Kbps modems were introduced, the performance improvement (they often only obtained 45 Kbps or worse) wasn't as dramatic as the difference between 14.4 Kbps and 28.8 Kbps (i.e., 100%). Consequently, many 28.8 Kbps modems are still in use today, but unlike 14.4 Kbps modems, which have almost completely vanished, 28.8 Kbps modems still comprise a significant (although decreasing) proportion of the Internet population. Many companies therefore use the 28.8 Kbps transmission speed as a basis for determining their Web site's performance requirements.

Table 7-11 lists some of the data transmission methods available today along with their corresponding speeds and file download times. The file download time listed in this table is based on the theoretical time required to download a single 10 Mbyte file using File Transfer Protocol (FTP). Page download time is based on the theoretical time required to download a 50 Kbyte Web page using HyperText Transfer Protocol (HTTP). In actuality, Web page download times are widely affected by the size of the Web page, number and size of graphic images per page, configuration of enabling hardware, and Internet traffic at any given time of day. That is, they are subject to extreme variations.

■■■■■■■■■■■■■■■■■

The following URLs provide more information on transmission speeds:

cablemodem.com
cablelabs.com
opencable.com
packetcable.com

While the download times listed in Table 7-11 are used for modeling purposes only, they are extremely valuable in predicting expected download times for other transmission speeds. Rather than configuring a computer with hardware capable of handling each of these transmission methods, it's possible to get a "ballpark" estimate for the other methods by accurately measuring just one. Then, using Table 7-11, you can estimate the transmission time required if the other methods were actually used. A 28.8 Kbps modem, for example, typically requires approximately 50% longer (46 minutes versus 30 minutes) to download than a 56.6 Kbps modem. Therefore, a file that requires 6 minutes to download over a 56.6 Kbps modem could be expected to require 9 minutes to download via a 28.8 Kbps modem.

Table 7-11 Data Transmission Methods, Speeds, and Times

Data Transmission Method	Transmission Speed	10 MB File FTP Download Time	50 KB Page HTTP Download Time
Dial-up Line	14.4 Kbps	N/A	12 seconds
Dial-up Line	28.8 Kbps	46 minutes	6 seconds
Dial-up Line	33.3 Kbps	40 minutes	N/A
Dial-up Line	56.6 Kbps (45.0 Kbps actual speed)	30 minutes	3 seconds
Integrated Services Digital Network (ISDN, 1-Line)	64 Kbps (1 line)	21 minutes	N/A
Integrated Services Digital Network (ISDN, 2-Line)	128 Kbps (2 lines)	10 minutes	1.3 seconds
Satellite (Direct PC)	400 Kbps	3 minutes	N/A
Local Area Network (LAN, Ethernet)	10 - 100 Mbps	N/A	N/A
Asymmetric Digital Subscriber Line (ADSL)	1.5 - 9 Mbps (receiving) 16 - 640 Kbps (sending)	9 - 53 seconds	N/A
Asynchronous Transfer Mode (ATM)	25 - 622 Mbps	N/A	N/A
Cable Modem	10 - 30 Mbps	3 - 8 seconds	N/A

(*Continued*)

Table 7-11　(*Continued*)

Data Transmission Method	Transmission Speed	10 MB File FTP Download Time	50 KB Page HTTP Download Time
Frame Relay (T-1 line)	1.544 Mbps	N/A	0.1 seconds
Frame Relay (T-3 line)	45 Mbps	N/A	N/A

Sources:　Brian Undercahl and Edward Willett, Internet Bible, IDG Books, 1998
　　　　　　MSN Site Inspection (msn.com), March 1999

ISP Tiers

An Internet Service Provider (ISP) is a company that provides individuals and other companies with access to the Internet and other related services, including Web site development and hosting. An ISP has the computer equipment and access to the communication lines required for points-of-presence (POPs) on the Internet for specific geographic areas. A POP is the physical location of an access point to the Internet.

Each POP has a unique Internet Protocol (IP) address so it can be identified and distinguished from other POPs. The size (i.e., capacity) of an ISP is sometimes measured by the number of POPs that it maintains.

In the United States, there are a handful of communication companies that own and maintain the high-speed interstate network connections that form the Internet backbone. These companies are commonly referred to as Tier-1 Internet Service Providers (ISP). Tier-2 providers do not have direct access to

■■■■■■■■■■■■■■■■■

For an extensive list of Internet Service Providers, visit:

thelist.internet.com

NOTE: Do not precede this URL with www.

■■■■■■■■■■■■■■■■■

U.S. Tier-1 ISPs currently include:

ATT.net
cablewireless.com
genuity.com
sprint.net
uu.net

the Internet backbone, but instead have to access this resource via a dozen or so Network Access Points (NAP). These often-congested hubs allow the various Tier-1 and -2 ISPs to exchange data packets that are destined for clients outside of their own networks. Tier-3 ISPs usually support specific cities and towns within a particular region and obtain indirect access to the Internet backbone and NAPs by leasing or purchasing bandwidth from larger, better connected ISPs.

The key point to remember is that Tier-1 providers have the most bandwidth and, hence, the fastest access to the Internet. Bandwidth decreases (and congestion increases) as you move down through Tiers 2 and 3 of the hierarchy. From a Web testing point of view, the number of hops (or Tiers) that a packet of data makes before reaching the backbone (Tier-1) can significantly affect performance. Specifically, the amount of time that a data packet requires to reach its final destination increases, and the probability that the packet will get lost or discarded along the way increases. Download times are also significantly affected by the connection speeds from both the backbone provider and the Internet Service Provider (ISP). The carrying capacity of any backbone provider and ISP varies substantially with Web traffic volume, available technology, capitalization, and many other factors.

Improvements in communications technology, however, have made transmission speeds in excess of 34 Gbps (OC-768) possible through fiber optics. Optical Carrier (OC) technology conforms to the American National Standards Institute (ANSI) standard for Synchronous Optical Networks (SONET). SONET establishes OC levels ranging from 51.8 Mbps (OC-1), which is approximately the same speed as a T-3 line, up to 34 Gbps and beyond.

Table 7-12 lists some of the data transmission methods used by ISPs today. The speeds for some of the more common high-end

■■■■■■■■■■■■■■■■■
Did you know...

The MS-DOS command Tracert can be used to trace the route and the hops of a packet request across the Internet.

NeoWorx (neoworx.com) offers a graphical route-tracing tool called NeoTrace.

connections are approximate values. For transmission methods that support multiple channels, each channel can be configured to carry voice or data traffic.

Table 7-12   ISP Data Transmission Methods and Speeds

Transmission Method	Transmission Speed
DS0 (T0)	64 Kbps (Digital Signal level 0 - 1 channel)
DS1 (T1)	2 Mbps (24 channels supporting 64 Kbps)
DS2 (T2)	6 Mbps (96 channels supporting 64 Kbps)
DS3 (T3)	45 Mbps (672 channels supporting 64 Kbps)
E1 (European T1)	2 Mbps
E2	8 Mbps
E3	34 Mbps
E4	139 Mbps
E5	565 Mbps
OC1 (Optical Carrier base)	52 Mbps
OC2	104 Mbps (2 times OC1)
OC3/STM1	156 Mbps
OC12/STM4	622 Mbps
OC24/STM8	1 Gbps
OC48/STM16	2 Gbps
OC192/STM64	10 Gbps
OC256	13 Gbps
OC768	34 Gbps

If you intend to conduct performance tests on a Web site currently hosted on a server outside of your organization's firewall (where access is via the Internet as opposed to a LAN), you may want to consider acquiring your own dedicated Internet access. Sharing Internet access with other departments (e.g., development) may result in inconsistent test results due to varying network demands placed on the Internet access point by other departments. Alternatively, you may need to run performance tests during off-peak hours (e.g., 4 a.m.) when the level of activity by the other departments is low, non-existent or at least predicable.

In an effort to avoid the congested "public" Internet, commercial organizations and academic institutions are developing a new high-speed (potentially private) Internet. Organizations with sufficient financial resources can pay to use these "private" backbones to ensure that their traffic travels faster and more directly than via the "public" Internet.

■■■■■■■■■■■■■■■■■
Did you know...

Zeus Technology Ltd. (zeus.co.uk) monitors the performance and availability of many of the leading ISPs in the United Kingdom.

Background Noise

Unless the production servers and network are dedicated to supporting your Web site, you should ensure that the servers and network in the system test environment are loaded with appropriate background tasks. When designing a load to test the performance of your Web site or application, you should identify additional activities that might need to be added to the test environment to accurately reflect the performance degradation caused by "background noise."

■■■■■■■■■■■■■■■■■
Did you know...

Background noise is sometimes also referred to as a *background load.*

Background noise can be caused by a variety of things, including other applications that will also be running on the production servers once the Web site or application under test is moved into production. Other network traffic can also consume network bandwidth and possibly increase the collision rate of the data packets being transmitted over the LAN and/or WAN (Internet). Some testing tools such as QALoad (compuware.com) include "white noise" in their generated load to try and simulate a real-life production environment.

User Geographic Locations

Due to network topologies, response times for Web sites vary around the country and around the world. Internet response times can vary from city to city depending on the time of day, the geographic distance between the client and the host Web site, and the local network capacities at the client-side. Remote performance testing can become particularly important if mirror sites are to be strategically positioned in order to improve response times for distant locations.

Currently, there continues to be significant variation in Internet performance by geographic location. Keynote Systems (keynote.com) measured the Internet performance of 27 major metropolitan areas within the United States during the week of June 5, 2000. Table 7-13 lists the response times required to download the same information from the slowest three and fastest three locations.

Table 7-13 Internet Performance in Selected Cities

U.S. City	Response Time
Portland, ME	7.56 seconds
Atlanta, GA	5.13 seconds
Detroit, MI	4.93 seconds
Seattle, WA	3.43 seconds
Minneapolis, MN	3.31 seconds
San Francisco, CA	3.26 seconds

It's important to note that the response times for some of the cities listed in Table 7-13 are less than half of others. This illustrates the importance of testing your Web site from multiple cities in order to get a realistic estimate of your Web site's national response time. You should determine similar estimates for other countries in which your organization conducts business.

But, how can you effectively test the performance of your Web site from locations that are thousands of miles away? There are several possible solutions:

- Use the services of a third party company that specializes in testing a Web site from different locations around the world.
- Utilize the different physical locations (branches) that your organization may already occupy, and coordinate the execution of your performance tests with coworkers at these offices.
- Use a modem to dial ISP telephone numbers in different cities and factor out the additional time for the cross-country modem connection.
- Buy an "around the world" airplane ticket for one or more of the Web site's testers.

Getting the Right Mix

When developing user profiles for the clients that will be used for performance testing, try to take into account as many of the previously mentioned parameters as possible. While a single parameter may only affect the test results by a few percent, the accumulation of several parameters may add up and have a significant impact of your test results. Table 7-14 provides a checklist of the various parameters that you should consider factoring into your test load and/or test results.

Table 7-14 B&D's User Profile Checklist

The following parameters have been factored into the test load and/or the test results:

Yes	No	Description
☐	☐	Number of concurrent users.
☐	☐	User activities.
☐	☐	Think times.
☐	☐	Site arrival rate.
☐	☐	Site abandonment rate.
☐	☐	Usage patterns.
☐	☐	Client platforms.
☐	☐	Client preferences.
☐	☐	Client Internet access speeds.
☐	☐	ISP tiers.
☐	☐	Background noise.
☐	☐	User geographic locations.

Acquiring the Test Data　■■■■■

Acquiring test data while running a performance test can be a challenge in itself. Some Web sites, for example, utilize dynamically generated session identifications. Reusing the same session id from the previous week or having all the clients use the same session id is likely to yield unrealistic results. However, there are several strategies that you can use to successfully acquire your test data:

♦ Generate the data by hand. That is, manually "cut & paste" data into the input files or directly type the data into a browser.
♦ Use existing Web logs as a starting point and then manually massage the data to fit the test requirements.

■■■■■■■■■■■■■■■■
Computer Associates (ca.com) offers a tool called TESTBytes that can be used to generate test data for relational databases.

♦ Use a tool to capture an initial template and then randomize the data.

If you're unable to identify the HTTP/HTML location of a Web page's variable input data, you should consider using a text comparison tool to locate the variable fields. Windiff.exe, supplied with the Windows Resource Kit, can be used to compare the HTTP/HTML scripts produced by two different users requesting the same Web page. The session id and other variable fields should show up as a "difference" between the two files.

In the event that test data is going to be run through the live production Web site to provide post-implementation monitoring, you may want to consider designing (into the Web site) the ability to "flag" or distinguish test data from real data.

Graphing Performance Results ■■■■■

In its raw form, performance data collected from your Web site can be overwhelming and confusing. When the data is graphed and interpreted, however, it can provide you with a clear understanding of the behavior of your Web site under various conditions. The graph shown in Figure 7-3 represents the performance data that B&D collected from its initial performance tests.

The graph illustrates how the response time for B&D's Web site increases as the load increases. For the purpose of this example, the load is defined as the number of transactions that B&D's Web site handles per second. Load may also be defined in terms of the number of concurrent clients, session initiations, or network throughput per second. The latter, however, may be more attuned to network bandwidth considerations than to the Web applications being tested.

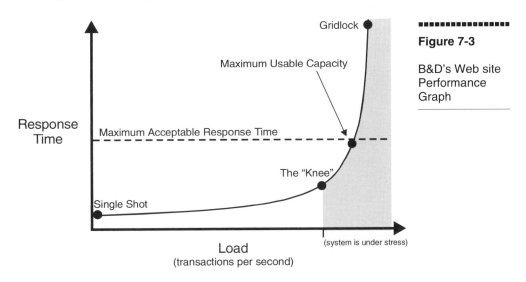

Figure 7-3

B&D's Web site Performance Graph

The performance graph begins with a load of only one client (i.e., "single shot"), which has a correspondingly short response time. As the load increases, the response time also increases and forms a linear-ish graph between the "single shot" and the "knee." The "knee" is the point at which system performance begins to degrade nearly exponentially. From this point forward, the system is considered to be "under stress," and in addition to performance degradation, functionality may also begin to degrade. It's not uncommon for a stressed system to lose requests from its queues. So, while things may appear to be working within acceptable performance bounds, the functionality of the system may actually be failing. The shaded region in Figure 7-3 represents the area where the system's functional integrity is especially in question.

■■■■■■■■■■■■■■■■■

Did you know...

The functionality of your Web site could be failing even though performance may fall within acceptable bounds.

The horizontal dotted line indicates the maximum acceptable response time for the system, based on B&D's Service Level Agreements (SLA). This value may change depending on the time of day (e.g., peak versus non-peak), security measures used (e.g., encrypted versus non-encrypted), and functionality of the Web page (e.g., home page versus database transaction). The maximum usable capacity is the point at which the load crosses the maximum acceptable response time. This point *potentially* represents the maximum capacity that the system can handle while still meeting its SLAs.

If the load continues to increase beyond the maximum usable capacity, the system may become so saturated that gridlock occurs. At this point, response time approaches infinity and the Web site is unable to process any transactions. Ideally, the Web site should never reach the point of gridlock. Instead, the Web site should be able to detect when it gets near gridlock and take preventive actions to avoid the situation.

Some performance testing tools allow you to vary the number of clients (and hence the load) "on the fly," while other tools require you to pre-plan how the number of clients will be varied prior to the start of the test run. If you do need to pre-plan the increase in the number of clients (or any other resource), ensure that the unit of increment is not so small that the volume of test results makes analysis needlessly lengthy and not so large that degradation points cannot be pinpointed.

Senior management may be more interested in the Web site's abandonment rate than its response times under different loads, because the abandonment rate is much more closely related to the amount of revenue that a Web site can be expected to lose under different load levels. Figure 7-4 illustrates the abandonment rate for B&D's Web site.

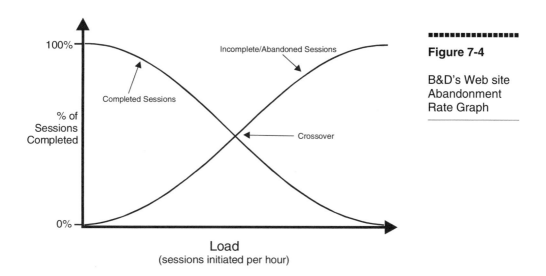

Figure 7-4

B&D's Web site Abandonment Rate Graph

In this graph, "Load" is measured as the number of users' sessions initiated per hour. As more users are attached to the Web site (perhaps through a marketing initiative), the Web site will start to slow down. As the Web site begins to slow, more people will become impatient and leave (i.e., abandon) the Web site before completing their original intention (i.e., actually buying something). "Crossover" refers to the point where 50% of all user sessions are being abandoned before completion. Check with your Marketing department to determine what level of abandonment is acceptable. It may be quite possible that this requirement is more rigorous than any "download response time" requirement that may or may not have been specified.

Margin of Error ■■■■■

No matter how realistically you design your testing environment and test scripts, they will probably not match the production environment exactly. So, how confident can you be of your test results? Your performance test plan should include an estimate of the margin of error (degree of uncertainty) associated with your test results. Figure 7-5 illustrates the margin of error for B&D's Web site performance graph.

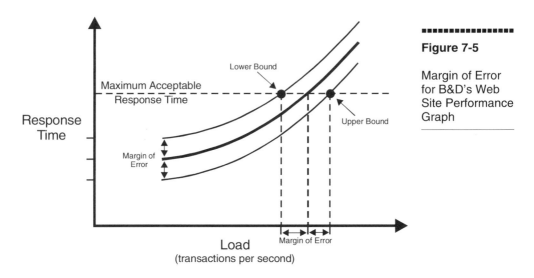

Figure 7-5

Margin of Error for B&D's Web Site Performance Graph

The margin of error is the range between the lower and upper bounds (refer to Figure 7-5). One method of estimating the margin of error is to revisit every assumption and parameter that was used to design and build the test load. Instead of selecting the most probable values, try selecting the most pessimistic and optimistic values. For example, if the normal mix of browsing clients versus purchasing clients is 75/25, then the most pessimistic (from a performance perspective) value would be a mix of 0/100, where every visitor is buying something. The most optimistic value would be 100/0, where no one buys anything. Once determined, the set of pessimistic and optimistic assumptions/parameters can be used to build your pessimistic and optimistic test loads. These loads can then be run against the test environment and compared with the results obtained using the probable test load.

The purpose of many of the extra features provided in performance testing tools is to make the test load as accurate as possible and thereby reduce your margin of error. While these features can be quite useful, the benefits may or may not outweigh the cost. Usability studies have shown that users are typically unable to distinguish between response times that differ by less than 10%. Before using the nth variable/feature to try to make your modeled test load more accurately represent the production load, you should estimate how much the margin of error would be reduced by utilizing this variable/feature. If the improvement is minimal, the return on investment for adding this parameter into your test load may also be minimal.

Spending too much time trying to model the real world exactly can become a moot point. The rapid growth and dynamic characteristics of the Internet mean that a Web site, which can be made to pass or fail a performance test by making a minor adjustment to the test environment, will probably fail when tomorrow's workload is applied to it.

Result Distribution   ■ ■ ■ ■ ■

Due to the unpredictability of the Internet, the same request for a specific Web page may take significantly more or less than the average time for the Web page to be downloaded. Indeed, depending upon the "time to die" setting in the IP protocol, some requests may never make it to the Web server and therefore have a response time of infinity as illustrated in Figure 7-6.

Realistic response time requirements should specify what percentage of requests should be returned within the required service level. B&D, for example, had a requirement that 95% of their Web page requests must be met within 10 seconds.

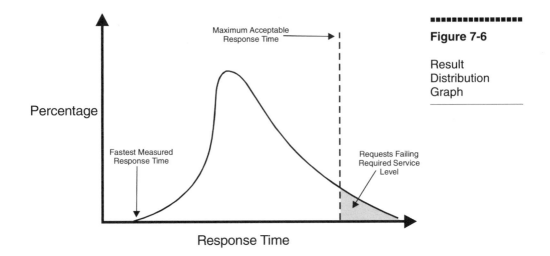

■■■■■■■■■■■■■■■

Figure 7-6

Result
Distribution
Graph

3 Ways to Improve Performance ■■■■■

There are basically three ways that the performance of a Web site can be improved (refer to Figure 7-7):

◆ The entry point (or "single shot") can be reduced, thereby reducing the response time for all loads. This could possibly be done by taking some of the frequently requested content out of the database and placing it in a "flat file" on a file server.

◆ The degree (or slope) of the degradation can be lowered, thereby slowing the rate at which the Web site degrades. One possible approach to accomplishing this is to increase the Web server's Internet network bandwidth from a T1 connection to a T3.

◆ The "knee" can be pushed further out, thereby postponing the point of drastic degradation. Typically, the "knee" can be pushed out by upgrading the resource that's causing the bottleneck (e.g., adding more memory to a Web server that's running at or near 100% utilization).

When deciding what test cases to build to assist in performance tuning, consider which of these three ways of improving the performance of a Web site would add "most bang for your buck" and then design your test cases accordingly.

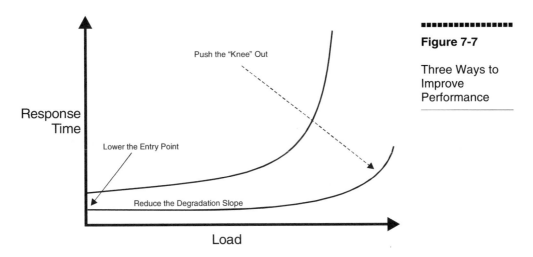

■■■■■■■■■■■■■■■■■

Figure 7-7

Three Ways to Improve Performance

Table 7-15 lists some of the performance tuning techniques that B&D's staff has employed on their Web site.

Table 7-15 B&D's Performance Tuning Checklist

Have all of these options been considered?

Yes	No	Description
☐	☐	Has reverse DNS lookup on the Web server(s) been turned off? Converting an IP address to a DNS address takes time. If the DNS name is only going to be stored in a Web log (which increases the size of the log), then the conversion can always be done later by a Web log analyzer.
☐	☐	Have the Web, Application, and Database servers' log files (large volume of write operations) been placed on separate disks from the static (e.g., HTML and JavaScript files) content (large volume of read operations)?
☐	☐	Do the servers have hard drives with the fastest possible seek times (this is typically not the largest disks available)? Using several small-capacity fast disks may provide better performance than a single large-capacity drive.
☐	☐	Do the servers' hard drives use the fastest controllers available? Currently, SCSI II controllers typically provide faster seek times than IDE or EIDE controllers, and a RAID configuration is preferable over a non-RAID configuration.
☐	☐	Have large files (video, audio, Java applets, etc.) been stored on a different file server than the small files (HTML, GIFs, etc.)? This would allow each file server to be tuned accordingly.
☐	☐	Have different servers (appropriately configured and tuned) been used to handle different network application protocols? For example, are there different servers for e-mail (SMTP), Web pages (HTTP), download files (FTP), and secure Web pages (HTTPS)?
☐	☐	Has the database been indexed and optimized?
☐	☐	Has frequently requested static database content been replaced with "flat files" (at the expense of creating redundant/duplicate data)?
☐	☐	Have frequently generated dynamic pages (e.g., ASP) been replaced with static HTML pages (at the expense of potentially increasing programming maintenance)?
☐	☐	Has static HTML content been placed on a separate Web server from dynamically generated content (e.g., ASP)?

(Continued)

Table 7-15 (*Continued*)

Have all of these options been considered?		
Yes	No	Description
☐	☐	Does the Web server have enough RAM to load all (or at least a large percentage) of the Web site's static content into memory?
☐	☐	Have the server's file permissions been optimized (and in some cases removed)? For example, script and execute permissions can be removed from directories that only contain static content.
☐	☐	Does the maximum data packet size (i.e., Maximum Transmission Unit - MTU and Maximum Segment Size - MSS) used by a Web server correspond to the settings that are used by the ISP that the Web server is connected to? Different settings will result in data packet fragmentation and add to network latencies.
☐	☐	Has the Web server been tuned correctly for the network latencies of a WAN (Internet application) or a LAN (intranet application)? LANs should have much smaller latencies. Excessively large numbers of WAN retransmissions may be the result of using settings that are more appropriate for a LAN. TCP settings that are tunable include: ♦ Listen queue length ♦ Retransmission delay ♦ Close/Wait interval ♦ Keep-Alive interval ♦ Receive window ♦ Slow start
☐	☐	Is the Web server (wherever possible) using HTTP 1.1 "Keep Alive"? This will allow the server to avoid having to generate numerous HTTP connections for each Web page transmission.
☐	☐	Have the most frequently used firewall rules been placed at the top of the rules list?
☐	☐	Have redundant/duplicate rules been removed? The more rules there are, the greater the demand on the firewall's CPU.
☐	☐	Have any comments/blank lines and superfluous tabs been removed from the production code? Although comments and "white space" may make debugging/maintenance easier, the production code will take longer to download.

When performance tuning a Web application, you should try to vary only one parameter at a time. Varying several parameters simultaneously will make it harder to determine the optimal settings for each variable.

Useful URLs ■■■■■

Table 7-16 Useful Web Sites

Web Site URLs	Description of Services
mindcraft.com and zdnet.com	Industry benchmarking applications.
internettrafficreport.com, mids.org, and statmarket.com	Internet traffic statistics.
cablemodem.com, cablelabs.com, packetcable.com, and opencable.com	Internet transmission speeds.
microsoft.com and neoworx.com	Internet route-tracing tools.
See Chapters 8 and 9 for more information.	Performance testing tools and services.
sqe.com/bdonline/	Case study Web site and downloadable test plans.

Chapter 8 – Scalability

Scalability is a system's ability to gracefully increase its capacity in order to accommodate future growth. Scalability can be measured as a ratio of the increase in system performance relative to the amount of new hardware and/or system software that you've added. If, for example, your system can achieve a performance level of 'x' with its current configuration and a level of $1.5x$ by doubling the amount of hardware, then your system has a scalability ratio of 50% (i.e., $0.5x / x$).

Given the dynamic characteristics of the Internet and the World Wide Web, the scalability of your system is a direct measure of its ability to respond to the rapid growth that surrounds it. Since the Internet itself is extremely scalable, your Web site should scale comparably. Consider, for example, HyperText Transfer Protocol (HTTP), one of the protocols used on the Internet. HTTP is a stateless protocol that opens and closes network connections in order to transmit small packets of data (e.g., parts of your Web page) across the Internet. Although HTTP isn't the most efficient network protocol, it is quite scalable. That is, additional servers can easily be added in order to accommodate increasing loads of requests. This is one of the fundamental differences between Web-based and client/server-based applications.

While it may have been possible to conduct small-scale performance tests manually – *"Everyone hit the Enter key at the same time,"* conducting scalability tests will almost certainly require the use of load generators and/or modeling tools. This chapter provides an overview of these tools and some of the more common technologies that organizations are currently employing to improve the scalability of their Web sites.

Scalability Testing Objectives ■ ■ ■ ■ ■

Sooner or later, a Web site will outgrow its existing hardware. Before that happens, the site should be tested to ensure that hardware upgrades can take place without interrupting service. For example, databases typically grow, but response times can initially be kept to modest increases by performing regular reorganizations. However, sooner or later, hardware or system software upgrades are likely to be the only way to maintain the database's response times. It is therefore important to accurately predict the database's performance degradation in order to schedule these upgrades at convenient/controlled moments.

Unfortunately, with potentially thousands of users conducting monetary transactions and insufficient time allotted for testing between releases, fixes/upgrades may possibly decrease performance with each subsequent release. It is extremely important that a Web site have a clearly defined upgrade path, not a performance *cul-de-sac*. The responsibility of ensuring sustainable growth normally falls upon the shoulders of the capacity planning team. However, in the event that your organization does not have a dedicated capacity planning team, the performance testing team is often asked to play this role, primarily because this is typically the only group with the tools and knowledge to conduct scalability tests. Table 8-1 lists the objectives that B&D's performance (and now scalability) testing team was asked to evaluate.

Table 8-1   B&D's Scalability Testing Objectives

Objective	Description
1	Will the current architecture scale as needed?
2	Ascertain the maximum capacity of the current system architecture.
3	Estimate the time period before maximum capacity is reached.
4	Determine the spare/unutilized capacity in various Web site components.
5	Identify any bottlenecks in the current architecture.
6	Evaluate performance improvement options.
7	Predict the impact of hardware and/or system software upgrades.
8	Predict the impact of application software changes.

Capacity Planning

Fortunately or unfortunately (depending on your point of view), Web sites have a habit of outgrowing their existing infrastructure. While a Web site may be able to handle today's workload, management is continually faced with the same two questions, "How much spare capacity do we presently have?" and "How long before we have to upgrade the existing infrastructure?" Capacity planning attempts to answers these questions.

Capacity planning is typically a two-step process. In the first step, you should attempt to predict when future load levels are expected to saturate your system. Second, you should determine the most cost-effective hardware and software upgrades that will allow your system capacity to expand as needed over a specified period of time. Capacity planning can provide your organization with the data needed to complete this process. Simply knowing

Do you know who handles capacity planning for your organization's Web site?

- ◆ The capacity planning team?
- ◆ The development team?
- ◆ The network support team?
- ◆ The test team?
- ◆ Nobody?

what the critical transaction volumes are for each of the different components of the Web site should allow the operations staff to be proactive. The operations staff will have the opportunity to implement mechanisms that can provide them with sufficient warning and thereby avoid major disasters.

The "three times" rule is a rule of thumb used by many engineers who build critical structures such as bridges or dams that must not fail. In essence, the structure is designed and built to withstand a load that is three times greater than the anticipated maximum load. While structures could be built with larger (or smaller) safety capacities, engineers have found that three times capacity provides a reasonable trade-off between safety and cost. Many organizations and Web performance consultants have adopted this centuries-old principle to provide capacity planning objectives. If B&D's Web site is expected to generate a maximum of 100 transactions per second, for example, can the current architecture handle 300 transactions per second without any significant alterations?

■■■■■■■■■■■■■■■■■■
Did you know...

The Web site for the National Center for Missing and Exploited Children went from 30,000 hits per day in 1996 to 2.4 million hits per day in 1998.

This is an 8,000% increase.

There are several approaches to acquiring a target test environment that can be used to conduct capacity planning tests in order to predict how the Web site will perform with *tomorrow's* workload. Some of these approaches will provide more accurate predictions than others:

♦ Use the Web site's decommissioned hardware and system software (i.e., *yesterday's* production environment) and adjust the test load accordingly in order to extrapolate the results to predict how the Web site will perform *tomorrow*.

♦ Build a scaled-down copy of *today's* production Web site to use as your test environment. Then, adjust the load accordingly in order to extrapolate the results to predict how the Web site will perform *tomorrow*.

♦ Build an exact replica of *today's* production Web site to use as your test environment.

- Use *today's* backup Web site as your test environment.
- Use *today's* production Web site as your test environment during off-peak hours (e.g., 4 a.m.).
- If a new architecture is currently being built (i.e., *tomorrow's* production environment), then it may be possible (and advisable) to run your capacity planning tests with this environment rather than *today's* or even *yesterday's* environment.

Once you've selected an approach (often based on budgetary constraints) for conducting your capacity planning tests, you need to decide how you'll actually generate the required test load. In-house or third party load-generating hardware and software is usually more effective than asking your entire staff to come in on a weekend to "hit the Enter key at the same time." A Miami-based company, for example, asked all of its employees to come in one weekend to help generate a test load. After calculating the expenses for overtime, pizza, and outside consultants' fees, the total cost exceeded $60,000 for a single weekend. Unfortunately, after analyzing the data, the test results were found to be inconclusive.

■■■■■■■■■■■■■■■■

Which approach would you use to generate your test load?

- Ask your entire staff to come in on a weekend.
- Use a load-generating tool.

Whichever approach is adopted, you should consider running a baseline or benchmark performance test against the old environment before tuning or implementing any system software or hardware upgrades. Then, compare the results with the new environment to help determine the Return on Investment (ROI) of the upgrade or tuning effort.

There are several alternatives to conducting full-scale capacity planning tests.

- Use sophisticated modeling/monitoring software to predict future capacity requirements. Unfortunately, many of these tools take excessive amounts of time to correctly calibrate and will generate significantly different predictions when given the same scenarios.

♦ Hire well-paid consultants with experience in equivalent Web sites and ask them to make educated guesses regarding your site's future capacity requirements. Of course, the risk here is that the well-paid consultant isn't very experienced.

♦ An extremely dubious approach is to use a pencil and paper or computer spreadsheet (e.g., MS-Excel, Lotus 1-2-3, Quattro, etc.) to extrapolate the results of small-scale tests in order to predict future capacity requirements. Unfortunately, due to the complex non-linear nature of performance test results, extrapolation is unlikely to generate accurate results and is therefore not recommended.

Table 8-2 lists representative capacity modeling tools.

Table 8-2   Sample Capacity Modeling Tools

Vendor	Product
AST Engineering Services (astes.com)	Qase
BMC Software (bmc.com)	Best/1
Clairvoyant Software (clairvoyant.com)	ForeCAST
Compuware (compuware.com)	EcoSYSTEMS
HyPerformix (hyperformix.com)	Strategizer
Imagine That (imaginethatinc.com)	Extend
Information Systems Manager (infosysman.com)	Perfman
Make Systems (makesystems.com)	Netmaker
Metron Technology (metron.co.uk)	Athene
Systems Modeling (sm.com)	Arena

API Routines vs. CGI Scripts ▪▪▪▪▪

One of the first bottlenecks that many Web sites experience is poor scalability of their CGI scripts. Many of the Web servers available today provide an alternative to CGI scripts called an Application Programming Interface (API). API routines address one of the major limitations of CGI scripts. That is, each time a client requests the execution of a CGI script, the Web server creates another copy of the CGI script or application to execute. Depending on the number of CGI requests that are received, this limitation can cause a significant drain on the server's resources as illustrated in Figure 8-1.

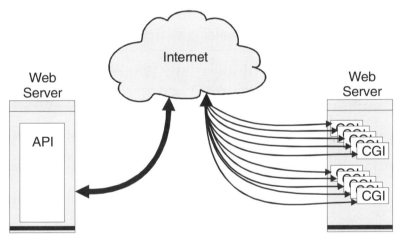

▪▪▪▪▪▪▪▪▪▪▪▪▪▪▪▪

Figure 8-1

API Routines versus CGI Scripts

By contrast, an API routine is only loaded once and is therefore much more scalable. The routine is designed to allow multiple threads to run within a single instance of the application. Using the provided API, developers can create loadable binary modules to add or replace heavily requested elements such as authentication, authorization, error logging, or content generation.

There are at least two instances in which an API can be particularly useful. The first instance is when a Web site has a routine that needs to be executed for nearly every visitor (e.g., login routines). When a Web site has a particularly code-intensive routine that needs to be executed, an API can provide a performance boost over CGI scripts.

Microsoft's Web server API is called Internet Server Application Programming Interface (ISAPI), Netscape's is called NSAPI, and the Apache organization's (apache.org) Web server API is simply referred to as the Apache API. B&D decided to evaluate which of these three APIs performed better on equivalent hardware and how each API compared to a CGI and a FastCGI implementation. Table 8-3 lists B&D's evaluation criteria.

■■■■■■■■■■■■■■■■■
Refer to the *User Interaction* chapter for an explanation of FastCGI.

Table 8-3 B&D's API Scalability Evaluation

	Determining Values	
Value	Description	
☐	Determine the maximum number of Transactions Per Second (TPS) that can be supported and still meet response time requirements.	
☐	Determine the average transaction response time under normal loads.	
☐	Determine the memory usage per transaction.	

Transaction Monitors

Transaction Monitors are often used to help a Web site scale, as they typically assist in load-balancing transactions, managing connections, multi-threading re-entrant code, and ensuring that a transaction that uses resources from several different areas is able to run to completion or roll back gracefully. Figure 8-2 shows the components that comprise a typical transaction monitor.

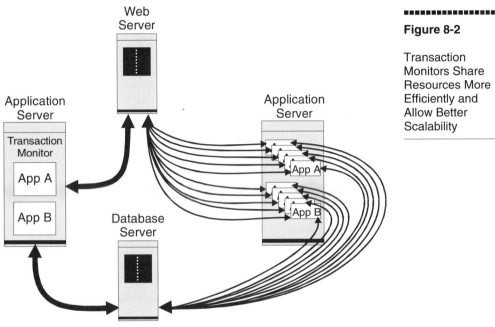

Figure 8-2

Transaction Monitors Share Resources More Efficiently and Allow Better Scalability

There are many Transaction Monitors/Application servers to choose from. Representative servers include Microsoft Transaction Server (MTS) (microsoft.com), Domino (IBM.com or lotus.com), and CICS from IBM, which has been enhanced to allow browsers to communicate to applications running under CICS. There are also various implementations of Enterprise JavaBeans (EJB) and Java Transaction Service (JTS).

EJB-test from Empirix/RSW (rswsoftware.com) is an EJB performance testing tool.

With so many EJB environments to choose from, B&D decided to evaluate which EJB implementation would best meet their needs if they decided to implement the next version of the Web site using JavaBeans. Table 8-4 lists the EJB implementations that B&D decided to evaluate.

Table 8-4   B&D's EJB Evaluation Shortlist

Product	Summary of Findings
Apptivity (progress.com)	
IPlanet (iplanet.com)	
IPortal (iona.com)	
Jrun (allaire.com)	
NetDynamics (netdynamics.com or sun.com)	
Netscape (iplanet.com or sun.com)	
Oracle Application Server (oracle.com)	
PowerTier (persistence.com)	
Sapphire/Web (bluestone.com)	
Sybase Application Server (sybase.com)	
WebLogic/Tuxedo (bea.com)	
Websphere (ibm.com)	

Server Scalability

Larger Web sites use multiple servers to handle their workload. Each server (tier) is typically dedicated to performing a specific task as illustrated in Figure 8-3. Each tier can be changed and scaled independently of the other tiers, thereby making the Web site more scalable. Possible upgrades could include installing system software upgrades/patches, implementing server hardware upgrades, integrating additional servers, upgrading network bandwidth, adding new load balancers, or implementing new caching strategies.

Can you implement a new version of system software or application software without taking your Web site off-line? Implementing standard housekeeping procedures on a 24x7

> If servers are shared by one or more departments, who decides what can be installed and uninstalled?

system that uses multiple servers can be extremely challenging. These systems are potentially more prone to errors (hence a greater need to test) than traditional client/server or mainframe systems, which can often be taken off-line for short periods of time without significantly affecting the business. It's especially important to ensure that each server can be easily upgraded if the servers have multiple applications running on them (i.e., shared servers).

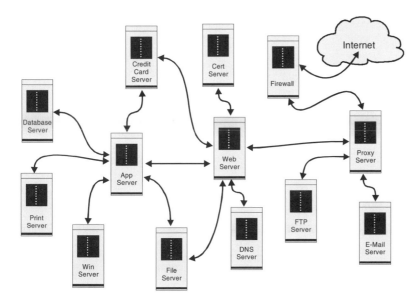

Figure 8-3

N-Tier Configuration

If multiple servers are used for each tier, one approach to handling live upgrades is to bring down half of the servers during a period of low usage (e.g., 3:00 a.m.) and upgrade them off-line. Once the first half have been upgraded successfully, the second half can be taken off-line and the process can be repeated.

In order to ensure that each of their tiers could be scaled up without interrupting the Web site, B&D decided to determine which tiers (servers) could be hot-swapped and/or have additional servers added without having to take the Web site off-line. Table 8-5 lists the tiers that B&D checked.

Table 8-5 B&D's N-Tier Scalability Testing Checklist

		Tiers to Check
Pass	Fail	Description
☐	☐	Firewall servers.
☐	☐	Proxy servers.
☐	☐	Web servers.
☐	☐	E-mail servers.
☐	☐	Application servers.
☐	☐	Database servers.
☐	☐	DNS servers.
☐	☐	Credit Card servers.
☐	☐	Win servers.
☐	☐	Digital Certificate servers.
☐	☐	FTP servers.
☐	☐	File servers.
☐	☐	Print servers.

Server Farms ■■■■■

There are various methods and many products that you can use to spread your Web site's workload over a "farm" of servers. Web server farms are often used to support highly scalable and highly available Web sites. There are several possible architectures for server farms. One popular solution is to build several independent clusters of servers (where each cluster is unaware of the other clusters) and then connect all of the clusters to the Internet via a single load balancer, as illustrated in Figure 8-4.

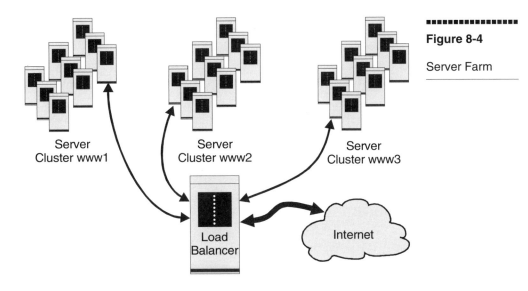

■■■■■■■■■■■■■■■■■

Figure 8-4

Server Farm
_____

Another possible architecture consists of a farm of Web servers that use replicated disk content. Unfortunately, this architecture has some drawbacks. Replicated disks are expensive and replicated content requires continuous synchronization. Whenever changes are made to the data, the changes must also be propagated to all of the clusters within the farm. If your system has a distributed database, then you should pay particular attention to how the clusters re-synchronize themselves in the event that one of the clusters temporarily loses its connection to the other clusters. In both of these architectures, each Web server has access to the entire content of the Web site. Therefore, any server can satisfy any client request.

■■■■■■■■■■■■■■■■■

Did you know...

Microsoft grew from using one Web server in 1994 to over 1,000 servers in 1999.
_____

Load balancing can be implemented in a number of ways. A hardware load balancer, for example, may be positioned between the Internet and the Web server farm. The load balancer can use a virtual IP address to communicate with the Internet router, and mask the IP addresses of each the individual servers in a cluster from the Internet. In other words, only the virtual address is advertised to the Internet, protecting the addresses of the individual servers. Load balancing can also be performed using software. Software load balancing on a cluster is typically the responsibility of a Domain Name System (DNS) server, which may use a technique called Round-Robin DNS. Round-Robin DNS attempts to distribute Internet access evenly between each of the servers in a cluster.

There are many tools available to help you test your server farm. Network Dispatcher from IBM (ibm.com) allows you to control IP multiplexing using a multiplexing router that is placed in front of the server farm. The domain name of the Web site is mapped to the IP address of this router, so all client requests send their packets to it. When the first packet from a client request arrives, the multiplexor selects a server or cluster of servers in the farm to forward the first packet and all subsequent packets in the same session. Distribution Director from Cisco (cisco.com) allows a Web site's DNS server to map a host domain name to a set of IP addresses and choose one of them for each client request. Jet Stream from WindDance (winddancenet.com) is an HTTP redirection tool that allows a Web server to respond to a client's request with a message that tells the client to resubmit its request to another Web server. IP version 6 implements a new service called *Anycast* that provides a more effective method of redirecting requests to another Web site than is currently available using IP version 4.

■■■■■■■■■■■■■■■■■

Did you know…

Editing a Windows-based client's "Hosts" file can direct a browser to different IP addresses (e.g., development, system test, West Coast production, Asia mirror site, etc.) for the same domain name.

Note the lack of the 3-letter filename extension.

One of the main problems with Web server farms is content management. Unfortunately, load balancing can interfere with a server farm's ability to efficiently utilize its available RAM. The popular Web page files tend to occupy RAM space in all the clusters, which can lead to redundant replication of popular content throughout the RAM of each of the clusters in the farm. Unfortunately, this will leave less available RAM for the rest of the content. Inefficient utilization of RAM can lead to degradation of overall system performance.

The ability to grow server farms incrementally over time provides a tremendous advantage for organizations whose capacity planning depends on many unknown variables. A farm of clusters can be used to increase the capacity and computing power of your system. Ideally, a farm of x clusters should be x times more powerful than a single cluster. However, content management and load balancing problems must be overcome in order to create an acceptable scalable solution.

Server farms present an interesting challenge. How can you generate enough traffic to test an entire farm? There are several possible approaches to this problem. One approach is to test each cluster individually, bypassing the load balancer entirely. If, for example, your server farm has 70 clusters and each cluster contains 15 or so servers, the "divide and conquer" strategy will ensure that each individual cluster has been installed and configured correctly, while also making your test cases more manageable. However, another approach will be required to test the load balancer configuration itself.

How you test a load balancer is extremely dependent on which load balancing and data replication strategies have been selected. For example, if your load balancer uses the client's IP addresses to distribute its load, you may need to "spoof" the load generator's IP address in order to make it look like the requests are originating from multiple sources. Alternatively, you can try to identify and modify the algorithm that the load balancer is using. Unfortunately, this approach means that you aren't testing the configuration that will actually be used in the production environment. Table 8-6 lists some of B&D's server farm test cases.

■■■■■■■■■■■■■■■■■
Did you know...

Some Web sites use the www, www1, www2, www3, ... prefix to designate each cluster in a server farm. Simply entering a different URL prefix will direct you to a different cluster.

Table 8-6 B&D's Server Farm Testing Checklist

Yes	No	Description
☐	☐	Has each cluster been correctly installed and configured?
☐	☐	Is the load balancer spreading the workload effectively?
☐	☐	Can the load balancer be taken off-line without impacting the Web site? This may happen if the balancer needs to be upgraded or replaced.
☐	☐	Is the load balancer compromising the integrity of the Web site's functionality? Special attention should be paid to business transactions that require the user to enter data on more than one Web page in order to complete the transaction.
☐	☐	Is the distributed database able to maintain consistency during normal operations?
☐	☐	Is the distributed database able to re-synchronize itself after one or more of the clusters are temporally disconnected from the others?

Web Site Replication - Mirroring ■ ■ ■ ■ ■

Many Web sites use *mirrors* that are geographically scattered throughout the world. A mirror Web site stores a copy of some or all of the primary site's information in an effort to improve response times experienced by visitors who are located far away from the primary site. B&D, for example, wanted to provide its European customers with fast access to New York stock prices. Consequently, B&D set up a mirror Web site in London, England, which is geographically closer to its European clients (refer to Figure 8-5). The mirror site has a local copy of all of the static components used by the Web site and requests updates for the dynamic components (e.g., stock prices) from the primary site at regular intervals.

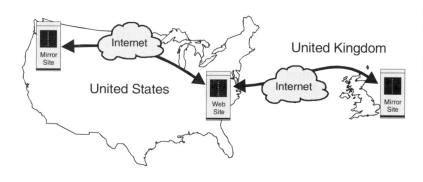

Figure 8-5

B&D's Mirror
Web Sites

One of the issues associated with mirror sites is deciding on the granularity of the replication. At the finest level, each Web page or page component can be individually managed. At the coarsest level, the entire Web site can be treated as a single entity. The question that Webmasters often ask themselves is "At what level should the data be replicated?" Some files may need to be replicated together in order to ensure that dynamic Web pages that are dependent on these files are generated correctly.

From a database perspective, a single federated database offers the advantage of centralized control. However, the reliance on a central Web site often requires compromises in accessibility, performance, and local autonomy over the business information. Dependency on the network and central site's proliferation of distributed databases often means a lack of consistent, timely, consolidated information at the corporate level. While the technology exists to support real-time concurrent updates to multiple databases across a WAN, the performance impact and availability risks often don't justify its use except in the most critical business transactions.

FreeFlow from Akamai (akamai.com) is a product/service that allows bandwidth-intensive Web page components (e.g., graphics or Java applets) to be hosted on numerous mirror sites around the world. A client visiting a Web site that uses

Did you know...

The National Institute of Standards and Technology (NIST) maintains a Web site (time.gov) that can be used to ensure that all of the server clocks at various mirror sites are synchronized.

For more information on distributing, synchronizing, and hosting mirror sites, visit:

exodus.com
f5labs.com
genuity.com
Inktomi.com
versant.com

FreeFlow would only need to download the dynamic portion of the requested page from the main Web server. Transparent to the visitor, the remaining static portions of the page would be downloaded from a local mirror site, which would reduce the visitor's wait time.

Table 8-7 lists some of B&D's mirror site test cases. You may want to add additional test cases based on your specific mirror site's requirements.

Table 8-7 B&D's Mirror Web Site Testing Checklist

Pass	Fail	Description
☐	☐	The static files on the mirror Web site are updated daily.
☐	☐	The databases are synchronized correctly through all mirror sites.
☐	☐	Visitors are correctly rerouted to the mirror site that is geographically closest to their location (e.g., a visitor from Paris is routed to the London site).
☐	☐	If the primary site goes down, mirror sites do not display time-sensitive information in order to avoid displaying inaccurate/old information (e.g., stock quotes).
☐	☐	If one mirror site goes down, traffic is rerouted to the closest mirror site.

Web Site Accelerators - Caching ■ ■ ■ ■ ■

Building a brand new dynamic Web page each time a different visitor requests the same Web page is clearly a waste of a Web site's resources and can create a needless drain on the performance of a Web server. Caching, however, can help alleviate this problem by storing a recently requested Web page in the memory (or cache) of any one of several different Web components as illustrated in Figure 8-6.

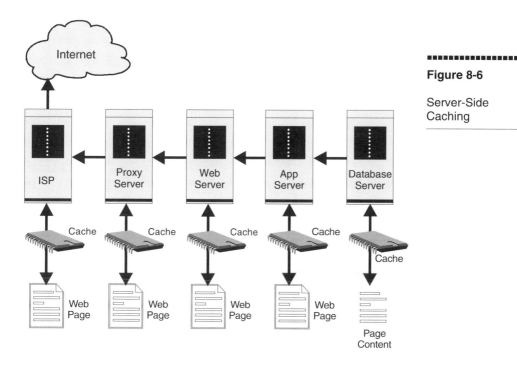

Figure 8-6

Server-Side
Caching

Consider, for example, a client who requests a particular Web page for the very first time. The Web page will typically "hop" from the Web server though several other servers and/or routers before being placed on the Internet and sent to the client. However, if a second client (or the same client) happens to request the same Web page within a short period of time, many of these network hops will be eliminated if one of the servers or routers already has the Web page stored in its cache memory.

Caching strategies were originally designed and optimized to handle static HTML Web pages that don't change very often but are requested by thousands of different users. Typically, a Web page is held in memory (on the Web server or the ISP's Proxy server) for a predetermined amount of time. If that page isn't requested again before the time period expires, then that Web page is purged from memory and replaced with a more popular

Web page. Dynamically generated pages can take a Web server up to 10 times longer to produce than a static page. Therefore, caching is even more important for dynamically generated Web sites than static ones. Unfortunately, due to the potentially large number of Web pages that can be generated by a dynamic Web site, implementing or optimizing a caching strategy for a dynamic Web site is significantly more challenging.

While the Webmaster may decide which caching strategy will be used, the team responsible for testing the Web site must ensure that the testing environment accurately reflects the production environment's caching strategy. This is particularly important if third party testing teams are responsible for remotely testing the Web site. The caching strategy used by the third party's ISP may distort test results, especially if the majority of the test load originates from only a few Internet entry points.

■■■■■■■■■■■■■■■■■

Inktomi.com provides more information on ISP-level caching.

It's highly probable that all of the components in an end-to-end test, including the routers on the Internet, are using caches. Consequently, all of these caches (wherever possible) should be flushed and any test run should be given an opportunity to "warm up" the various caches. That is, allow each of the caches to reach its normal operating capacity. If caches are used, it's particularly important that the test input data be sufficiently randomized in order to ensure that the caches are able to swap out Web pages at a rate equivalent to that of the production system. If the hit rate in the test environment is too high, the test results may be better than what could actually be achieved in the production environment. If it's not possible to generate sufficient volumes of randomized data, you should consider using alternate methods to degrade the performance of the test environment caches to the equivalent performance level of the production environment. For example, you can physically reduce the size of a cache or alter the system's software settings.

Table 8-8 lists B&D's pre-test run caching checklist for the test environment.

Table 8-8 B&D's Test Environment Caching Checklist

Is the test environment page hit rate equal to the rate achieved in production?		
Yes	No	Description
☐	☐	Database servers.
☐	☐	Applications servers.
☐	☐	File servers.
☐	☐	Web servers.
☐	☐	Proxy servers.
☐	☐	Web site's ISP routers.
☐	☐	Client-side ISP router. This typically only applies if the test load is originating from a small number of physical locations.

Load Generation Options ■■■■■

There are several different strategies that can be employed to generate a sufficient workload to test a Web site. Perhaps the easiest to implement is the manual approach, which entails bringing in the whole staff on a weekend to have them all "hit the Enter key at the same time." Unfortunately, this approach doesn't scale well, is typically unrepeatable, and can be extremely expensive for larger tests (e.g., 100+ users).

A comparatively rare approach to generating a test load entails running shareware, freeware, or in-house developed load generating software on in-house load generators. While this approach provides maximum control over the workload and may save money on the purchase of a testing tool, it often involves high learning curves and the tools typically need continual maintenance. In the case of freeware and shareware, the high learning curves are often due to little or no documentation.

Probably, the most common approach used today is to purchase load-generating software and run the tools on in-house load generators. These tools typically include extensive functionality, which requires that upgrades be handled by the original software vendor (for a maintenance fee). Unfortunately, buying all the software and hardware needed for this solution can be costly.

A growing trend among many organizations is to purchase the tools but use someone else's load generators. Companies that offer to hire out their load generators are typically referred to as Application Service Providers (or ASPs). This approach can potentially save money and may also make the testing environment more realistic. Using this approach, the test load will typically travel many miles over the Internet rather than the short loop that an in-house environment often dictates. However, one word of warning is necessary before adopting this strategy. You should check that your organization's security administrators are willing to allow the test load through the firewall or be prepared to host the Web site that you're testing outside of the organization's firewall.

The final strategy involves hiring not only the load generators, but also the testing tools, from an ASP. Using this approach can be quick to implement and reduces the investment risk. Abandoning an ASP solution is much cheaper than abandoning purchased software, since tool vendors typically don't give refunds. Hiring is typically more cost-effective than purchasing when a large amount of a particular service is only needed for a short period of time (e.g., hiring a moving van or hiring a reception hall for a wedding).

Perhaps the most cost-effective strategy of all is to use a combination of load generation options. Initial testing (1 or 2 users) should be done manually. If this step goes well, a larger-scale test (5 to 100 virtual users) can be conducted using purchased software and hardware. Finally, a large-scale test (100 to 10,000+ virtual users) can be conducted using an ASP.

Performance Tool Configuration ■■■■■

Rather than using several thousand physical computers to create a test load for a Web site, several high-end servers can be used to mimic the interactions of many more computers. These multiple "simulated" user interactions created by the load generators are typically referred to as *virtual clients* or *virtual users*. These clients or users don't really exist as true standalone computers, only as virtual loads as illustrated in Figure 8-7.

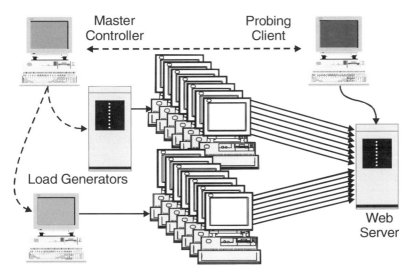

Figure 8-7

Virtual Clients

There are three major components involved in setting-up a large-scale performance test: load generators, probing clients, and the master controller. Probing clients are individual virtual users that measure the exact values of the test scripts that are executed during a test run. The master controller acts like a conductor, processing the information that it receives from the probing clients and load generators, which create virtual clients for the Web server. Unfortunately, load generators are typically only able to report average values for the virtual client requests that they create. Even these values can be somewhat suspicious, due to the load generator itself being stressed by the resource-intensive task of managing all of the virtual users. This makes it necessary to have probing clients. Table 8-9 lists representative performance testing tools and services.

Table 8-9   Sample Performance Testing Tools and Services

Vendor	Product
Compuware (compuware.com)	QALoad
Cyrano (cyrano.com)	OpenSTA and WebTester
Envive (envive.com)	Prophecy
Five Nine Solutions (fiveninesolutions.com)	RemoteCog
IBM (IBM.com)	TPNS-2-go
Keynote Systems (keynote.com)	KeyReadiness
Mercury Interactive (merc-int.com)	LoadRunner, Astra LoadTest & ActiveTest
Microsoft (microsoft.com)	Web Capacity Analysis Tool (WCAT) and Web Application Stress Tool (Homer)
Radview (radview.com)	WebLoad
Rational (rational.com)	Performance Studio and SiteLoad
RSW (rswsoftware.com)	e-Test Suite and EJB-test
Segue (segue.com)	SilkPerformer, SilkRealizer, and eConfidenceScale
Software Research (soft.com)	eValid

Since each virtual client uses resources on the load generator, you will need to calculate the total hardware resources needed to generate the required test load. Suppose, for example, the performance testing tool that you're considering using needs 2 MB of RAM to store the test script for each virtual user and you have four (4) test computers, each with 64 MB of available RAM.

■■■■■■■■■■■■■■■■■■
Did you know...

Testing tools vary significantly in the amount of RAM that each virtual client needs.

(4 Computers x 64 MB) / 2 MB = 128 Virtual Clients

You may discover that 128 virtual clients may not be enough if you're expecting several thousand concurrent users. It's important to remember that it may be possible to generate more virtual clients than can fit in the amount of available RAM that you have. Unfortunately, the load generator will be forced to swap virtual clients out to disk (virtual memory). The time taken to swap virtual clients in and out can make any test results meaningless.

There are also many other factors that can affect the amount of resources that each virtual client requires: the size of the test script being executed, whether or not cookies are used, and whether or not encryption is used. You should remember to consider these factors when configuring your load generators. Table 8-10 shows the steps that B&D's performance testing team followed in order to estimate how much hardware and software they needed to purchase and install.

Table 8-10 B&D's "Back of an Envelope" Resource Requirements

Step	Description
1	During normal business hours, the Web site's log indicates that the average number of page requests (not Web site hits) equals 100 per second.
2	Assuming the "think time" between page requests is 30 seconds on average, the estimated number of concurrent users that will be needed to test the Web site will be at least 3,000 (30 x 100). This figure will be confirmed through detailed analysis of the Web site logs.
3	Using brand X performance testing tool, most of the test scripts required between 500 KB and 1.5 MB of RAM per virtual user.
4	Assuming an average virtual client resource requirement of 1 MB, the test environment would need 3,000 MB of RAM.
5	While experimenting with installing different amounts of RAM on a load generator, the team found that after 256 MB, the load generator did not significantly improve performance by adding more RAM. The reason was that the load generator's CPU was running at near 100% utilization. It's important to note that the LAN connection was established via a 1 GB Ethernet connection and the WAN was a dedicated T3 line. Consequently, neither of these components constrained the load generators.
6	The team decided to use each load generator to generate 200 virtual clients, theoretically leaving 56 MB for the operating system and a few other basic utilities.
7	The B&D performance testing team therefore estimated that using brand X to test their Web site would require 15 (3,000 / 200) load generators.

Virtual Client Caching ■ ■ ■ ■ ■

Why does each virtual client require its own resources (e.g., RAM)? Some of these resources are used by the load generator to track the location of where each virtual client resides in the test script and the settings of any global/environmental variables that each virtual client may be using. However, a large portion of a virtual client's resources is consumed by the virtual client's simulated browser cache. Each virtual client should have its own cache memory (Figure 8-8), which is managed independently from every other virtual client running on the same server. Since each virtual client attempts to simulate a single user using a separate browser, it's important that each virtual client's cache remember which files have already been displayed and, hence, don't need to be requested again. For example, if all of the virtual clients access a graphics file called *logo.gif* on every Web page, then that file should be retrieved once (and only once) for each iteration of a virtual user's test script.

■ ■ ■ ■ ■ ■ ■ ■ ■

Did you know...

Real (not virtual) browsers have two levels of cache: memory (RAM) and disk.

Many load generating tools don't differentiate between these two levels and will attempt to store everything in memory.

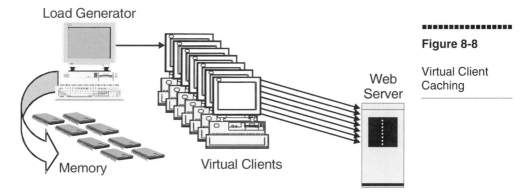

Load Generator

Memory

Virtual Clients

Web Server

■ ■ ■ ■ ■ ■ ■ ■ ■

Figure 8-8

Virtual Client Caching

Ideally each virtual client's cache should be cleared after each iteration of a test script. Some test tools refer to a complete iteration of a test script as a *round*.

Some performance testing tools "listen" to the HTTP traffic that is generated by a browser in order to generate a test script. If you're using such a tool to generate your initial test script, make sure that the browser's cache is cleared before recording your script. This will ensure that any file (e.g., graphic, HTML, etc.) that the browser requests for the first time will result in a corresponding HTTP request being generated. Failure to clear the cache could prevent the test script from detecting the request and cause subsequent playbacks to ignore this file.

It's important to remember that some visitors may choose not to enable caching in their browsers. In order to correctly mimic these visitors, some of your virtual clients should have their caching ability restricted or turned off. Switching off caching will generally slow down the execution of a test script and increase the workload on the Web server and network.

Some performance tools may require that each virtual client run as a separate process on the load generator, especially if the Web site is using session cookies to handle state management. Having to run each virtual client as a separate process, as opposed to multi-threading each virtual client through a single process, may improve the integrity of the results but will also have a significant impact on the amount of resources that each virtual client needs.

Table 8-11 summarizes the resource evaluation tests that B&D's performance testing team followed in order to estimate how much RAM brand X performance testing tool would need for each virtual user.

Table 8-11 B&D's Virtual Client Memory Resource Evaluation

RAM Required	Description
+ _____KB	Standard test script - all options enabled.
– _____KB	RAM freed up by disabling strong encryption.
– _____KB	RAM freed up by disabling all encryption.
– _____KB	RAM freed up by disabling cookies.
– _____KB	RAM freed up by turning off caching.
– _____KB	RAM freed up by ultra-short test script.
+ _____KB	Additional RAM need for extra-long test script.
+ _____KB	Additional RAM needed to run virtual clients in their own process.

Load Tool Calibration

Using the maximum number of virtual clients that a software license permits may not actually generate the largest workload. Depending on the capacity of the load-generating computer, the load generator may be spending too much time juggling the various virtual clients in and out of memory instead of actually processing their requests. Therefore, at some point, adding more virtual users may in fact slow down the total number of requests that can be generated, as shown in Figure 8-9.

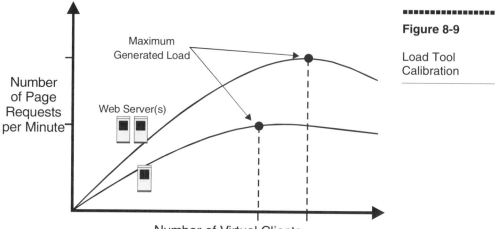

■■■■■■■■■■■■■■■■

Figure 8-9

Load Tool
Calibration

Before conducting any Web server measurements, it's important to calibrate your load generators and determine what percentage of degradation will be attributable to the load generators being stressed. You should also determine the point at which the load generators will reach maximum capacity.

By monitoring the number of Web page requests and/or the volume of network traffic generated, it should be possible to identify the effective capacity of a load generator. Failure to adequately calibrate the generators may result in the load generator being asked to handle too many virtual clients and, as a result, spending too much time juggling virtual users. Under these conditions, the load generator wouldn't generate an appropriate test load, thereby causing the Web site to appear to be capable of handling a much larger workload than it can actually handle.

When selecting a load-generating tool, it's important to understand the total cost of ownership. You shouldn't overlook or under-budget the cost of purchasing any additional hardware

■■■■■■■■■■■■■■■■

IBM has a product called TPNS-2-Go designed specifically to generate huge volumes of Web traffic to load test Web sites.

This package features a network-ready IBM S/390 Mainframe preloaded with IBM's software.

and system software needed to utilize the software license of the performance tool.

Table 8-12 summarizes the calibration tests that B&D's performance testing team performed in order to estimate the maximum usable capacity of the load generators.

Table 8-12   B&D's Load Generator Calibration Checklist

Value	Description
☐	Maximum number of usable virtual clients per load generator.
☐	Maximum number of transaction per second that each load generator can produce.
☐	Maximum number of HTTP connections that the load generator can support.
☐	Confirm that the load generator's network bandwidth utilization is less than 30%, thereby avoiding artificially high network traffic collision rates.

Intrusive vs. Non-Intrusive Tests

When both the Web site under test and the testing tool that's used to test or monitor the Web site reside on the same hardware (e.g., database server or Web server), the Web site under test will need to share computer resources with the testing tool, as illustrated in Figure 8-10. These kinds of tools are typically called *intrusive* tools because they use resources from the systems that they are attempting to measure. Intrusive tools can alter the behavior of the system they are trying to measure and cause the system that is being tested to under-perform.

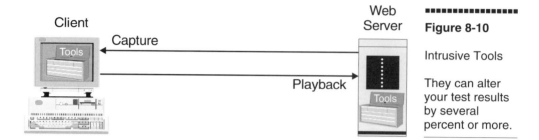

■■■■■■■■■■■■■■■■■■

Figure 8-10

Intrusive Tools

They can alter
your test results
by several
percent or more.

In many situations the amount of under-performance may be
minimal. However, unless the load generators and reporting
agents are calibrated beforehand, the degree of intrusiveness and
the corresponding degree of error in the test results will be
unknown.

Intrusive tools tend to cost less than non-intrusive tools. Before
purchasing a testing tool, consider asking the tool vendor how
much the tool mis-reports the true performance of the system
under test due to the tool's own overhead. Beware of vendors
who insist that their tool will not affect your performance results
at all, even though the tool is intrusive.

■■■■■■■■■■■■■■■■■■

Did you know...

Many tool
vendors claim
degradations of
between 1% and
5%.

Theoretically, the ideal testing tool would be non-intrusive and
platform independent, as illustrated in Figure 8-11.

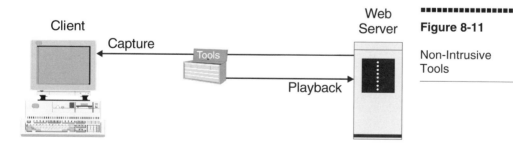

■■■■■■■■■■■■■■■■■■

Figure 8-11

Non-Intrusive
Tools

Because non-intrusive tools must reside outside of the system being tested, they must treat the system under test as a black box. Unfortunately, a black-box approach is less useful when trying to identify the exact cause of an under-performing Web site. In contrast, intrusive tools often possess white-box monitoring features that provide the tool with the ability to "drill down" into a Web site's components in order to help identify bottlenecks. Examples of non-intrusive tools include: Ferret (azor.com), Solutions Evaluation Tool - SET (IBM.com), and TestRunner (qronus.com).

Table 8-13 summarizes the calibration tests that B&D performed in order to estimate how much testing tool brand X would affect the test results. B&D wanted to know how much the subsequent results obtained using brand X should be modified in order to compensate for the intrusive nature of the tool.

■■■■■■■■■■■■■■■■■■
Did you know...

Intrusive tools are sometimes referred to as *native* tools.

Table 8-13 B&D's Testing Tool Intrusion Checklist

Percentage of Intrusion	Description
_____%	On the firewall server, determine how much the additional traffic and rules that allow system resource utilization data to be passed back to the testing tool affect results.
_____%	On the Web servers, determine how much the additional network traffic caused by monitoring agents affects results.
_____%	On each of the Web site's servers, determine how much CPU degradation and memory usage due to additional system resource monitoring processes being active affect results.
_____%	Estimate the total percentage of Web site under-performance that is due to monitoring activities.

White- vs. Black-Box Monitoring ■ ■ ■ ■ ■

Some performance testing tools require *agents* to be installed on the servers that are being tested. The testing tool is able to poll these agents and gather detailed statistics on each of the servers under test. Some tools rely on a server's built-in performance management and reporting capabilities, while others aren't able to incorporate any direct measurements from the server into the test results.

Tools that are able to see inside a system are commonly referred to as *white-box* tools. Alternatively, tools that are unable to "look under the covers" and have no idea what is actually taking place behind the scenes are referred to as *black-box* tools. The difference between white-box monitoring tools and black-box tools is illustrated in Figure 8-12.

Built-in O/S performance monitoring utilities include:

Netstat (UNIX)
Perfmeter (UNIX)
Perfmon (Windows)
Rstatd (UNIX)

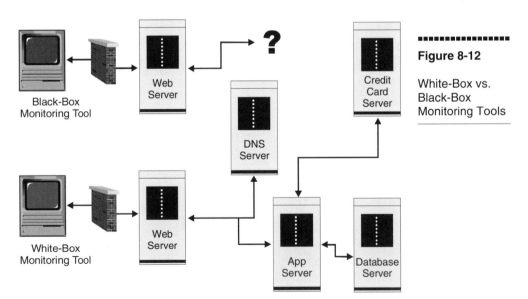

Figure 8-12

White-Box vs. Black-Box Monitoring Tools

Before setting up a test execution that requires a load generator outside of the organization's firewall, check with the engineer who administrates the firewall's security policies to ensure that the load generator's traffic will be permitted through the firewall.

In the event that the testing tool is not able to gather statistics from behind a firewall (due to security reasons or the capability of the tool), you should consider developing special diagnostic Web pages that the probing clients (as opposed to load generators) can execute. These pages can help you determine the exact response times for transactions that utilize different resources, thereby allowing you to pinpoint the potential bottleneck without the benefit of white-box monitors.

Table 8-14 lists some of the measurements that a black-box performance testing tool might be expected to collect.

Table 8-14   Black-Box Performance Measurements

Measurement	Description
1	Network throughput measured in bytes per second (bps).
2	Actual connection speeds (e.g., 28.8 Kbps, etc.).
3	Number of successful virtual client script executions (in terms of absolute number and % of total script executions).
4	Number of unsuccessful virtual client script executions (in terms of absolute number and % of total script executions).
5	Total number of virtual client script executions.
6	Number of successful page requests, sometimes referred to as transactions per second or TPS (in terms of absolute number and % of total script executions).
7	Number of unsuccessful page requests (in terms of absolute number and % of total script executions).

(Continued)

Table 8-14 (*Continued*)

Measurement	Description
8	Total time for a virtual client script execution.
9	Number of successful HTTP requests (in terms of absolute number and % of total script executions).
10	Number of unsuccessful HTTP requests, broken down by return code (in terms of absolute number and % of total script executions).
11	HTTP connection time. This is the time between a virtual client requesting an HTTP connection and the establishment of the connection.
12	Send time. This is the time it takes a virtual client to make an HTTP request. This is useful for calibrating a load generator.
13	Response time. This is the time from when the Web site finishes receiving a page request to the time when the last item has been downloaded to the virtual client. This is quite possibly the most important measurement.
14	Response data size. This is particularly useful for detecting when the wrong page is being transmitted (e.g., a default 404-error page).
15	Process time. This is the time it takes a virtual client to digest an HTTP response. This measurement is useful for calibrating a load generator.

In addition to the default monitors that come with a server's operating system, there are many specialized server monitoring packages that can provide additional statistics on many "behind the firewall" measurements. Table 8-15 lists a few of these measurements.

Unfortunately, all of the white-box monitors will utilize some of the server's resources and, consequently, degrade the performance of the server. While some degradation cannot be avoided, it's important to determine how much degradation is attributable to the monitor so this under-performance can be factored into the predictions for the server's performance after the monitoring software is turned off or removed.

Table 8-15   White-Box Performance Measurements

Measurement	Description
1	Server status.
2	Printer status.
3	CPU utilization.
4	Memory utilization and leakage.
5	File system size, utilization, and fragmentation.
6	Database size, utilization, and fragmentation.
7	Analysis of system and application logs.
8	Analysis of critical system messages (e.g., security violations).
9	Number and duration of users logged on.
10	Hits per domain, Web page, and Web page component.

A memory monitor is an example of a white-box monitoring tool. Memory problems such as "blown" arrays can be caused when an application reads or writes over an array's boundary, thereby corrupting the contents of an adjacent array. Memory monitors can be used to check arrays and help you determine if your Web application has accessed unauthorized portions of memory that are typically reserved for the operating system. Table 8-16 lists some of the measurements that a memory monitor could take as it monitors a server's memory usage.

Table 8-16 Memory Monitor Measurements

Measurement	Description
1	Memory utilization with warnings before critical levels are reached.
2	Memory leaks. Leaks are caused when a portion of memory that was once allocated has been "lost" because no currently active process is using it and the operating system has not freed it.
3	Blown arrays. They are caused by either reading or writing over an array boundary.
4	Reading unutilized/unallocated memory.
5	Accessing unauthorized portions of memory (e.g., memory reserved for the operating system).

Some Web testing tools differentiate themselves by the ability to automatically synchronize server-side (white-box) measurements with client-side (black-box) measurements, rather than relying on the performance testing team to make manual comparisons. These types of tools can save you a considerable amount of time when analyzing the test results.

Outsourcing Performance Testing ■■■■■

Due to the complexity and size of the resources required to set up massive performance tests, many organizations decide to outsource some or all of their performance testing. It's typically easier to outsource tests that don't require intimate knowledge of your business (e.g., performance tests). Functional tests, on the other hand, may be more difficult to outsource because they often require first-hand knowledge of your organization's business rules, polices, and procedures.

If expensive consultants are brought into your organization, you should make sure that your initial set of test scripts are ready to be run *before* they arrive.

If performance tests are going to be conducted remotely while your Web site is still in development (i.e., behind your organization's firewall), you should conduct an early feasibility test to ensure that personnel working from remote locations are able to pass through your company's firewall to access the site. Tables 8-17 and 8-18 list just a few of the many companies that are now offering to assist organizations with their Web site performance testing.

Table 8-17   Sample Performance Testing Providers (U.S.)

Provider URLs	Provider URLs
aptest.com	norteksolutions.com
benchmarkqa.com	nstl.com
betasoft.com	psw.com
compaq.com	quest.com
computacenter.com	readytestgo.com
compuware.com/optimal.com	realitycorp.com
data-dimensions.com	responsenetworks.com
envive.com	revlabs.com
exodus.com/servicemetrics.com	rstcorp.com
fiveninesolutions.com	segue.com
grci.com	sqp.com
gresham-computing.com	superioris.com
ibm.com	systest.com
iq-services.com	tescom-usa.com
inspect.com	testpros.com
interim.com/spherion.com	tritonic.com
keylabs.com	turnkeysolutions.com
keynote.com	vanteon.com
merc-int.com	veritest.com

Table 8-18 Sample Performance Testing Providers (European)

Provider URLs	Provider URLs
evolutif.co.uk	mission-testing.com
gresham-computing.co.uk	ocs-consulting.com
imagoqa.com	onion.it
iquip.nl	simgroup.co.uk
isintegration.co.uk	sqs.de
magicgroup.com	testcom-intl.com
mercury-eur.com	

Useful URLs ■■■■■

Table 8-19 Useful Web Sites

Web Site URLs	Description of Services
astes.com, BMC.com, compuware.com, clairvoyant.com, hyperformix.com, imaginethatinc.com, infosysman.com, makesystems.com, metron.co.uk, and sm.com	Capacity modeling tool vendors.
akamai.com, exodus.com, f5labs.com, genuity.com, inktomi.com, starfishsoftware.com, and versant.com	Background information on mirror sites.
compuware.com, cyrano.com, IBM.com, merc-int.com, microsoft.com, radview.com, rational.com, rswsoftware.com, segue.com, and soft.com	Performance testing tool vendors.
azor.com, IBM.com, and qronus.com	Non-intrusive testing tools.
sqe.com/bdonline/	Case study Web site and downloadable test plans.

Chapter 9 – Reliability and Availability

If a transaction that was working fine when it was originally put into production starts to fail (from a functional or performance perspective), who is responsible for noticing the problem and diagnosing the approximate area of failure? All too often the answer is "Nobody."

Reliability Testing Objectives

Reliability is often measured by the Mean Time To Failure (MTTF), Mean Time To Repair/Recover (MTTR), or the number of outages that last for a certain interval during a specified period of time. For example, some organizations may measure reliability as "the number of outages that exceed 1 hour each month."

Alternatively, the degree of "acceptable" failure for a particular resource can be specified. Organizations define the degree of "acceptable" failure in a variety of ways. "Memory leakage on any server must not exceed 10 KB per day," or "At any given moment in time, not more than 2% of external links can be broken," or "No more than 5% of network data packets can be lost." The definition of acceptable failure depends on the policies and procedures of each organization.

Table 9-1 lists some of B&D's reliability and availability testing objectives.

■■■■■■■■■■■■■■■■■
Case Study

Review the following *Case Study Test Plans* to see an example of how the topics covered in this chapter can be utilized to test a Web site:

* System
* Post Implementation

Visit:
sqe.com/bdonline/

■■■■■■■■■■■■■■■■■
Did you know...

Many Web sites have an availability goal of providing acceptable performance 99.999% of the time.

This goal is sometimes referred to as the *five 9's* and equates to a total downtime of less than 9 hours per year.

Table 9-1   B&D's Reliability &Availability Objectives

Objective	Description
1	Ensure the Web site can still operate under adverse conditions.
2	Detect rare defects.
3	Estimate Web site reliability and availability.
4	Ensure Web site performance levels are maintained.
5	Q/A the Web site's recovery procedures.
6	Diagnose performance problems.

Categories of Reliability Testing ■■■■■

Web sites that have been running in production for a reasonable period of time often eventually fail for a variety of reasons. An accumulation of small resource leaks can ultimately cause a Web site to run out of a particular resource. If strange or unexpected input data is submitted, the server may be unable to handle the condition. An unusually heavy load placed on the Web site may cause a failure, or one or more hardware components may fail. There are several categories of reliability and availability tests that seek to reduce or at least estimate the frequency with which a Web site (or component) will fail.

Some people refer to reliability testing as *continuity testing*.

Low-Resource Testing

Low-resource stress testing is a type of reliability/robustness testing that seeks to verify that an application can continue to function correctly (although more slowly) under reduced system resources such as low memory. Due to the extreme conditions under which many Web sites have to remain operational, applications that require large amounts of resources to operate correctly have a higher probability of failure. These applications should be viewed as potential candidates for redesign.

As part of its Software Development Kit (SDK), Microsoft (microsoft.com) provides several facilities to degrade the performance of your Windows operating system. The Stress utility (stress.exe), for example, allows you to allocate system resources and see how your application behaves under low-resource conditions. You can allocate resources such as global memory, user and GDI heap memory, file handles, and disk space. The CPU Stress utility (cpustres.exe) is useful for demonstrating the effects of priority levels on system performance. It can also be used to load the microprocessor so you can test your application while the system is under a heavy load.

Endurance Testing

Endurance testing is a simplified variation of load testing or stress testing that is run for an extended period of time (e.g., several days). The purpose of running such a test is to identify defects that are slow to appear. Due to the amount of time required to run an endurance test, it's normally only performed after the Web site has demonstrated its ability to perform acceptably under short-term load and stress testing.

■■■■■■■■■■■■■■■■■
Endurance testing is sometimes referred to as *soak* testing.

A very small memory leak is an example of a problem that can usually only be diagnosed through endurance testing because it develops over a long period of time. For example, a CGI script that leaks 1 KB of memory every time it's invoked will ultimately cause any Web server to fail, but may not show up for several days.

Memory leaks occur when a software application asks the server to allocate blocks of memory for a specific purpose, but later loses all references to those blocks, leaving them unusable. This is often caused by applications that don't correctly release their resources after they're done using them. Crashes due to memory leaks are difficult to diagnose because the server may crash at apparently random time intervals depending on usage. A crash could occur during hours of peak usage or at times of low traffic when you would least expect it. It all depends on when the last block of available memory is exhausted.

Memory monitors can be used to monitor the memory usage of a Web site's servers and help detect and pinpoint where the memory leak is occurring. Analysis of memory utilization patterns can provide an advance warning of potential problems before your server reaches critical levels and performance begins to degrade.

Memory leaks are not the only type of problem that an endurance test might uncover. There are a variety of other problems that may take a while to surface. Running out of disk space for logs or data files is a common problem. Some transactional Web sites may even run out of sequential numbers. The millionth transaction may fail because the field used to store the transaction-id was only designed to hold six digits. Long-running or dormant processes may be terminated by the operating system.

■■■■■■■■■■■■■■■■■
Memory leaks most commonly occur in new business logic or system features.
_____

■■■■■■■■■■■■■■■■■
In general, Java applications are far less prone to memory leaks than C or C^{++} applications.
_____

■■■■■■■■■■■■■■■■■
Did you know...

If restarting your Web server significantly improves performance, you may have a memory leak.
_____

Volume Testing

Volume testing is typically used as a form of load testing where extremely large volumes of input data are submitted to the Web site under test in order to see how it performs. However, a byproduct of volume testing is its ability to uncover rare functional errors. A large volume of data, for example, may contain instances of input data that someone who is performing regular functional testing may not have considered (or had time to test). Processing this input data could uncover rare defects that normally might not have occurred until the Web site was in production. In this situation, the purpose of running a volume test is not to gauge a Web site's performance, but rather to provide an additional form of functional testing. Volume testing typically entails executing a large number of tests (often duplicates), which are based on actual input data rather than assumed or manually generated input.

If a copy of an entire day's input is used to test the Web site and no errors are detected, it's reasonable to assume that the Web site will have (on average) less than one outage per day due to functionality problems. Input data can typically be obtained from the Web site logs. Increasing the amount of input data that the Web site is tested with to a week or even a month without incident will have a corresponding effect on the estimate of the Web site's functional robustness.

Consider the following example where volume testing might have uncovered a defect that B&D's testing missed. Shortly after going into production, B&D's main settlement program crashed unexpectedly. Upon investigation, the source of the problem was discovered not to be a typical load spike or gradual deterioration of some key resource, but rather a single input record. After analyzing the Web site's logs, the input record (a regular sell order) was discovered to have a realized capital gain of $0.00. That is, the sell price minus handling fees equaled the purchase price plus commissions. Unfortunately one of the program's routines used this field in a division calculation. Since computers don't perform "divide by zero" calculations very well, this record caused the program to crash. However, if a large enough volume of data had been used to test this function before the Web site went into production, a trade with a zero profit might have occurred and subsequently uncovered the defect during testing.

From a test execution perspective, endurance testing and volume testing could be combined into a single test run rather than two separate test runs, thereby saving considerable resources.

Peak Loading

Peak loading can be used to help estimate the frequency with which a Web site will crash due to load spikes and, hence, the reliability and availability of the Web site. For example, if the Web site is able to handle the typical daily peak load without a problem, the chances of the site failing more than once a day due to the volume of traffic is relatively small. If the Web site is also able to handle the type of peak load that typically only occurs once a month, then the Web site is not likely to suffer an outage due to traffic volume more than once a month, and so on.

If a full stress test has already been executed, it may be possible to use the results of the test to estimate the failure rate of the Web site due to large volumes of requests, with some degree of accuracy. The failure rate can be estimated based on how infrequently a load greater than the maximum load that the Web site can handle (determined by the stress test) will occur.

Table 9-2 lists some basic test cases that B&D included in its reliability and availability testing checklist.

Table 9-2 B&D's Reliability and Availability Testing Checklist

Pass	Fail	Description
☐	☐	The Web application can function correctly (although very slowly) on servers with minimal available resources.
☐	☐	The Web application is able to run for long periods of time (i.e., at least one week) without any noticeable deterioration in resource utilization.
☐	☐	Restarting any of the servers did not significantly improve performance. Performance improvements are often symptomatic of "leaky" servers.
☐	☐	The Web application was able to successfully process an entire week's worth of input data.
☐	☐	The Web application was able to handle (although very slowly) the worst load that can be expected to occur at least once a month.

Web Site Monitoring ■ ■ ■ ■ ■

While a Web site may provide acceptable levels of service on the day it goes live, there's no guarantee that the same level of performance will be maintained. Performance could degrade for any number of reasons. The Web site may get more hits than expected, database files may become disorganized, the server may run out of free disk space, the RAM on the server's motherboard may fail, or network congestion between the server(s) and the Internet backbone may increase. These are just a few of the unknown variables.

Monitors that are installed outside of the organization firewall are typically only able to measure Web site response times and functional correctness. However, additional monitors can be installed "behind the firewall" to provide much more detailed

■■■■■■■■■■■■■■■■■
Did you know...

It can be especially hard to troubleshoot network congestion if a third party ISP is hosting the Web site.

information, while only marginally degrading the Web site's performance.

The goal of Web site monitoring is to detect a system failure before it becomes critical. That is, the Web site's support team should be given enough time to fix the problem before it has a significant effect on performance.

Table 9-3 lists some representative monitoring tools and services. Many of the vendors that provide performance testing services also offer availability testing services.

Table 9-3 Sample Monitoring Tools/Services

Vendor	Product
Cisco (cisco.com)	Netsys
Coast Software (coast.com)	WebMaster Pro
Compuware (compuware.com)	EcoSYSTEMS & PointForward
CrossKeys Systems (crosskeys.com)	Resolve
Envive (envive.com)	Sensory
Freshwater Software (freshwater.com)	SiteReliance, Siteseer & SiteScope
HostWatcher (hostwatcher.com)	HostWatcher Pro
Keynote (keynote.com)	Lifeline, Perspective & Red Alert
Lucent (lucent.com)	VitalSuite
Mercury Interactive (merc-int.com)	Topaz & ActiveWatch
Quest Software (quest.com)	Foglight
Rational (rational.com)	Purify
Segue (segue.com)	SilkMonitor
TeamQuest (teamquest.com)	TeamQuest Suite
Tivoli (tivoli.com)	Various
Visual Networks (visualnetworks.com)	Visual Uptime
Web Site Watchers (websitewatchers.co.uk)	WatchMyWeb

Web Site Fail-Over Testing   ■ ■ ■ ■ ■

The process by which a backup system takes over the responsibilities of a production system is referred to as *fail-over*. Fail-over testing is concerned with ensuring that the fail-over process that was put in place (assuming one exists) works as specified.

There are several different methods of establishing a backup Web site. Generally speaking, the quicker the backup Web site is able to take over the work of the "live" Web site, the more costly the backup Web site is to implement. The cost may be measured in terms of money or the degradation in performance of the "live" Web site.

Most backup Web sites fall into one of the following categories: hot, warm, cold, or none. Each of these approaches has its advantages and disadvantages. For example, implementing a "hot" backup Web site may reduce the performance of the database component of the Web site to a degree that the live Web site fails to meet one of its performance objectives. Database performance is degraded because the live Web site must "commit" in unison with the backup Web site using a distributed database. On the other hand, implementing a "warm" solution may mean that a Web site becomes unavailable for short periods of time and potentially even loses an occasional completed transaction.

Since there is no fail-over strategy that works best for all Web sites, you should ask yourself, "Is the implemented fail-over strategy the best strategy for this Web site?"

■■■■■■■■■■■■■■■■■
Did you know...

Fail-over or recovery testing is sometimes referred to as a form of *robustness* testing.

■■■■■■■■■■■■■■■■■

Companies such as Comdisco (comdisco.com), IBM (IBM.com), and Sungard (sungard.com) offer disaster recovery and business continuity services.

Hot Backup Web Sites

As each transaction on the "live" Web site occurs, a replica of the transaction is made on the backup site. The live Web site "commits" in unison (two-phase commit) with the backup Web site, thereby guaranteeing that the data on the backup site is identical to the data on the live site.

Hot backups can be implemented at a number of levels. Hardware RAID (Redundant Array of Inexpensive Disks) storage devices, for example, allow data to be duplicated by the disk controller. Fault-tolerant operating systems allow CPU calculations to be duplicated. Enhanced Database Management Systems allow data to be duplicated by the DBMS.

When using a hot backup Web site, visitors should not be able to detect that the live site has gone down. In fact, the backup site may even run faster than the live site (assuming they have the same hardware, etc.) because the backup no longer needs to stay synchronized with the primary system.

Warm Backup Web Sites

Transactions on a live Web site are "committed" to the live database without gaining assurance from the backup site that the transaction has actually been backed up. Instead, changes are queued (or buffered) for processing by the backup site. Depending on how "far behind" the backup site is in processing the data, the completed transaction may sit in the queue for a few seconds or even a few hours. Unfortunately, if something happens to the live site that causes it to crash, it's quite possible that some of the completed transactions that are held in the

■■■■■■■■■■■■■■■■
Did you know...

It's not uncommon for a warm Web site to run 20-30 minutes behind the live site.

queue may be lost, in addition to any partially completed transactions.

The average and maximum lengths of the queue are key factors in determining whether a Web site can meet its Service Level Agreements (SLA). Suppose, for example, that a completed transaction typically has to wait 15 minutes in a queue before being processed by the backup site. In the event that the live Web site goes down, the backup site will need at least 15 minutes to process all of the transactions siting in the queue (i.e., catch up) before it can start processing new transactions in lieu of the live site. This is acceptable if the SLA only requires that the backup Web site be up and running to process new transactions within 30 minutes of the live site going down. Unfortunately, this may be unacceptable if the SLA requirement is less than 15 minutes.

■■■■■■■■■■■■■■■■■
Did you know...

If non fail-over periods exist for the Web site and a warm backup site has been implemented, then the warm backup site might make an ideal system test environment.

Cold Backup Web Sites

Full or incremental backups of the live Web site are made periodically and stored on mediums such as network drives, tapes, or Zip™ drives. In the event of a failure, the Web site could be brought back online by using the organization or a third party's previously dormant Web site infrastructure. This infrastructure should contain a complete restore (as near as possible) from the cold backups and possibly the live Web site's transaction logs.

From a disaster recovery perspective, even if an organization has a hot or warm backup site, it makes sense to make regular cold backups, which are physically stored off-site (i.e., a backup for the backup). Many ISPs provide 20 MB (or more) of free disk space with a standard Internet access account. Rather than using this space to host a Web site, it can be used as a cost-effective

■■■■■■■■■■■■■■■■■
Companies such as Iomega (iomega.com), Seagate (seagate.com) and Veritas (veritas.com) provide more information on backup servers and tape drives.

Companies such as @Backup (backup.com) and driveway (driveway.com) offer remote storage services.

way of storing (compressed and encrypted) program and data files off-site, especially if the backups are duplicated at several different ISPs.

Many senior managers believe they have a hot backup Web site (cold or even warm backup just doesn't sound politically correct). True hot backup Web sites are relatively rare, partly because a hot backup site will typically slow down the live site. Instead, many organizations typically have a Web site that can be immediately made available for use in the event of a failure in the live site. Unfortunately, this doesn't mean that the backup Web site will be functioning immediately. In essence, these organizations have a very fast cold backup Web site.

No Backup Web Site

Cold backups are made, but no backup hardware other than the current live system is available to restore the data to. In the event of a failure, the Web site would be brought back online by restarting the live site and doing a restore using the cold backups and possibly the live site's transaction logs.

If the live system must be used to restore a cold backup Web site, you should pay particular attention to ensuring that an exact replica of the system software (together with configuration settings) and application software are also backed up, in addition to the live Web site's data. All too often, an organization finds that their most recent backup data files are unusable until the last several weeks of application and system software bug fixes and enhancements have been reapplied.

■■■■■■■■■■■■■■■■■

When was the last time your organization performed a complete restore from backup?

In other words, when were the backup procedures actually tested?

LAN vs. WAN Backup Web Sites

There is a trade-off between LAN (Local Area Network) backup sites and WAN (Wide Area Network) backup sites. With today's generation of highly reliable server hardware, when LAN computers do crash, they often go down at the same time as the other computers on the same LAN. This is typically because these computers depend on shared resources such as file systems, domain name servers, administrative staff, power supplies (either at the room, building, or city block level), and proximity to potential disasters (e.g., rivers, earthquakes, road construction, etc.). When one of these shared resources fails, it affects many or all of the servers that depend on it.

Locating the backup Web site at a geographically distant location removes many of the problems associated with having the backup site co-located on the same LAN (i.e., shared dependencies). Unfortunately, WAN-to-LAN communication is less reliable and more problematic to implement than LAN-to-LAN communication. Consequently, a WAN backup may not be any more reliable than a LAN backup. The net effect is that neither solution in isolation is perfect. If money is no object, an organization may want to consider implementing both solutions.

Table 9-4 lists B&D's Web site fail-over and recovery Q/A checklist.

Table 9-4   B&D's Web Site Fail-Over and Recovery Q/A Checklist

Yes	No	Description
☐	☐	Has the most appropriate fail-over strategy been implemented?
☐	☐	Are fail-over and recovery procedures adequately documented and followed? For example, is there a pager schedule in place? If a backup site needs to be brought online, is there a process in place to ensure that network traffic is redirected to the new IP addresses?
☐	☐	Is there a process in place to ensure that any software with an expiration date is renewed ahead of time?
☐	☐	Can the fail-over and recovery take place within the required time period (based on the SLA)? Can this occur when the Web site is operating under stressful conditions?
☐	☐	After a server is unexpectedly restarted, are all of the transactions that were midway through being processed rolled back or aborted cleanly?
☐	☐	Can the Web site handle one or more of the servers being saturated to the point at which either the server automatically reboots itself or becomes completely locked up?
☐	☐	Can the Web site handle individual servers (e.g., the load balancer) being unexpectedly turned off or rebooted without warning?
☐	☐	Can the system handle multiple server failures?
☐	☐	Are data, system software, and application software files being backed up off-site at locations that have sufficient capacity to handle the continually growing requirements of the Web site?
☐	☐	Are the data, system software, and application software files all restorable?
☐	☐	Does the Web site have an Uninterruptible Power Source (UPS)? Is a process in place to ensure that the UPS is tested regularly?

Server Fail-Over Testing ■■■■■

Larger Web sites use multiple servers, each server typically dedicated to performing a specific task (i.e., tier). Unfortunately, this specialization can often make the Web site more vulnerable to random events. A single failure on any one of the servers, for example, could bring down the entire Web site. Therefore, fail-over systems are often put in place so that if one server goes down, the work shifts to another server.

The more complicated the system, the more things there are that can go wrong. It's usually safe to assume that despite all of the integration testing that may have been performed on a Web site, it's still likely that some random event (e.g., disk crash) will take down one or more services. Consequently, test cases should be added to the system test plan to help ensure that the Web site is capable of recovering from such random events.

Hardware components typically fail at one of two points: the beginning of their life (due to manufacturing errors) or at the end of their life (due to the product wearing out). Therefore, many organizations not only install a standard software "footprint" on any new server, but also "burn-in" the server before it's put into service in order to minimize the possibility of failure at the beginning of its life. By analyzing the failure of existing production hardware, it may be possible to predict the failure of other hardware components in the same batch. For example, if two servers from a cluster of 15 identical servers that entered service at the same time fail at approximately the same time, it wouldn't be unreasonable to expect some of the other 13 servers to also fail in the near future. As a minimum, you should consider adding the test cases listed in Table 9-5 to your system test plan.

Table 9-5 B&D's Server Fail-Over Q/A Checklist

Yes	No	Description
☐	☐	Can the server be unexpectedly turned off/on or rebooted without interrupting service?
☐	☐	Can individual services running on the servers be stopped and restarted (e.g., the HTTP service on a Web server or MTS on a Windows application server) without interrupting service?
☐	☐	Can the hardware components be replaced, swapped out, or reconfigured without having to reboot the computer (e.g., hot swappable hard drives and controllers)?
☐	☐	Does the server use redundant hard drives such as mirrored disks, stripping, or a Redundant Array of Inexpensive Disks (RAID)?
☐	☐	Does the server use redundant controllers for its hard drives?
☐	☐	Was the server "burned in" to increase the probability that it will not fail unexpectedly shortly after entering service?
☐	☐	Was the manufacturer's factory-installed software overwritten with the standard B&D server software installation?

Diagnosing Performance Problems ■■■■■

If a Web site fails the end-to-end performance testing criteria, how can you diagnose which component is causing the problem? Since a performance bottleneck could be in any one, or several, of the components shown in Figure 9-1, a systematic approach to isolating the problems should be adopted. In this particular case, the performance bottleneck occurred between the Application server and the Web server.

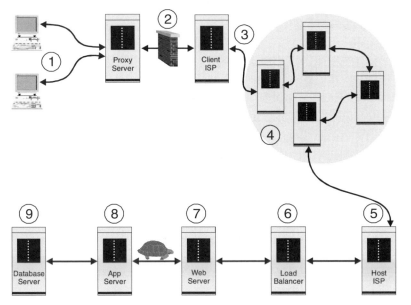

Figure 9-1

Systematic
Approach to
Diagnosing
Performance
Problems

The ability to troubleshoot a poorly performing Web site and identify the location of a performance bottleneck is often an overlooked objective. Being able to identify the cause of a performance problem down to the "area of responsibility" is extremely important. A poorly performing product such as a Web site, which crosses not only departmental responsibilities but also company ones, is especially susceptible to the "it's not my problem" mentality and subsequent lack of action.

While these activities are really diagnosis and debugging, rather than pure testing, the performance testing team often does them because they typically have the equipment (i.e., spare hardware and testing tools) and the knowledge to conduct this kind of testing and debugging. Once the under-performing component (e.g., LAN, DBMS, or Web Server) has been identified, the appropriate performance expert or consultant can be brought in to help tune or redesign the problematic area.

Did you know...

Western Digital (WDC.com) offers a diagnostic service called *Data Lifeguard* for troubleshooting hard drives via the Internet.

Troubleshooting Strategies ■ ■ ■ ■ ■

There are several strategies that you can use to systematically identify your Web site's performance problems. These strategies can be implemented individually or in combination with one another, depending on the scope of the problem.

Onion Skin Strategy

The onion skin strategy (Table 9-6) requires that you begin testing with the component that resides at the very core of your Web application and work your way out until the under-performing component is found.

Table 9-6   Onion Skin Diagnostic Strategy

Step	Description
1	Starting with the component at the very core of the Web application (e.g., database server), test the performance of each component.
2	If the response time is found to be acceptable, add the next layer of the application (e.g., application server) and retest these components together.
3	If the response time is found to be acceptable, continue this process until the final layers (e.g., Web browsers on the client) are added and retest all of these components together.
4	If the response time is unacceptable at any point in this process, you will have identified which component is not performing adequately.

A drawback to this strategy is the need to build multiple test harnesses before isolating the under-performing component. In addition, a clear understanding of realistic performance requirements for each layer that you will be testing is required.

Drill-Down Strategy

Some performance measurement tools and monitors provide you with the ability to "drill down" into the performance data while it's being captured by the tool. The drill-down approach (Table 9-7) works well when only a few transactions repeatedly under-perform in comparison to most of the other transactions. For example, the performance testing tool that B&D used allowed them to drill down into the test results and discover that the "Buy a Stock" transaction was significantly slower than the "Sell a Stock" transaction.

Table 9-7 Drill-Down Diagnostic Strategy

Step	Description:
1	List all of the performance-sensitive transactions that the Web application handles.
2	Develop a set of test scripts that will execute all of the identified transactions.
3	Run the test scripts using a performance testing tool.
4	Drill down into the test results collected by the tool. This will allow you to pinpoint the cause of the problem.

Unfortunately, only components that are being directly measured by the performance tool or monitor can be analyzed.

Bad-Apple Strategy

The bad-apple strategy (Table 9-8) assumes that the performance problem is caused primarily by a single component. This strategy also assumes that each component can (has the ability to) be swapped out and replaced by a known "good" component.

Table 9-8 Bad-Apple Diagnostic Strategy

Step	Description
1	Identify all of the components (and alternatives) that the Web site utilizes (e.g., database server, application server, Web server, firewall, proxy server, etc.).
2	Monitor the performance of each of these components.
3	One at a time, swap out each component with an alternative (e.g., swap out MS IIS for Apache, or vice versa) to see if performance improves.
4	Repeat this process until all of the "bad apples" have been identified and replaced with alternatives.

Unfortunately, swapping out components may be easy in some cases, but not in others.

Christmas Tree Lights Strategy

Sometimes, performance problems are caused by more than one component. Unfortunately, some testing strategies don't work well when more than one component is causing the problem. Consider a string of Christmas tree lights, for example. If two or more bulbs are burned out, simply replacing each bulb on the string one at a time won't necessarily identify the problematic bulb. A better approach is to take each suspect bulb and add it to a known good string of lights. If the good string suddenly starts to fail, then it's safe to assume that the most recently added suspect bulb is the cause of the problem. This strategy (Table 9-9) requires a backup or mirror Web site that can be used as the reference set of good components. This strategy also assumes that each component has the ability to be swapped out.

Table 9-9   Christmas Tree Lights Diagnostic Strategy

Step	Description
1	Build, buy, or borrow a Web site that is known to perform well.
2	Benchmark the well-performing Web site.
3	Take each suspect component and add it to the known good Web site (e.g., swap out MS SQL Server with Oracle, or vice versa).
4	Compare the new performance level with the baseline.
5	If the new performance level is the same as (or even better than) the baseline, return the component to the original Web site. If the performance level is worse, then the suspect component is a candidate for replacement.
6	Repeat the process until all of the suspect components have been compared.

B&D's Strategy

The B&D troubleshooting (SWAT) team decided to use a variation of the bad-apple strategy (Table 9-10) to isolate their Web site's performance problems. Starting from the outermost point (i.e., the browser on a client PC), each component was swapped out and replaced with an equivalent alternate component. The response times were then compared. Components with significantly different response times were turned over to the appropriate experts for further investigation.

■■■■■■■■■■■■■■■■■■
Did you know...

The computer acronym "PING" was contrived to match the submariners' term for the sound of a returned sonar pulse.

Table 9-10   B&D's Diagnostic Strategy

Step	Description
1	*Client software* - Try to recreate the same response time using a different brand/version of browser, thereby eliminating the browser component.
2	*Client hardware* - Try to recreate the same response time using a different PC in the same office, thereby eliminating the client hardware component. It's important to remember that PCs store recently used IP addresses in a local Address Resolution Protocol (ARP) cache. In order to obtain a true performance baseline, this cache may need to be flushed prior to testing. Also review the PC's network and host name files (typically called *networks* and *hosts*) for the symbolic names of any of the IP addresses that are to be used as baselines and flush them.
3	*Client LAN* - Try to recreate a comparable response time using a dial-up modem to the same client ISP, thereby eliminating the client LAN and proxy server components.
4	*Client ISP* - Try to recreate a comparable response time using a dial-up modem to a second client ISP, thereby eliminating the client ISP component.
5	*Internet* - Try to determine what proportion of the bottleneck is attributable to the Internet itself. Count the number of Internet hops that a data packet makes and how long each hop takes. By comparing these results to previously recorded benchmarks (or even a mirror Web site if one is being used), it may be possible to identify the network node(s) causing the problem. Unfortunately there is only one Internet, which can't easily be replaced. Private internets exist, but can be cost prohibitive to use. However, some information can be obtained about the path taken by each packet by using several MS-DOS prompt commands: ping, tracert, route, arp, and winipcfg. Additional help is available through your computer by typing these commands at a DOS prompt without any parameters.
6	*Host ISP* - Try to recreate a comparable response time using a second Web site hosted by the same Host ISP. By running a series of performance checks against this second Web site and comparing the results with known benchmarks, it should be possible to determine whether the hosting ISP is having problems with its own Internet connection or local LAN.

(Continued)

Table 9-10 (*Continued*)

Step	Description
7	*Web site* - Try to recreate a comparable response time using a collection of diagnostic Web pages specially created to perform a single task and thereby exercise a specific feature of the Web site. Some of these tasks may include displaying a graphic, displaying a secure (encrypted) Web page, running a basic CGI script, running a Java servlet, accessing a single database record, inserting a new record into the database, and building a dynamic Web page. It's important to note that these diagnostic Web pages are hidden from the public and accessible only by site administrators. It may be possible to identify the cause of the performance problem by creating a benchmark (or baseline) for each of these Web pages during normal operation of the Web site. Then, compare these values with the times achieved during a problematic period.

Useful URLs ■■■■■

Table 9-11 Useful Web Sites

Web Site URLs	Description of Services
agilent.com, chevin.com, cisco.com, compuware.com, crosskeys.com, envive.com, flukenetworks.com, freshwater.com, ganymede.com, hostwatcher.com, keynote.com, lucent.com, merc-int.com, microsoft.com, quest.com, rational.com, segue.com, teamquest.com, testmart.com, tivoli.com toast.net, visualnetworks.com and wg.com	Diagnostic tools and services.
comdisco.com, IBM.com, and sungard.com	Disaster recovery and business continuity services.
backup.com, driveway.com, iomega.com, myspace.com, seagate.com, and veritas.com	Backup tools and services.
ontrack.com and WDC.com	Recovery tools and services.
sqe.com/bdonline/	Case study Web site and downloadable test plans.

Chapter 10 – Emerging Technologies

Web technology has achieved incredible growth and diversity since the mid-1990s, when graphical browser interfaces first started to become widely available. New technology creates new opportunities, but also generates new problems, and that's where Web testing comes in. Web testing doesn't stop when the Web application goes into production because it's unlikely that development stops once the Web application is "live." Marketing can be expected to dream up new business models, and developers are sure to continually enhance the application using newer and (presumably) better technologies.

There are several newer technologies that are becoming more widely adopted. The Extensible Markup Language (XML), for example, is being used as a more flexible way of transferring data between applications than traditional proprietary file formats. Other advances include providing Internet access to wireless users or rewriting the source code that resides on a Web site's application server using an Object-Oriented language such as Java in order to allow greater reuse of existing code and site scalability. B&D is currently evaluating these technologies and expects to implement them in the near future. Unfortunately, like many other organizations, B&D is still trying to figure out the best way to implement and subsequently test these technologies. Consequently, they have not yet developed their emerging technologies testing checklists. If you're in a similar situation, this chapter might not provide you with all of the answers that you're looking for, but it will hopefully provide you with many clues that will point you in the right direction.

■■■■■■■■■■■■■■■■

Web testing is never completely done because technology continues to evolve.

This chapter examines some of these evolving technologies including:

♦ XML
♦ Wireless
♦ Java

Extensible Markup Language

The World Wide Web Consortium (W3C.org) defines the Extensible Markup Language (XML) as the universal format for displaying structured documents on the Web. By "structured documents" they mean everything from spreadsheets, address books, and financial reports to technical drawings. Or to put it another way, XML is a set of rules, guidelines, and conventions for designing text formats for data in a way that produces unambiguous, platform-independent files that are easy for a computer to generate and read.

Programs that produce structured data often store the information in a binary file that contains the data along with its corresponding formatting information or a text-only file that excludes all formatting. The text-only file allows you to look at the data without executing the program that originally produced it. XML is a set of standard rules for reformatting these text-only documents and presenting them via any computer system, independent of platform.

XML is a close cousin of HTML, as illustrated in Figure 10-1. Both languages are derived from the same META Language, Standard General Markup Language (SGML ISO-8879). However, XML differs from HTML in that XML is a META language whereas HTML is an actual language defined using SGML. Basically, XML is a subset of SGML that has been streamlined specifically for the Web. Like HTML, XML makes use of tags (words bracketed by '<' and '>') and attributes (in the form of name="value"). While HTML specifies the meaning of each tag and attribute, XML uses tags only to delimit pieces of data and leaves the interpretation of the data to the application that reads it. The tag "<p>" in an XML file, for example, isn't

Did you know...

More information on XML can be found at:

xml.com
xml.org
xmlecontent.com
xmlmag.com
xml-zone.com
w3.org/xml

The University of Cork provides a good FAQ page on XML at:

ucc.ie/xml

Bluestone (bluestone.com) provides information on XML servers.

necessarily interpreted as a new paragraph. Depending on the application that reads it, "<p>" might be interpreted as something entirely different, such as pounds, pence, or simply the letter "p."

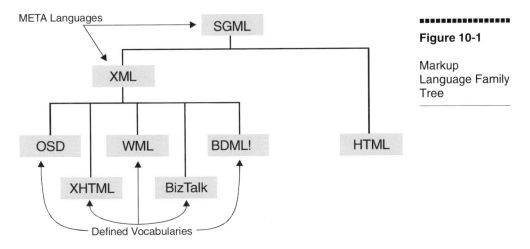

Figure 10-1

Markup
Language Family
Tree

XML is also an abbreviated version of SGML that makes it easier for authors and developers to define their own document types (languages). XML omits the more complex and less used features of SGML in exchange for some important benefits. XML applications are easier to write, easier to understand, and better suited to delivery and interoperability over the Web. Since XML is still SGML, XML files can still be parsed and validated using the methods that you would apply to any SGML files. Unfortunately, the number and range of SGML- and XML-aware tools are much smaller than are available for HTML.

Depending on the development tool or programming style that was used to originally create the HTML code for your Web site, it may be possible to convert the existing HTML to an XML document type. Why would you want to convert your documents? XML allows your documents to be formatted differently depending on the viewing audience. The amount of work involved in the conversion will typically depend on how "white space" is handled in your document and how "sloppy" the HTML tags are. XML typically handles white space differently than HTML. XML doesn't allow missing tags, whereas HTML is far more forgiving.

XML is still in its infancy and, while these standards are still evolving, it may be a while before this technology makes its debut in the mainstream Information Technology (IT) market. Indeed, Microsoft and Netscape have hardly implemented XML and there is already talk of a replacement. Object-oriented concepts may be used to allow a language to include data validation and business rules in addition to presentation (markup) information. Table 10-1 lists just some of the XML-defined languages that are emerging.

Table 10-1   Some XML-Defined Languages

Language	Description
Open Software Description (OSD)	Joint effort between Microsoft and Marimba to create an XML-based software distribution system.
Open Financial Exchange (OFE)	Used to support financial transactions across the Internet.
BizTalk	Microsoft's common vocabulary for software communication across any platform or application.
Resource Description Framework (RDF)	Used to define the structure of data used for indexing, navigating, and searching Web sites.
Mathematical Markup Language (MathML)	Allows mathematicians to specify extremely complex mathematical notations for accurate viewing via a browser.
Wireless Markup Language (WML)	An XML-compliant language that is used specifically for wireless applications.
Extensible HyperText Markup Language (XHTML) 1.0	HTML 4.0 defined using XML instead of SGML. You can convert HTML documents into XHTML using the W3C's (W3C.org) HTML Tidy tool.

Testing XML pages may initially prove to be problematic, as some of the major browsers currently don't fully support it. However, since anyone can define his or her own Web language using XML semantics, perhaps a greater challenge will be building competency in the many new and continually evolving XML-defined languages that have and continue to appear. For example, BDML (in Figure 10-1) is B&D's own internal language that is used to define how information is passed between B&D's back-office applications.

Business-to-Business (B2B) XML

Many Business-to-Business (B2B) Electronic Data Interchange (EDI) layouts that were originally specified using the ANSI X12 standard are now being rewritten to use XML. Consider B&D, for example. Figure 10-2 shows how XML data can be passed between the New York Stock Exchange and B&D's Web site using a Document Type Definition (DTD) defined by the Securities and Exchange Commission (SEC).

■■■■■■■■■■■■■■■■■

The Data Interchange Standards Association (DISA.org) provides more information on EDI and the ANSI X12 standard.

■■■■■■■■■■■■■■■■■

Figure 10-2

B&D's B2B XML Application

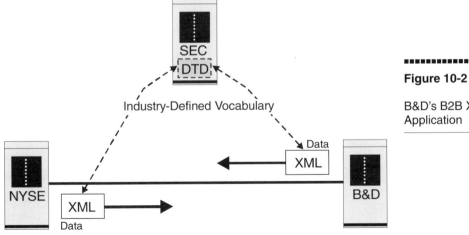

By defining industry standard DTD files, businesses are able to exchange common information over the public Internet without the need for expensive customized or proprietary EDI solutions.

There are two levels of checking available to automatically validate an XML document. The first level of checking involves the structure of XML itself. Unlike many browser interpretations of HTML, XML tags must be structured precisely correctly. Tags, for example, must be paired and attributes must be properly quoted. An XML file that is correctly structured is considered *well formed*. You can verify that an XML document is well formed by simply opening it with an XML-compliant browser. The Web browser should automatically identify any errors in the file. Figure 10-3 shows an example of an XML file used by B&D's Web site. Notice this file refers to another file called *Trade.dtd*, which defines the format of the data that is contained in the XML file.

■■■■■■■■■■■■■■■■■

Did you know...

Computer Data Interchange Format (CDIF) was a previous attempt by the computer industry to create a standard format to exchange data syntax/semantics between different software vendors' tools.

```
Trade.xml
<?xml version="1.0" standalone="no"?>
<!DOCTYPE BDTrade SYSTEM "Trade.dtd">

<BDTrade VERSION="1.0.0">
  <Trades>
    <Trade ID="BD1295" CustomerId="AF34567" BuySell="S"
TickerSymbol="IBM" NumberShares="100" Price="105"/>
    <Trade ID="BD1296" CustomerId="AF45678" BuySell="B"
TickerSymbol="CPQ" NumberShares="400" Price="25"/>
    <Trade ID="BD1297" CustomerId="AF67893" BuySell="B"
TickerSymbol="MSFT" NumberShares="10000" Price="80"/>
    <Trade ID="BD1298" CustomerId="CC45978" BuySell="S"
TickerSymbol="INTC" NumberShares="500" Price="120"/>
  </Trades>
</BDTrade>
```

■■■■■■■■■■■■■■■■■

Figure 10-3

Example XML File

The second (optional) method of validating an XML document is to use an XML Document Type Definition (DTD). The XML DTD specifies the permitted syntactical layout for the information that will be interchanged in the XML data file. A XML file that meets the requirements of its associated DTD file is considered *validated*. Again, the simplest way to validate an XML file and associated DTD file is to open the XML file with an XML-compliant browser. The browser will read the rules defined in the DTD file and check that they are all being complied with by the data in the XML file. Figure 10-4 shows an example DTD file used by B&D's Web site.

```
Trade.dtd
<!ELEMENT BDTrade        (Trades)>
<!ATTLIST BDTrade         VERSION CDATA #IMPLIED >
<!ELEMENT Trades         (Trade*)>


<!ELEMENT Trade          (#PCDATA)>
<!ATTLIST Trade          ID ID #IMPLIED
                         REFID IDREFS #IMPLIED
                         CustomerId CDATA #IMPLIED
                         BuySell CDATA #IMPLIED
                         TickerSymbol CDATA #IMPLIED
                         NumberShares CDATA #IMPLIED
                         Price CDATA #IMPLIED >
```

Figure 10-4

Example DTD File

XML data files tend to be more verbose than traditional EDI data files and, therefore, may consume more network bandwidth to transfer the same information. Consequently, if an existing EDI interface is being replaced by an XML interface, you should consider running some performance tests to ensure that the reformatted data can still be transferred with the existing network infrastructure.

Business-to-Customer (B2C) XML

XML allows authors and developers to define their own language and store information in this language on the server-side. In theory, a client-side XML-capable browser would be able to download the data contained in the XML file and, using either a traditional CSS file or an XSL file, present the information in the format that the author or developer had intended.

The Extensible Style Language (ESL or XSL) is a specification for separating style from content when creating HTML or XML Web pages. XSL provides greater control over document styles than Cascading Style Sheets (CSS). XSL allows developers to have more control over the way Web pages are printed, and strict specifications allow XML documents to be transferred across different applications. Consider, for example, an XML file that contains data such as a stock's last trade price, day's range, bid, ask, and volume. Using XSL, you could tell the Web browser to display the day's range of a stock, where to display it, and what font to use. XSL provides you with the tools you need to describe exactly which data fields in an XML file to display and exactly where and how to display them. Like any style sheet language, XSL can be used to create a style definition for one XML document or reused for many other XML documents. XSL style sheets can be used to specify the presentation of a *class* of XML documents. This is accomplished by describing how a single instance of the class is transformed into an XML document that uses the formatting vocabulary.

▪▪▪▪▪▪▪▪▪▪▪▪▪▪▪▪▪

Did you know...

XSL is based on and extends the Document Style Semantics and Specification Language (DSSSL) and the Cascading Style Sheet (CSS, Level 1) standards.

Extensible Linking Language (XLL) will eventually provide considerably more powerful and flexible linking capabilities than are presently available through HTML. However, XLL will not break existing HTML linking conventions, since XLL provides a superset of HTML linking. Features such as multidirectional links, links with multiple destinations, and link databases that can track updates automatically are only a few examples of XLL's capabilities. Figure 10-5 illustrates a typical Business-to-Consumer XML application that uses XLL to cross-reference the data in the Web server.

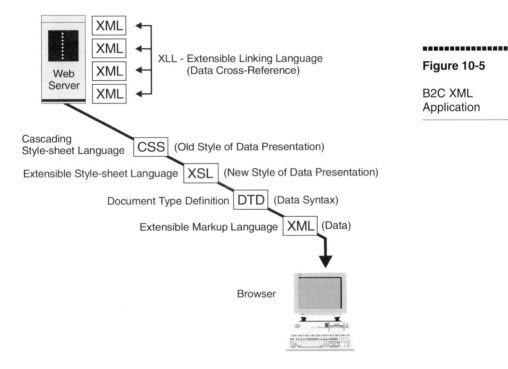

Figure 10-5

B2C XML Application

In 1998, the World Wide Web Consortium (W3C.org) split XLL into two parts: XLink and XPointer. XML Linking Language (XLink) specifies constructs that may be inserted into XML resources to describe links between objects. Resultant structures define simple (current HTML) unidirectional hyperlinks as well as more sophisticated multi-ended and typed links. XML Pointer Language (XPointer) describes how to construct specific references to elements, character strings, and other parts of XML documents, whether they bear an explicit ID attribute or not.

XSL Clients

By separating the data (XML) from the presentation (XSL), it's possible to display a single data file completely differently depending on the client. The Web server would detect the display type (i.e., the agent) of the client and select the most appropriate XSL file to send along with the XML file. An XSL client may be a desktop or laptop computer, home appliance, cellular phone, portable digital assistant (PDA), television, or many other devices, as illustrated in Figure 10-6.

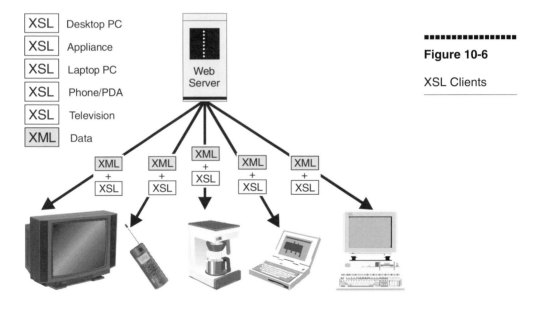

■■■■■■■■■■■■■■■■■

Figure 10-6

XSL Clients

Information and Content Exchange

The Information and Content Exchange (ICE) protocol allows one organization to send data to another organization's Web site, and have it appear automatically in the recipient's format. ICE builds upon two existing Web standards: the Extensible Markup

Language (XML) and the Open Profiling Standard (OPS). By using ICE, the originator of the information only needs to transmit the content along with the appropriate tags (via XML) that describe the kind of information that is being transmitted, as illustrated in Figure 10-7. The recipient Web site has complete control over how the information will be displayed, thereby "dovetailing" the information into its own Web site.

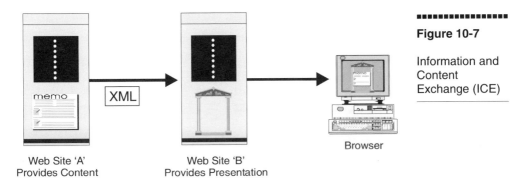

Web Site 'A'
Provides Content

Web Site 'B'
Provides Presentation

Browser

Figure 10-7

Information and Content Exchange (ICE)

The ICE protocol was submitted to the World Wide Web Consortium (W3C.org) in October of 1998, and is backed by over 200 high-tech companies including National Semiconductor (national.com), Adobe (adobe.com), Microsoft (microsoft.com), and Sun Microsystems (sun.com).

Client-Side Language Evolution

While every Web application will not evolve as illustrated in Figure 10-8, the current trend is for the functional and presentational logic residing on the client to become more complex. Some Web sites may skip steps, while others may begin their evolution with technology that's more complicated than basic HTML.

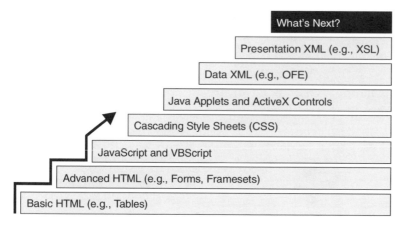

Figure 10-8

Possible
Evolution of a
Web Site

Wireless Application Protocol

The Wireless Application Protocol (WAP) is a specification for a set of communication protocols that standardizes the way that wireless devices, such as cellular telephones and radio transceivers, can be used for Internet access. The WAP includes specifications for e-mail, Web pages, newsgroups, and Internet Relay Chat (IRC). While Internet access via wireless devices has been possible in the past, different manufacturers have used various incompatible technologies. WAP seeks to standardize wireless communication and thereby allow devices from different manufactures to inter-operate.

A WAP-compliant device can display the content of a Web site using either of two methods, as illustrated in Figure 10-9. A traditional HTML application can be used to generate the content and a filter is applied to convert the HTML into WML (WML is defined later in this chapter). The filter may reside either at the host Web site or at another site somewhere between the host site and the WAP device. Another approach is to use a WML

■■■■■■■■■■■■■■■

Did you know…

Palm (palm.com)
provides a tool
that can emulate
a Palm PDA on a
PC.

Nokia
(nokia.com)
provides a tool
that emulates a
Web-enabled
phone.

application to generate the Web content in WML format. If the content is sent to the WAP device via the Internet, the hosting Web site will use various Internet protocols (e.g., HTTP, TCP, IP, etc.) to transmit the content to a WAP proxy. The proxy will then convert the content from the Internet set of network protocols to a wireless set. If the WAP proxy also converts the HTML content into WML content, it's typically referred to as a *WAP gateway*.

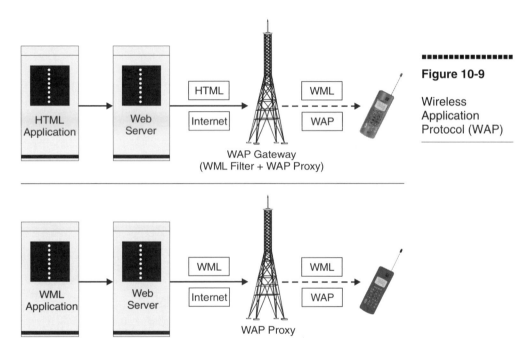

Figure 10-9

Wireless Application Protocol (WAP)

The WAP consists of five communication layers: application, session, transaction, security, and transport as illustrated in Figure 10-10. Other services and applications can access the features of the WAP through a set of well-defined interfaces. External applications can access the communication layers directly. The WAP is designed to compensate for differences among carriers. Applications that communicate with the WAP device directly using WAP (i.e., the data does not travel across

Visit wap.com for a good FAQ page on WAP and WML.

the Internet) are referred to as Wireless Transport Applications (WTA).

Layers

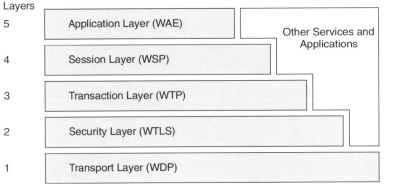

Figure 10-10

WAP Architecture

The WAP was originally conceived by Ericsson (ericsson.com), Motorola (motorola.com), Nokia (nokia.com), and Unwired Planet (now called phone.com). To a large degree, the future direction of the WAP will be shaped by organizations such as the WAP Forum (wapforum.org). Meanwhile, Microsoft is developing an alternative to WAP called *Microsoft Mobile Explorer*. I-MODE from Nippon Telegraph & Telephone DoCoMo (nttdocomo.com) is another competing standard to WAP that uses standard HTML tags to build Web pages. Bluetooth (bluetooth.com) is a WAP-related standard that specifies how Personal Digital Assistants (PDA), mobile phones, and desktop computers can transfer data between devices from different manufacturers over short distances (i.e., 10 to 100 meters) using a Wireless Personal Area Network (WPAN).

Did you know…

In early 2000, the Gartner group (gartner.com) predicted that by the year 2003, approximately 40% of all e-commerce links will be made via mobile devices.

The Wireless Markup Language (WML) is a language specified using XML and is the successor to the Hand-held Markup Language (HDML), which was a customized version of HTML. WML provides a way of encoding and optimizing Web pages for very small screens on mobile devices. Currently, mobile phone WAP browser displays cannot exceed a 96 x 65 pixel resolution, and wireless Internet access runs at speeds slower than outdated

Did you know…

IBM's (IBM.com) Websphere product line has the ability to translate HTML documents into WML-compliant documents.

14.4 Kbps landline modems. While this may not be a major handicap given the small size of most WAP screens, WAP carriers are working to improve their network data capabilities, including capacity and speed. In addition to screen resolution and speed considerations, there are also several mobile phone operating systems that you should consider when developing your wireless test plan. Ensure that your wireless compatibility testing includes checks for several (or all) of the most common mobile phone operating systems used in the geographic area (potentially the entire world) that your Web site is expected to be accessed from. Table 10-2 lists some of the most common operating systems currently used by mobile phones.

■■■■■■■■■■■■■■■■■

For more information on the operating systems used by cellular phones and carriers in the U.S., visit:

point.com

Table 10-2   Mobile Phone Operating Systems

Operating System	Description
Advanced Mobile Phone Service (AMPS)	Developed by AT&T in 1983, this O/S uses an analog signal with a frequency range between 800 and 900 MHz. This is still the most widely deployed cellular system used in the United States.
Time Division Multiple Access (TDMA/TDMA-edge)	Used in digital cellular communication. Divides each cellular channel into three time slots in order to increase throughput. Operates between 850 MHz and 1.9 GHz.
Code Division Multiple Access (CDMA/CDMA2000)	Used in narrow-band digital cellular communication. Multiple calls are overlaid on a single channel. Spreads the data over the entire bandwidth that is available.
Global System for Mobile Communication (GSMC)	Widely used in digital cellular communication throughout Europe. Digitizes and compresses data, then sends it down a channel with two other streams of user data. Operates in either the 900 MHz or 1800 MHz frequency band.
Wide-band Code Division Multiple Access (WCDMA/UMTS)	Similar to CDMA, but utilizes wide-band communications.

Source: Derived from Point.com, Inc. (point.com)

Object-Oriented Code

With object-oriented code, developers define not only the type of data contained in a data structure, but also the operations (e.g., functions) that can be applied to that structure. Consequently, the data structure becomes an *object* that includes both data and functions. These objects can inherit characteristics from other objects, so developers are able to form relationships between objects. A major advantage of using object-oriented code over procedural code is its ease of modification.

Objects are a mixed blessing when testing Web applications. When implemented correctly, the encapsulation and data abstraction aspects of objects provide a clean interface between objects. This makes identifying and setting up test cases straightforward. Unfortunately, the black box nature of objects also makes it harder to identify the root cause of a problem once a defect has been found.

Many developers use "design patterns" (flexible blueprints) to design objects, object interactions, and object collaborations. Before developing the test strategy for testing the objects on your Web site, you should clarify if you need to test the objects for reusability. In other words, was the object designed in such a way that it will be easy (and likely) to use in future development? If so, then designing a standard set of test cases around a design pattern effectively creates a "test pattern" which should increase the reusability of your test cases. Unfortunately, object collaborations often result in parallel actions (e.g., non-sequential code execution), which may yield different results when you run the same test case with different workloads. This is especially true if key objects (e.g., the object request broker or the DBMS interface) are experiencing heavy usage. Therefore,

Over the years, Microsoft has renamed its object-oriented technology several times:

- DDE (Dynamic Data Exchange)
- OLE (Object Linking and Embedding)
- OLE2 (Object Linking and Embedding 2)
- Network OLE (Network Object Linking and Embedding)
- OCX (Object Linking and Embedding Custom Control)
- COM (Common Object Model)
- COM+ (Common Object Model Extension)
- DCOM (Distributed Common Object Model)
- ActiveX

it's important to make sure that object collaborations undergo stress testing as well as functional testing.

Deploying objects in a production environment can be very challenging for developers as well as testers. Since access permissions can be assigned at the object level rather than the file level, your testing strategy will require a much more granular deployment. Although there are many benefits (e.g., saving time and money) to reusing your test cases, it's up to you to decide whether the benefits outweigh the stringent testing requirements.

Class Hierarchies

In object-oriented programming, a class is a category of similar objects. For example, the objects *John Smith* and *Mary Doe* both belong to a group (or class) called *Investor*. Objects may be visual, such as a stock graph on the client-side, or non-visual, such as a market maker running on the server-side. Methods are things that can be done to an object in a particular class. Consider for example, a class called *Person* (Figure 10-11) that contains attributes (data) such as *Name*, *Age*, *Social Security Number*, etc. and methods such as *Change Address* or *Mark Deceased*. B&D needs to store information on several different types of people, rather than defining the classes *Investor*, *Broker*, *Fund Manager*, and *Accountant* from scratch. B&D's developers simply inherited (or reused) the common attributes and methods from the *Person* class.

Inheritance can be beneficial for both developers and testers. Suppose, for example, that a new attribute called *Tax Status* needs to be added. Simply adding this attribute once to the *Person* class will result in all of the inherited classes being updated as well. Ultimately, this saves programming time and

■■■■■■■■■■■■■■■■■
Did you know...

Most people use the term *class* to refer to a group's name (e.g., City) while the term *object* is typically used to refer to a specific instance of the group (e.g., Boston).

also reduces the possibility that one of the classes might be missed.

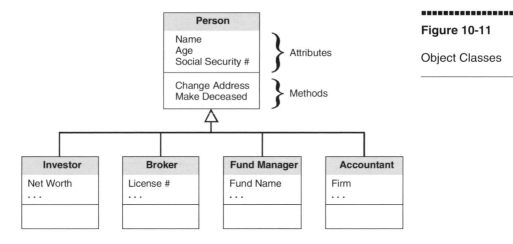

Figure 10-11

Object Classes

Some programming languages (e.g., Visual Basic) only allow single inheritance. Other languages (e.g., C^{++}), however, allow multiple inheritance, where classes can be inherited from more than one parent. You should be especially wary of code that uses multiple inheritance, because it can behave unpredictably if the parents have inconsistent attributes or methods. This can create a scenario that's extremely challenging to test. Consequently, some organizations have discontinued the practice of multiple inheritance because of the problems associated with testing these classes.

Having access to your Web site's class hierarchy diagram (assuming that it's accurate or that it even exists) can save valuable testing time. A class hierarchy diagram can help you identify an object's true inheritance and help you determine which test cases are appropriate. For example, there is little need to retest a function if it has already been exhaustively tested while testing another object. Classes that are only used to build other classes are referred to as abstract classes (Figure 10-12). Abstract classes can be difficult to test because they typically

Did you know...

When testing a class hierarchy, start testing from the top. By moving progressively downwards, test cases designed for the higher classes can be reused.

aren't designed for execution, and they may require developing special test harnesses in order to adequately test all of their methods. While it may be good object-oriented design to use several levels of abstract classes, a Java applet with excessive levels of classes can become needlessly large and subsequently cause performance problems when the "bloated" applet is downloaded over the Internet.

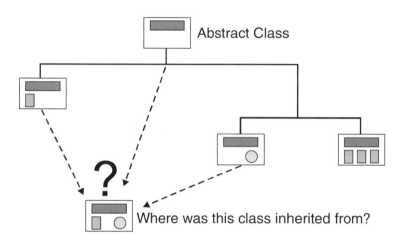

Abstract Class

Where was this class inherited from?

■■■■■■■■■■■■■■■■■
Figure 10-12

Without access to source code, how do you know which class(es) a class was inherited from?

One alternative to executing live tests is to use static testing practices such as walkthroughs, inspections, and reviews. This approach allows you to test an object without having to develop a test harness to exercise the object in a run-time environment. If, however, you choose to use a test harness to test classes (abstract or not), you should consider developing a generic test harness that can be reused to test many different objects. In the long run, this can save considerable testing time and increase the reliability of the testing environment. Alternatively, objects can be developed with test hooks embedded within them. These hooks (methods) could be exposed as public methods during testing and then redefined as private methods prior to production.

The higher a class is in the hierarchy, the greater the need for regression testing in the event that the class is modified.

Therefore, it's important to ensure that your test plan specifies when, how, and why an object in a class hierarchy (or library) can be changed. This will help you determine how much regression testing should be performed and help ensure that none of the object's descendants are adversely affected.

Class Libraries

A class library is a collection of frequently used classes (groups of objects) that can be easily accessed and reused. There are many commercially available class libraries. Microsoft's (microsoft.com) Foundation Class (MFC), for example, provides a hierarchical library of C++ classes for Windows-based applications. Hewlett-Packard's (hp.com) *e-speak* provides components designed specifically for e-commerce applications. Sun Microsystems (sun.com) provides developers with the Java Foundation Class (JFC/Swing), Abstract Windowing Toolkit (AWT), and Java Development Kit (JDK). PowerSoft (sybase.com) offers its own library of classes called the PowerBuilder Foundation Class (PFC).

As an alternative to purchasing one of the many commercially available class libraries, some developers may choose to design their own. There are several variations of the "design your own" approach. In one approach, developers may build a class library before starting a project. While this approach may help ensure that everyone is using the same class library, it may not be feasible because developers can't anticipate every component that will be needed to complete the project. Consequently, this approach may actually delay the start of a project, as developers create the library and the application sequentially. Alternatively, developers can build the application and class library simultaneously. However, this "make-it-up-as-you-go-along" approach can lead to configuration management nightmares and is, therefore, typically not recommended. Another possible approach is to build the library at the end of the first project based on the knowledge that was gained. Using this approach, developers have more experience than they did at the beginning of the project. However, this obviously means that the library can't be used for the first project.

Whether your organization chooses to purchase a class library or develop one, you should identify a standard and comply with it. Developers, testers, and Webmasters who use different versions of a class library while working on the same Web application are often the cause of many post-production incidents. Therefore, you should ensure that your organization includes class library versions in its standards and configuration management procedures, and that the testing and production environments accurately implement these standards.

Java

Java™ is an object-oriented programming language defined by Sun Microsystems. Java is similar to the C/C++ family of languages, but has been modified to eliminate certain facilities that cause common programming errors. Java provides numerous features that make it well suited for use on the World Wide Web. Small Java applications called *Java applets*, for example, can be downloaded from a Web server and run on a client's computer via a Java-compatible Web browser (e.g., Netscape Navigator or Microsoft Internet Explorer). Compiled Java code can run on most computers because Java interpreters and run-time environments, called Java Virtual Machines (JVMs), exist for most operating systems including UNIX, Macintosh, OS/2 and Windows.

■■■■■■■■■■■■■■■■■
Did you know...

Java was originally called *Oak* and was designed for handheld devices and cable television boxes.

Java Virtual Machines

A Java Virtual Machine (JVM) is a self-contained operating environment that behaves as if it were a separate computer. One of Java's most touted benefits – "write once, run anywhere" – is accomplished by using a JVM installed on the computer that will be used to run the program.

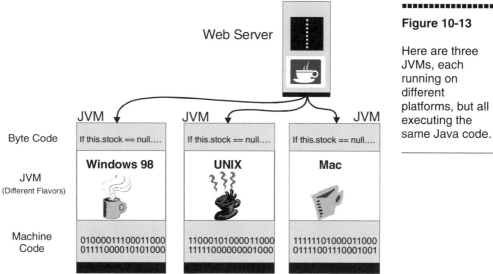

Figure 10-13

Here are three JVMs, each running on different platforms, but all executing the same Java code.

A Java applet, for example, that runs on a JVM has no access to the host computer's operating system. This provides both system independence and security. The Java applet will run nearly the same on any JVM, regardless of the configuration of the host computer. Each platform, however, needs a separate JVM customized and optimized for the underlying operating system. Ideally, each JVM would convert the byte code into machine code that, although different, would appear to execute identically to the user. Unfortunately, each JVM may behave slightly differently. This is partly because the various JVMs are

Did you know…

Jserv from Apache (apache.org) is a Java servlet engine that allows Java servlets to potentially run on any version 1.1 compliant JVM.

written by different organizations and the underlying operating systems and hardware architecture have different capabilities. To minimize these differences, JavaSoft (javasoft.com) attempts to certify each JVM as being 100% compliant.

Java Dialects and Flavors

Unlike most computer languages, Java is not defined by a standards committee but is still owned by Sun Microsystems. One advantage to this model is that new features or extensions can be added to the language relatively quickly. Of course, from a testing perspective this can make the task more difficult. As the number of versions of Java increases, so does the number of Java/browser combinations. Fortunately, Sun implemented a program called *100% pure Java* that allows companies to have their code certified to prove that it's pure Java. This means that the code doesn't contain any native (e.g., Windows only) methods and should therefore run correctly on any Java-compliant platform.

Rather than use Sun's implementation of Java, which runs on many platforms, Microsoft decided to create its own language called J^{++}. Microsoft's J^{++} is very similar to Java, but includes some features that only operate on Windows platforms. While developers are free to ignore these Windows-only features, it's not always clear which aspects are Java compatible and will run on Macs, UNIX, or even OS/2, and which are Windows specific.

An object that conforms to Sun Microsystems' definition of how a Java object should interact is called a *JavaBean*. Any object that meets this specification can then be utilized by any application that understands the JavaBean's format. The principal differences between a JavaBean and an ActiveX control (Microsoft's equivalent) is that ActiveX controls can be

■■■■■■■■■■■■■■■■■

For more info on Sun's 100% pure Java program, visit: javasoft.com

For more information on Java politics, visit: java.sun.com microsoft.com javalobby.org

■■■■■■■■■■■■■■■■■

Did you know...

Java comes in several dialects and flavors:

Dialects include:
♦ JavaSoft (1.0, 1.1, 1.2, 1.3)
♦ Visual J++ (1.0 through 6.0)

developed in any programming language but can only be executed on a Windows 32-bit platform. JavaBeans, on the other hand, can only be developed in Java but can potentially run on any platform.

Java Applets and Servlets

Java applets are client-side programs designed for execution through other applications. Due to their small file size and cross-platform compatibility, applets are well suited as small Internet applications. Unlike traditional software, however, applets cannot be executed directly from an operating system. Instead, they are executed via a JVM-equipped browser. A Java servlet is similar to an applet, with the exception that it's designed to run on the server-side. Java servlets are becoming an increasingly popular alternative to CGI programs, which don't scale as well as servlets.

If your Web site uses Java applets, you should identify which dialect(s) and version(s) were used to create them and then execute your test cases accordingly. For example, if J^{++} was used, extra testing on non-Windows platforms would be well advised. Of course, this wouldn't apply if the Web site is an intranet and the entire network is composed of Windows-based machines. Alternatively, if Sun's JDK version 1.2 was used for development, then additional compatibility and robustness tests may be needed to ensure that any supported browsers that contain a JVM that was built with an earlier JDK (e.g., version 1.1.x) are still able to execute the Java applet correctly.

In theory, a Java applet that works on one JVM should work exactly the same on another JVM. In reality, however, programs may run differently across platforms. Consequently, all Java applets should undergo compatibility testing with all (or some,

■■■■■■■■■■■■■■■■■

Did you know...

The JavaOS software is an optimized, Java technology-based operating system designed specifically for information appliances such as Web phones, set-top boxes, and handheld computing devices.

■■■■■■■■■■■■■■■■■

Did you know...

Sun's Java uses the Abstract Windows Tool (AWT) for its base class library, while Microsoft's J^{++} uses the Windows Foundation Class (WFC).

depending upon business risk) of the JVMs that may be used to interpret them. Unfortunately, testing Java applets can also present some interesting challenges. Depending on the version of Java used, for example, the applet under test may not be able to print to a file on the host machine. Instead, this information must be sent back to a Web server for later analysis and review. Another challenge lies in testing Java applets for browsers that don't support Java, or have it turned off. If a client has turned off Java support or the browser being used doesn't support Java, the Web site should degrade gracefully. One approach to handling this scenario may be to place equivalent HTML functionality between the <applet> tags. This HTML code will be ignored if Java is turned on, but executed if Java is turned off. As a bare minimum, the <applet> tag should at least include an error or warning message coded in HTML to explain why the Java applets are not running.

Java Applications

A Java application is a stand-alone program that doesn't need to run inside a browser. In fact, it may not even be part of a Web site. However, a Java application still needs a Java interpreter (e.g., JVM) or a compiler to convert its byte (or source) code into machine (or object) code that can be executed on the desired platform. Although the machine code created by a Java compiler would no longer be able to run anywhere, it would run faster on the platform for which it was compiled than a non-compiled version.

Java Tools

There are many testing and monitoring tools available to help you test your Web site's Java applications. Browsers typically come with a Java Console, which can be used to help trace and debug Java applets that are executed via the browser's JVM. Table 10-3 lists some of the other tools that are available.

Table 10-3　Sample Java Testing/Monitoring Tools

Vendor	Product(s)	Description
Intuitive Software (optimizeit.com)	OptimizeIt	Performance testing tool.
KL Group (klgroup.com)	Jprobe	Performance testing and tuning suite.
McCabe & Associates (mccabe.com)	McCabe Test	Code coverage tool.
Rational (rational.com)	Pure Coverage and Quantify	Code coverage and performance profiling tools.
Reliable Software Technologies (rstcorp.com)	AssertMate, DeepCover, TotalMetric, and WhiteBox	Code coverage and analysis tools.
Empirix/RSW (rswsoftware.com)	EJB-test	Functionality and performance testing tool.
Software Research (soft.com)	TCAT for Java	Code coverage tool.

ActiveX Controls

ActiveX controls may run differently across platforms, but the number of different platforms that support ActiveX controls is comparatively small (e.g., Native Windows and Windows emulation O/S's). Consequently, all ActiveX controls should undergo compatibility testing with all (or some, depending on business risk) of the environments that may be used to execute them. If your Web application uses ActiveX controls, check your Web application using a browser that doesn't support ActiveX. Your Web site should either degrade gracefully or supply the equivalent functionality using an alternative technology.

B&D initially offered their stock charts via GIF images. Later, they added the option of viewing these charts via ActiveX controls. Unfortunately, some versions of Netscape and non-Windows users (at that time, approximately 50% of their audience) were unable to display the ActiveX charts. B&D subsequently replaced their ActiveX offerings with Java applets.

Useful URLs ■■■■■

Table 10-4 Useful Web Sites

Web Site URLs	Description of Services
bluestone.com, xml.com, xml.org, xmlecontent.com, xmlmag.com, xml-zone.com, ucc.ie, and w3c.org	Information on XML.
bluetooth.com, ericsson.com, motorola.com, nokia.com, nttdocomo.com, palm.com, phone.com, point.com, wap.com, and wapforum.org	Information on wireless Internet access.
apache.org, apple.com, hp.com, ibm.com, javasoft.com, microsoft.com, and sun.com	Information on Java and JVMs.
klgroup.com, mccabe.com, optimizeit.com, rational.com, rstcorp.com, rswsoftware.com, and soft.com	Java testing tools.

Chapter 11 – Post Implementation

The only criterion that Julie Sold, B&D's Vice President of Marketing, specified other than the time scale was that the Web site must "look cool." However, it wasn't long before Julie wanted to know if the Web site had been a success. How can you quantify success? Specifically, what metrics can you provide that demonstrate how successful your Web site really is?

There are many possible metrics available for measuring the success of your Web site. Metrics about your site visitors will be of great interest to your Marketing department, as metrics about banner ads that appear on your site can make or break potential advertising revenue. Commonly used measures include total Web site *hits* per day, unique visitors per day/month, or number of click-throughs per day. These kinds of metrics are easily derived using Web log analysis tools, although the results may vary slightly from tool to tool.

Technically speaking, a *hit* is basically a request to the Web server for a file. If the home page contains 10 separate graphics, then each time the home page is viewed, the Web server will register 11 or more hits (1 for the HTML file and 10 for the graphics files). Since the number of hits per day can be easily manipulated by merely adding or removing graphics files, many advertisers regard *hits* as a meaningless measure and have started to regard page views as a better gauge.

Many Web sites add a visible (on-screen) counter to their home pages, so their visitors can easily get a feel for how popular (or unpopular) the Web site is. Since these counters can easily be manipulated to display any value that a Webmaster desires, their

■■■■■■■■■■■■■■■■■
Case Study

Review the following *Case Study Test Plans* to see an example of how the topics covered in this chapter can be utilized to test a Web site:

- Unit
- Post Implementation

Visit: sqe.com/bdonline/

■■■■■■■■■■■■■■■■■
Did You Know...

Your Web logs can tell you which Web sites your visitors are leaving to come to your Web site.

displays should always be taken "with a grain of salt." Netscape provides a tool called *Hitometer* (hitometer.com) that provides an analysis of how many people visited your Web site, who visited your site (in terms of type, country, and domain), when the visitors came, and which search engine they used to find your site. Web Side Story (hitbox.com) and FXWeb Web Technologies (fxweb.com) provide similar hit counter services.

Many Web sites use *cookies* to help track the frequency with which anonymous visitors frequent their Web sites. Unfortunately, secretly gathering marketing information about your visitors has significant public relations issues. When you consider the fact that many visitors turn off their cookies, the Return on Investment (ROI) may become so low that using cookies may be undesirable.

Feedback buttons provide another means for measuring the success of your Web site. Simply ask your visitors to send their comments and suggestions to your Webmaster via e-mail. B&D's marketing department, for example, enticed their customers to respond to their online survey by offering a 50% discount on a stock trade. Alternatively, live interaction can be used to solicit feedback from visitors to the Web site. Companies such as LivePerson (liveperson.com) and LiveHelper (livehelper.com) provide technology that allows visitors to instantly communicate their comments via a browser to a live customer service representative. LiveHelper is actually able to take control of a visitor's browser in order to help a customer support person see the problem that a visitor might be having. Unfortunately, it doesn't take much imagination to realize how the same technology could be used by another Web site with more devious intentions.

Traditional surveys can also be conducted via telephone or "snail mail" with potential clients, using contact information available through various marketing firms or derived from your own organization's customer databases. The phone approach could require at least two or more calls: one cold call to ask the online investor to look at the Web site and a second call to obtain feedback.

There are several independent approaches that you can take to obtain generalized information about the traffic through your Web site. Companies such as Media Metrix (mediametrix.com), NetRatings (netratings.com), and PC Data Online (pcdataonline.com) provide a variety of basic Internet traffic statistics. Web sites such as bizrate.com, scorecard.com, and shopperconnection.com provide ratings for some of the more popular Web sites.

Another effective, but sometimes overlooked, method for measuring the presentation of your Web site is to ask employees' teenage children to critique and rate your site. After all, teenagers are often regarded as the connoisseurs of "what's cool" on the Internet. Table 11-1 lists the criteria that B&D decided it would use to determine whether or not their Web site was successful.

Table 11-1 B&D's Success Measurements

Within 3 Months of Going Live		
Pass	Fail	Description
☐	☐	Attracts at least 10,000 unique visitors per day.
☐	☐	Generates 500 click-throughs for business partners per day.
☐	☐	50% of registered users visit the Web site at least once a week.
☐	☐	Scores "above average" or better for quality of service, as registered via the online survey.
☐	☐	Rates in the top 50% of online brokerage Web sites, as measured by scorecard.com.
☐	☐	Less than 10% of e-mails to the Webmaster are complaints.
☐	☐	The VP of Marketing thinks the Web site looks *cool*!

Domain Names ■ ■ ■ ■ ■

The best-designed Web site in the world is worthless if no one can find it. Owning as many as possible of the domain names that are associated with your organization and the products or services that your organization provides will make it easier for potential clients to find your Web site and, consequently, be able to do business with you. Too many businesses register a single obscure domain name and believe that their Web site is successful because they are attracting x number of visitors per day. It never occurs to them that by registering multiple domain names they might be able to attract two or three times more visitors. Although B&D had a late start getting into e-business, they decided to acquire as many related domain names as possible, partly to increase Web traffic, but also as a defensive measure to protect the good name of Brown & Donaldson. In the past, some of B&D's competitors have tried to mislead potential or existing clients into believing that their Web sites are somehow related to B&D and could therefore be trusted.

Until recently, Network Solutions (networksolutions.com), also known as InterNic (internic.net), was the only registrar for U.S. non-government domain names. Today, domain names are available and administered through several registrars. Organizations such as ComNetwork promote the sale, lease, and development of domain names. Registrars are accredited through the Internet Corporation for Assigned Names and Numbers (ICANN.org). ICANN is a non-profit corporation formed by the global Internet community to assume responsibility for certain Internet domain name system functions as set forth in the U.S. Government's Statement of Policy (i.e., white paper). Information about ICANN and ICANN's registrar accreditation process is available at icann.org.

Did You Know...

According to a survey conducted by Network Solutions (networksolutions .com) in August 2000, the average length of a domain name is 11 characters.

In December 2000, there were over 33 million registered domains worldwide.

Other interesting statistics on domain names can be found at:

cybergeography.org
domainstats.com
isa.org

While many US organizations are familiar with "dot com," there are many more domain names that are available. While the .com, .net, and .org domains were originally intended for commercial organizations, Internet network providers, and non-profit organizations respectively, they are now available to any person or organization worldwide and are often referred to as *global* or *international* domains. *Country-specific* domains, on the other hand, were created for the use of individual countries. Table 11-2 lists some sample top-level extensions.

■■■■■■■■■■■■■■■■■

Did You Know...

While the *.us* extension is typically used by state, county, and city government bodies, any organization or individual can apply for a *.us* domain.

Table 11-2 Top-Level Domain (TLD) Name Extensions

Country	Top Level Extensions with Their Original Intended Usage
Global	.com for commercial enterprises
	.int for international treaty organizations (e.g., UN.int)
	.net for Internet network service providers
	.org for non-profit organizations
Australia	.au
Canada	.ca
Germany	.de
Japan	.jp
Norway	.no
Sweden	.se
United Kingdom	.uk
United States	.edu for colleges and universities offering 4-year degrees
	.gov for federal government departments and agencies (except military)
	.mil for military establishments
	.us for US geographic locations (typically state and county governments)

Each country is free to optionally define its own second- or even third-level domains. For example, the United Kingdom has multiple second-level domains as shown in Table 11-3. Eligibility is determined by an organization's legal status such as Public Limited Company (.plc), Limited Company (.ltd), and so on.

■■■■■■■■■■■■■■■■■
For more info on country domain name extensions, visit nic.*xx*, where *xx* is the 2-letter country code.
_____

Table 11-3 Second-Level Domain Name Extensions

Second-Level Extension	Description
.ac.uk	for academic establishments
.co.uk	for commercial enterprises
.gov.uk	for government bodies (except defense)
.ltd.uk	for Limited companies
.mod.uk	for Ministry of Defense (MoD) establishments
.net.uk	for Internet network service providers
.nhs.uk	for National Health Service (NHS)
.org.uk	for non-commercial organizations
.plc.uk	for Public Limited companies
.police.uk	for police forces
.sch.uk	for schools

Contrary to popular belief, being the first to register a domain name doesn't guarantee that you have the right to use it (e.g., the name may be trademarked). Network Solutions now has a Domain Name Dispute Policy to resolve conflicts in domain names that are registered through their organization. However, using this or any other legal means to acquire a domain name from another organization or individual is almost certainly going to cost more than registering the name yourself. And, the outcome of your legal action may be uncertain.

Figure 11-1

Acquiring a
Domain Name
through
comnetwork.com

There are many examples of well-known companies that didn't register domain names for their products or services and later discovered that the most obvious domain names were already taken. Time Warner, for example, didn't register roadrunner.com (the name of one of their cartoon characters and Internet cable service) first, and later sued the Internet Service Provider (ISP) located in New Mexico that owned the registration. Interestingly, NASDAQ (NASDAQ.com) decided to register NASDAQ-uk.com as well as NASDAQ.co.uk for their UK stock exchange Web sites. IBM registered IBM.com and IBM.net, but not IBM.org, which is currently owned by an AOL user. At the time that this book was published, the domain name internationalbusinessmachines.com was still available, perhaps due to its length?

Consider "Ask Jeeves" as another example. Since this phrase can be spelled several ways (e.g., askgeeves.com, askgeves.com, askjeeves.com, askjeves.com, aj.com, ask.com, etc.), the company decided to register several different spellings of their URL and made them all point to the same Web site.

Did you know...

Many domain names aren't owned by the companies that you would think:

AAA.org
(not the Automobile Association of America)

Amazom.com
(not Amazon.com)

BigBlue.com
(not IBM computers)

NewYorkYankees.com
(not the baseball team)

TomHanks.com
(not the actor)

Pornographic Web sites, as another example, are often concerned with increasing the number of hits they receive in order to meet the requirements of their advertisers. Consequently, these Web sites register common misspellings and typos of some of the most popular Web sites (e.g., micosoft.com, infoseekk.com) in order to get more hits. The Internet is filled with opportunities, which often present themselves in the form of domain names. If you don't take advantage of these opportunities, chances are that someone else will.

Domain name lookup services (e.g., networksolutions.com and easyspace.com) can help you determine if the domain name that you selected is available. If it's not available, these Web sites may suggest alternatives that are available.

Table 11-4 lists the domain names that B&D considered acquiring.

Table 11-4 B&D's Domain Name Checklist

		Domain names should be registered for each of these cases
Pass	Fail	Description
☐	☐	All of the formal ways that visitors might refer to Brown & Donaldson (e.g., brownanddonaldson, browndonaldson, and brown-donaldson).
☐	☐	All of the informal ways that visitors might refer to Brown & Donaldson (e.g., bandd, bd, and b-d).
☐	☐	All common misspellings of Brown & Donaldson (e.g., browndonoldson, browndonoldson, and brown-donoldson, etc.)
☐	☐	All of the Brown & Donaldson specific products (e.g., brownbonds, brown-bonds, collegehelper, college-helper, and retiremax, etc.).

(Continued)

Table 11-4 *(Continued)*

Pass	Fail	Description
Domain names should be registered for each of these cases		
☐	☐	The generic names of products that Brown & Donaldson offers (e.g., bonds, stocks, mutualfund, and mutual-fund, etc.).
☐	☐	For each of the identified domain names, global extensions (e.g., .com, .net, and .org) have been reserved.
☐	☐	For each of the identified domain names, international extensions (e.g., .de, .uk, and .us) have been reserved in the countries where B&D has existing or potential customers.
☐	☐	All domain names are registered in Brown & Donaldson's corporate name and not the name of any B&D employee or third party such as an ISP.
☐	☐	All technical and administrative contact information for all of the registered domain names contains non-employee-specific information (e.g., sales@ instead of john.smith@) in order to avoid having to update this information if the employee leaves the organization or changes jobs.
☐	☐	All registered domain names are automatically redirected to the primary B&D domain name.
☐	☐	All of the B&D Web servers have been configured to accept domain names prefixed with and without the www identifier.

Search Engines and Directories ■■■■■

A search engine is a program that searches Web pages for specific keywords and returns a list of the URLs that point to the locations where these keywords can be found. Some search engines utilize indexing software agents often called *robots* or *spiders*. These agents are programmed to constantly "crawl" the Web in search of new or updated Web pages. When visiting a Web site, an agent will typically record the full text of every page (home and sub-pages) within the Web site. By registering your site (URL) with a particular search engine, you are providing that search engine with a "heads-up" that you have a site worth crawling to.

A directory is a special file used to organize other files into a hierarchical structure. In Internet terms, a directory is a Web site that contains links to other Web sites in some organized format. Directories, however, are quite different from search engines. Normally, directories will not find your Web site unless someone tells the directory that your Web site exists. Directories don't use automated indexing software. They typically require additional information (e.g., keywords) about your Web site, which means more work for you and more time to process. It's important to remember, however, that most directories only allow one listing per Web site, while search engines typically allow multiple pages from the same Web site to be listed.

There are numerous companies that can submit your Web site to hundreds of different search engines and directories for a fee. For example, doog.com currently offers to submit your site to over 600 search engines and directories for a nominal fee. There are also many other companies (e.g., scrubtheweb.com and businessweb.com.au) that will submit your registration to a few search engines and directories free of charge. When submitting your Web site to a search engine or third party placement service, you may want to use a "black hole" e-mail address. This e-mail address will typically receive auto-responses from many of the search engines and, subsequently, be sold to many e-mailing lists.

Search engines vary significantly in the features that they support which, in turn, can affect how they rank your Web site. Search engines use agents that are programmed to constantly "crawl" the Web in search of new or updated Web pages. *Deep crawling* search engines will typically list many pages from a

■■■■■■■■■■■■■■■■■■
Did you know...

Speechbot from Compaq (compaq.com/ speechbot) is an experimental search engine that indexes audio files, as opposed to traditional search engines, which index text.

single Web site. Some search engines will instantly index any Web page that you submit to them. This means that your Web site will usually appear in their lists within a day or two after submission. Some search engines can follow links within frames and image maps, while others can't. Most search engines can determine the popularity of a Web page by analyzing the number of links that point to the page from other pages. And, some search engines can even track how often your Web page changes.

Other common components of search engine ranking algorithms include keyword density and position, coordination of marketing messages with page titles and descriptions, and even actual manual reviews of the submitted page. However, since each search engine uses distinct algorithms to determine a Web site's placement, it's easy to hurt your rating in many engines by focusing your efforts on matching the requirements of a specific search engine.

All of the major search engines say that they index the full visible body text of a Web page. However, they exclude *stop words* that have been predetermined to be unnecessary (e.g., *a*, *the*, *their*) in order to save time and storage space. Also, not all search engines support META, ALT, or TITLE tags.

All of the major search engines penalize, reject or "blackball" Web sites that they suspect are unfairly trying to influence the search engine's rankings (typically referred to as "spamdexing" or "spamming the bot"). Examples of such techniques include using tiny text to increase the number of times that critical search keywords appear on your Web pages, or hiding large amounts of text from viewers of your Web page simply by making the text the same color as the background. Alternatively, a less risky technique is to add a link to a search engine on your Web site. In some cases, this will result in that particular search engine promoting your Web site near the top of its list.

So, how do you determine where your company's Web site ranks in comparison with your competitors? Some companies (e.g., site-see.com and webpromote.com) offer to analyze your Web site's position on various search engines free of charge. Other companies such as marketposition.com, northernwebs.com, notess.com, positionagent.com, searchenginewatch.com, seekhelp.com, selfpromotion.com, and webposition.com offer tools to determine your position and/or provide suggestions on how to influence these ratings.

B&D developed a list of keywords that, when submitted to the main search engines (e.g., Yahoo, Excite, etc.), would ideally result in B&D's Web site being displayed near the top of the list of search results. Some of the keywords that they selected were stock, equity, Brown +Donaldson, broker, shares, stock +market, NYSE, and NASDAQ. B&D obtained a measure of their Web site's overall ranking by counting the number of times that B&D's Web site appeared on the first page of a search engine's results. Table 11-5 shows B&D's site recognition testing checklist.

Table 11-5 B&D's Site Recognition Testing Checklist

Pass	Fail	Description
☐	☐	B&D's Web site is listed on all of the major search engines and directories.
☐	☐	B&D's Web site appears on the first results page for at least half of the major search engines and directories when the following keywords are submitted: online +broker, brown +donaldson, and online +trading

(Continued)

Table 11-5 (*Continued*)

Pass	Fail	Description
☐	☐	B&D's Web site appears on the first results page of at least one major search engine and directory when the following keywords are submitted: stocks, bonds, NYSE, and NASDAQ
☐	☐	A process is in place to continually monitor B&D's search engine ratings and, if necessary, resubmit the Web site to the major search engines and directories. This is especially important if the Web site has been redesigned.

There are many tools available to assist you with testing your Web site. META search engines, for example, can be used to search many other search engines for specific keywords. You can enter some of your Web site's keywords and see how many different search engines list your Web site in their results. Askjeeves.com, dogpile.com, internet2.com, and metafind.com are all examples of META search engines. Search engine rankers (e.g., site-see.com) allow you to check how your Web site ranks in comparison to other Web sites that are listed with various search engines and directories.

META Tags ■ ■ ■ ■ ■

META tags are small pieces of code placed at the top of a Web page that provide additional information on the content of the Web page. META tags have a wide variety of uses, but are especially useful for search engine robots that are "spidering" a Web site and trying to figure out the focus of a Web site's content. Short of directly paying search engines or directories to boost your Web site's ranking, META tags provide a low-cost and effective method of improving a Web site's ranking. Perhaps the most effective method of improving your Web site's ranking is to make frequent and regular manual page submissions to the leading search engines.

Two META tags, "description" and "keywords" are used to provide a brief overview of the Web page and a list of keywords that would ideally result in the search engine including your Web page in its results. Because of the huge impact that META tags can have on a Web site's ratings, many organizations require all of their Web site's META tags to be independently inspected by someone other than the developer or Webmaster who coded them. A simple syntax error or an overzealous Webmaster attempting to spam a search engine could result in disastrous search engine ratings.

Figure 11-2 shows the "description" and "keywords" META tags used in Brown & Donaldson's original Home page.

```
<HEAD>
<TITLE>Brown & Donaldson</TITLE>
<META name="description" content="The best online trading
site for individual investors">
<META name="keywords" content="stocks, bonds, mutual
funds, trade stocks, buy, sell, quote">
</HEAD>
```

■■■■■■■■■■■■■■■■■

Figure 11-2

B&D's Home Page Description and Keywords META Tags

Table 11-6 lists some of the other META tags that can be used.

Table 11-6   Commonly Used META Tags

META name=	Description
"author"	Used to identify the Web site's author.
"copyright"	Used to store any copyright information that pertains to your Web site.
"formatter/generator/publisher"	Often added automatically by authoring tools to indicate the tool used to build the Web site.
"robots"	Provides assistance to search engines that are "spidering" (scanning) your Web site.
"rating"	Indicates the suggested viewing age for your Web site (e.g., general, mature, fourteen years, or restricted). This META tag is often used by software that allows parental control over which Web sites can be accessed.

The "robots" META tag warrants further explanation. One of the features of this tag is that it allows you to specify a particular page within your Web site that should not be indexed by a search engine. This is useful when you want to block the contents of certain pages (e.g., frequently changing content) from being indexed by a search engine. Unfortunately, not all search engines support this tag. Alternatively, most (if not all) search engines support the "robots.txt" convention of index blocking. You can indicate which parts of your Web site should not be visited by a robot by listing the Web pages that should be skipped in a TXT file located in your Web site's root directory.

META tags with an HTTP-EQUIV attribute are equivalent to HTTP headers. Typically, they control the action of browsers and may be used to refine the information provided by the actual headers. Tags using this form should have an equivalent effect when specified as an HTTP header. In some cases, these tags

■■■■■■■■■■■■■■■■■■
Did you know...

While many Web sites have META tags on their home page, non-home/index pages that are feasible entry points into the Web site should also have their own set of META tags.

may be translated into actual HTTP headers automatically or via a pre-processing tool. Table 11-7 lists some of the more common HTTP-EQUIV META tags.

Table 11-7   HTTP-EQUIV META Tags

META HTTP-EQUIV=	Description
"content-type/content-disposition"	Provides character set information.
"content-script-type/content-style-type/content-language"	Defines the default scripting language, style sheet and "human" language.
"cache-control"	Controls the action of cache agents.
"expires"	The date and time after which the Web page should be considered expired.
"pragma"	Controls caching in HTTP 1.0. Value must be set to "no-cache" to prevent caching. Issued by the browser when it receives a request to reload.
"refresh"	Specifies a delay (in seconds) before the browser automatically reloads the Web page. Optionally, specifies an alternative URL to load.
"window-target"	Specifies the named window of the current page. Can be used to stop a page from appearing in a frame with many (but not all) browsers.

There are many different strategies used by various search engines to interpret your Web site's META tags. Since these strategies are continually changing, trying to "tune" a META tag for a specific search engine may prove to be a waste of time or even cause other search engines to disqualify your site.

Some Web sites (e.g. searchenginewatch.com, site-see.com, submitit.com, submitplus.com, theweb.com, vancouver-webpages.com, and webposition.com) offer background information, tools, and tips for optimizing your Web site's META tags. Metabot from Watchfire (watchfire.com) and

■■■■■■■■■■■■■■■■■
Did you know...

META tags that are successful in improving your Web site's rank with some search engines may actually lower your Web site's rank with others.

WebPosition Gold from FirstPlace Software (webposition.com), for example, both provide syntax checking for many of the more common META tags.

Companies will often change their Web site's META tags in order to improve their rankings in search engine results. CloakMaster (cloakmaster.com) provides a tool to hide META tags from everyone except bonafide search engines. This helps prevent competitors from copying successful keyword combinations from your Web site. It's important to keep abreast of what your competitors are doing. Just because your Web site ranks above a competitor's site today doesn't mean you'll stay there tomorrow.

Table 11-8 lists some of B&D's test cases for validating their Web site's META tags.

■■■■■■■■■■■■■■■■■
Did you know…

Compaq (compaq.com/alta vista.com) found that from a sample of 500 million search requests, only 32% of viewers looked past the first page of results.

Table 11-8 B&D's META Tag Testing Checklist

		Meta Tag Validation
Pass	Fail	Description
☐	☐	Pages contain no META tag or HTTP-EQUIV META tag syntax errors.
☐	☐	Pages contain the copyright META tag.
☐	☐	Pages within the Web site that are feasible entry points have appropriate "keyword" and "description" META tags defined.
☐	☐	Pages that should not be indexed by search engines (e.g. they contain frequently changing information) contain the "expires" and "robots" META tags and are listed in the robots.txt file. In addition, these pages should not have "keyword" or "description" tags defined.
☐	☐	META tags do not contain other companies' trademarks, brand names and/or copyrighted phrases.

Maintenance Testing

Web testing doesn't stop when the application goes into production – it's not a bounded-interval event. Instead, Web testing is a regular process that continues as long as the application is alive.

There are many maintenance testing activities that should be performed on a regular basis. Table 11-9 lists some of the most common maintenance testing activities. Unfortunately, some of these activities may be outside of the Web developers' or testers' control. Consider, for example, the content of Brown & Donaldson's Web site. B&D once ran a "Stock Pick of the Hour" section on their Web site. Unfortunately, it became too much of a burden to keep updating and re-testing this feature, so they eventually dropped it. This was a management decision that the developers and testers had no control over. As another example, consider the importance of maintaining your Web site's administrative contact information. B&D's Web site and e-mail system was down for several hours because the credit card that their domain name renewal fee was being billed to eventually expired and the contact information that the Domain Name Registrar had on file was out of date. With proper documentation and planning, this situation could have been avoided. The point to remember is that Web testing is never completely done. It's an ongoing process that requires continual attention to obscure details.

Web testing is never completely done. Do you know who's responsible for testing your Web site after it goes live?

Did you know…

In November 1999, NTSL (NTSL.com) found that Windows NT/2000 servers on average ran more than 50% faster once their hard drives had been de-fragmented.

Table 11-9   B&D's Maintenance Testing Checklist

Pass	Fail	Description
☐	☐	The Web site has passed all test cases for new brands and versions of browsers.
☐	☐	The Web site has passed all test cases (e.g., performance, functionality, navigation, etc.) for new server-side system software upgrades or patches.
☐	☐	There are no broken internal or external links.
☐	☐	Links to your Web site from other Web sites (e.g., business partners) are not broken.
☐	☐	The content displayed on the Web site is not out of date.
☐	☐	Old Web site components are removed when they're upgraded, enhanced, or dropped.
☐	☐	E-mail addresses are departmental (rather than using specific individuals) and still valid. Note that departmental e-mail addresses can be auto-forwarded to specific individuals.
☐	☐	Mailboxes for e-mail addresses are not full, and a process is in place to warn B&D's IT department when any mailbox becomes more than 80% full.
☐	☐	Contact names and telephone numbers displayed on the Web site are still valid.
☐	☐	The database is reorganized regularly in order to maintain optimal performance.
☐	☐	File and directory structures are de-fragmented on a regular basis in order to maintain optimal performance and ensure data integrity.
☐	☐	Sufficient free space is maintained for all databases and file servers.
☐	☐	Audit records are created, archived, and purged from the production system in accordance with the guidelines defined by B&D's auditors.

(Continued)

Table 11-9 (*Continued*)

Pass	Fail	Description
☐	☐	Archived audit records are destroyed in accordance with the guidelines defined by B&D's auditors. B&D typically keeps its archives for a period of 7 years.
☐	☐	Security groups are maintained, especially after a new version of the Web application or system software is installed.
☐	☐	Existing and potential clients are able to easily find B&D's Web site through the majority of the leading search engines and directories.
☐	☐	A process is in place to ensure that when the Web site's content changes significantly, the Web site is resubmitted to the leading search engines and directories.
☐	☐	The ISP providing Internet connectivity for the B&D Web site meets or exceeds the service levels specified in their Quality of Service (QoS) contract. QS measures include network availability, effectiveness of network throughput, network packet loss, network latency, and network latency variation (referred to as "jitter").

There are several different types of tools available to help you with your maintenance testing. HTML spell checkers can scan the content (ignoring HTML tags) of your Web site for spelling mistakes. Microsoft FrontPage, for example, can check a Web site for correct spelling based on U.S. English or a number of other languages. Other tools such as LinkBot from Watchfire (watchfire.com) can search a Web site for orphaned Web pages that typically can't be reached by following the links from the Web site's home page. WebCheck from Compuware (compuware.com) identifies Web pages that have been changed in the past *x* number of days (where *x* is user-definable) by reading the header codes returned by the server when a page is requested.

Configuration Management

Configuration management is the process of identifying, controlling, tracking, and reporting the components of a Web site (e.g., hardware, system software, application software, data/content, documentation, processes and relationships between them) at discrete points in time. The purpose of doing this is to maintain the integrity of the system and provide a means of tracing the life cycle of the system.

It's impossible to effectively develop or maintain a reasonable Web site without implementing some kind of configuration management process. Environment configuration management can become a nightmare if developers, testers, or even programs start downloading/uploading plug-ins, service packs, or beta versions over the Internet on an ad-hoc basis (some programs automatically refresh themselves!). However, a configuration management process should not be so obtrusive, bureaucratic, or all-encompassing that it has a net negative effect on productivity or makes it difficult for developers or testers to comply with its terms.

For many Web sites, it may make sense to break up the configuration management duties into two processes: structural code (e.g., the HTML used to build a Web page) and content (the data used to populate a Web page). Generally speaking, content changes are more frequent than code changes, but often have less impact on the testing effort. Unfortunately, content changes may generate huge numbers of "false positives" during regression testing.

Failure to break out the content changes from the code changes may mean that, in the event of a serious failure, it may be

---

Configuration management consists of the following activities:

- identification (what)
- control (library management)
- audit (who and when)
- status reports (who cares)

The following Web sites provide more information on content management:

ca.com
chasebobko.com
interwoven.com
merant.com
microsoft.com
rational.com
vignette.com

impossible for a Web site to "roll back" to an earlier release. Consequently, many sites have found that the pace of content and code changes on a Web site is so fast that they are never able to back out a version once it goes into production.

Useful URLs ■■■■■

Table 11-10 Useful Web Sites

Web Site URLs	Description of Services
accrue.com, ilux.com, netgen.com, sane.com, serverwatch.internet.com, uu.se/Software/Analyzers, webtrends.com, and yahoo.com	Web log analysis tools.
fxweb.com, hitbox.com, and hitometer.com	On-screen hit counters.
livehelper.com and liveperson.com	Live interactive feedback services.
bizrate.com, mediametrix.com, netratings.com, pcdataonline.com, scorecard.com, and shopperconnection.com	Web site rating services.
apnic.net, ICANN.org, networksolutions.com, and ripe.net	Domain name usage.
cybergeography.org, domainstats.com, and isa.org	Domain name statistics.
cmg.co.uk, consumeronsite.com, cyberatlas.com, domainstats.com, emarketer.com, forrester.com, glreach.com, nsol.com, nua.ie, statmarket.com, un.int, and zonaresearch.com	Internet usage statistics.

(Continued)

Table 11-10 (*Continued*)

Web Site URLs	Description of Services
marketposition.com, northernwebs.com, notess.com, positionagent.com, searchenginewatch.com, seekhelp.com, selfpromotion.com, site-see.com, webposition.com, and webpromote.com	Search engine analysis.
askjeeves.com, dogpile.com, internet2.com, and metafind.com	META search engines.
cloakmaster.com, searchenginewatch.com, site-see.com, submitit.com, submitplus.com, theweb.com, vancouver-webpages.com, watchfire.com, and webposition.com	META tags.
execsoft.com, raxco.com, and symantec.com	De-fragmentation tools.
ca.com, chasebobko.com, interwoven.com, merant.com, microsoft.com, rational.com, and vignette.com	Configuration management.
sqe.com/bdonline/	Case study Web site and downloadable test plans.

Appendix A – Internet Architecture

Remember that the key to understanding many of the principles behind Web testing lies in comprehending the technology used to implement your Web site. If you can understand how your organization's Web site works, then you're in a much better position to develop a comprehensive test plan for the Web site.

Uniform Resource Locator (URL) ■■■■■

A Uniform Resource Locator (URL) is a general-purpose naming scheme used to specify Internet resources. URLs aren't limited to pointing to just files. A URL can also point to queries, documents within databases, or just about anything else. A typical URL consists of five parts: a protocol scheme, a server address, a port number, a target resource, and a query string. Figure A-1 shows a sample URL and its components.

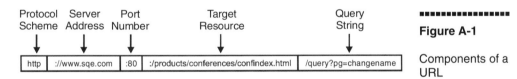

Protocol Scheme	Server Address	Port Number	Target Resource	Query String
http	://www.sqe.com	:80	:/products/conferences/confindex.html	/query?pg=changename

■■■■■■■■■■■■■■■■■

Figure A-1

Components of a URL

The protocol scheme tells the Web browser which Internet protocol to use when accessing a resource on a server. Common Internet protocols include HTTP, HTTPS, and FTP. The server address is a host domain name that identifies a specific Web site. The port number identifies a program that runs on a specific server. If you don't specify a port number in your URL, the browser automatically directs your requests to a default port.

The target resource in a URL is a directory path that leads to a specific resource. More often than not, this path leads to a HyperText Markup Language (HTML) file. Table A-1 lists typical port assignments for a Web server.

Table A-1 Typical Web Server Port Assignments

Port Number	Internet Service
21	File Transfer Protocol (FTP)
23	Telnet
25	Simple Mail Transfer Protocol (SMTP)
70	Gopher
79	Finger
80	HyperText Transfer Protocol (HTTP)
110	Post Office Protocol Version 3 (POP3)
139	Network Basic Input/Output Systems (NetBIOS)
143	Internet Message Access Protocol (IMAP)
161	Simple Network Management Protocol (SNMP)
443	HyperText Transfer Protocol Secure (HTTPS)

Network Protocols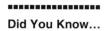

To reduce network design complexity, most modern network protocols are organized as a series of layers or levels. Each layer builds upon the functionality and capabilities offered by the layer immediately below it. Consider an analogy from the desktop computer world, for example. User-developed MS-Office macros utilize the functionality of MS-Office, which in turn uses the Windows operating system, which in turn utilizes the Desktop's BIOS. Early versions of Windows used DOS as an additional layer between the operating system and the Desktop's BIOS.

The number, name and purpose of each network layer varies from protocol to protocol, which can make interfacing networks that use different protocols problematic. In an effort to try to make network protocols more standard and easier to integrate, the International Standards Organization (ISO.ch) proposed the Open Systems Interconnection (OSI) model. This model breaks down the various tasks that need to be performed by a network into seven (7) reference layers, where each layer is responsible for a set of specific functions.

The Application layer is where the World Wide Web (WWW) resides. The Application layer uses specific programs to provide file, print, message, and application database services. This layer controls how these services are performed. Once the proper service has been identified, the user's request is processed. Examples of Internet Applications include FTP, TelNet, SMTP, DNS, HTTP, and S-HTTP.

OSI Layer 7

Application

The Presentation layer transforms data into a mutually agreed-upon format that each application can understand. Additionally, it compresses large data and encrypts sensitive information. The Presentation layer provides translation services when two computers are speaking different languages.

OSI Layer 6

Presentation

The Session layer opens a dialog between the sending and receiving computers. It makes sure that communications continue by using three simple steps: connection establishment, data transfer, and connection release. Once the session dialog has been established and data transfer has begun, the system moves its focus to the Presentation layer. Secure Sockets Layer (SSL) is typically considered to be an OSI Session layer because it utilizes the functionality provided by the Transport layer to enhance the service available to the higher-level Application layer protocols.

OSI Layer 5

Session

The Transport layer organizes datagrams into segments and delivers them to upper layer services. A datagram is an independent, self-contained message sent over the network whose arrival, arrival time, and content are not guaranteed. If the segments are not delivered to the destination device correctly, the Transport layer can retransmit the segments or inform the upper layers of the problem. The Internet uses two Layer 4 protocols: TCP and UDP. Unlike TCP, UDP is a connectionless protocol, which means that it can typically send data faster but can't guarantee that the data is received. UDP is typically used for streaming video and audio, where losing a few packets here and there is a small price to pay for increased network speed. Web pages, on the other hand, typically use TCP as a means of ensuring that the entire page is received correctly.

■■■■■■■■■■■■■■■■■■

OSI Layer 4

Transport

The Network layer provides logical network-to-network communications by organizing Data Link frames into datagrams. Remember that the data field from the Data Link layer becomes the entire packet (i.e., a datagram) at the Network layer. The Network layer and Transport layer work together in providing OSI network functions. The layer 3 protocol used by the Internet is called IP (Internet Protocol).

■■■■■■■■■■■■■■■■■■

OSI Layer 3

Network

The Data Link layer organizes electronic bits into logical chunks of data called *packets*. A packet (Figure A-2) is a contiguous series of data with a common purpose. Packets allow the network to organize bits into a logical data unit and transmit them to the correct computer.

■■■■■■■■■■■■■■■■■■

OSI Layer 2

Data Link

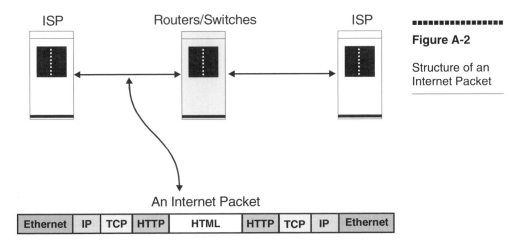

ISP   Routers/Switches   ISP

An Internet Packet

| Ethernet | IP | TCP | HTTP | HTML | HTTP | TCP | IP | Ethernet |

Figure A-2

Structure of an Internet Packet

In the Physical layer, data is represented as electronic bits in the form of zeros and ones. Data travels over a physical medium (e.g., copper wire) using specific transmission devices such as modems, routers, hubs, switches, and other devices. Common layer 1 and 2 protocols include Asynchronous Transfer Method (ATM), Ethernet, ISDN, Token Bus, Token Ring, Frame Relay, and ARCNET.

OSI Layer 1

Physical

The network protocol used by the Internet is called IP (Internet Protocol) and corresponds to layer 3 in the OSI model. Its specification can be traced back to a 1960's U.S. Department of Defense network research project called *ARPANet*. In order for a computer to be directly connected to the Internet, it must use IP as its layer 3 (network) protocol. However, it may potentially use any number of lower-level protocols (e.g., Data Link and Physical) to support the various high-level protocols. Figure A-3 shows how the architecture of the seven-layer OSI model can be mapped to the Internet model.

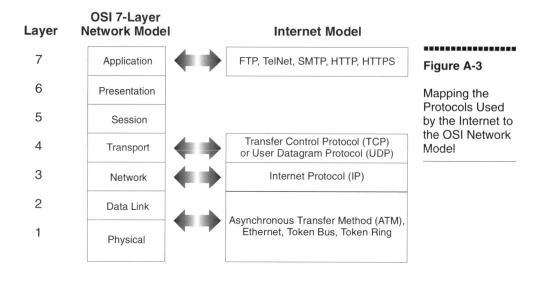

Layer	OSI 7-Layer Network Model	Internet Model
7	Application	FTP, TelNet, SMTP, HTTP, HTTPS
6	Presentation	
5	Session	
4	Transport	Transfer Control Protocol (TCP) or User Datagram Protocol (UDP)
3	Network	Internet Protocol (IP)
2	Data Link	Asynchronous Transfer Method (ATM), Ethernet, Token Bus, Token Ring
1	Physical	

Figure A-3

Mapping the Protocols Used by the Internet to the OSI Network Model

Internet Protocol (IP)

Along with its URL, every Web site is assigned a unique Internet Protocol (IP) address. The current IP address format (version 4) is comprised of a 32-bit field that uniquely identifies each network and node connected to the Internet. IP version 4 was designed to handle up to 4 billion addresses. Unfortunately, at the current rate of growth, the Internet will run out of unique numbers in only a few more years.

A new IP address format (version 6) seeks to address the potential shortage of IP addresses by increasing the number of bits used to identify a network node from 32 to 128. This is a sufficiently large enough number to guarantee 1,500 unique IP addresses for every square meter of the Earth's surface. Unlike IP version 4, version 6 identification numbers will most likely be assigned geographically, similar to the assignment of telephone area codes. Version 6 identification numbers will also be backward compatible with version 4 and have built-in encryption capability.

Figure A-4 shows the format of an IP version 4 header. Notice that each tick mark in the diagram represents one bit position.

```
 0                   1                   2                   3
 0 1 2 3 4 5 6 7 8 9 0 1 2 3 4 5 6 7 8 9 0 1 2 3 4 5 6 7 8 9 0 1
+-+-+-+-+-+-+-+-+-+-+-+-+-+-+-+-+-+-+-+-+-+-+-+-+-+-+-+-+-+-+-+-+
|Version|  IHL  |Type of Service|         Total Length          |
+-+-+-+-+-+-+-+-+-+-+-+-+-+-+-+-+-+-+-+-+-+-+-+-+-+-+-+-+-+-+-+-+
|         Identification        |Flags|     Fragment Offset     |
+-+-+-+-+-+-+-+-+-+-+-+-+-+-+-+-+-+-+-+-+-+-+-+-+-+-+-+-+-+-+-+-+
| Time to Die   |   Protocol    |        Header Checksum         |
+-+-+-+-+-+-+-+-+-+-+-+-+-+-+-+-+-+-+-+-+-+-+-+-+-+-+-+-+-+-+-+-+
|                        Source Address                         |
+-+-+-+-+-+-+-+-+-+-+-+-+-+-+-+-+-+-+-+-+-+-+-+-+-+-+-+-+-+-+-+-+
|                      Destination Address                      |
+-+-+-+-+-+-+-+-+-+-+-+-+-+-+-+-+-+-+-+-+-+-+-+-+-+-+-+-+-+-+-+-+
|             Options                   |        Padding         |
+-+-+-+-+-+-+-+-+-+-+-+-+-+-+-+-+-+-+-+-+-+-+-+-+-+-+-+-+-+-+-+-+
```

Figure A-4

Format of an IP Version 4 Header

Table A-2 describes in more detail each of the fields contained in the IP version 4 header.

Table A-2 IP Version 4 Header Fields

Field	Description
Version	This 4-bit field always has a value of 0100 (binary) or 4 (hex). IPv4 will eventually be replaced with a more complex version, IPv6, in order to solve addressing and security issues.
IHL (Initial Header Length)	Indicates the length of the IP header. The length of the header is always 20 bytes, unless options are present.
Type of Service	Provides hints to the router on how a packet of information should be routed to its destination.
Total Length	Represents the total length of the IP datagram once the packet has been reassembled.

(Continued)

Table A-2 (*Continued*)

Field	Description
Identification	A unique ID number that identifies the entire packet of information. It distinguishes the fragments of one datagram from the fragments of another. All fragments of a packet carry the same ID.
Flags	There are two flags that control fragmentation. The DF (Don't Fragment) bit tells the routers not to fragment the packet. The MF (More Fragments) bit tells routers that this is not the last fragment in the packet.
Fragment Offset	Tells the receiver the position of a fragment in the original datagram. The fragment offset and length determine the portion of the original datagram that is covered by this fragment.
Time to Die	This field indicates how many hops (routers) the packet can pass through before being discarded. Each router that forwards the packet decrements this field by one.
Protocol	Indicates the next protocol header that occurs immediately after the IP header.
Header Checksum	Validates the information contained in the IP header.
Source Address	This is the IP address of the originator (sender) of the packet. This is included in every packet so the receiver knows where to send errors or other information.
Destination Address	This is the IP address of where the packet is going. Each router along the way compares this address to its routing tables in order to determine which direction to send it.
Options	Additional information that can affect the way the packet is routed.
Padding	IP headers must be aligned on even 32-bit boundaries. In order to accommodate this, null bytes are sometimes added.

Source: *Voice and Data Communications Handbook*, McGraw Hill, 1998

The IP protocol field "Time to Die" is particularly interesting because it specifies how many "hops" an IP packet can take before it's discarded from the Internet. Modifying this value may increase your packet delivery success rate. It also helps explain why some Web page requests go unanswered (i.e., the packet died before making it to the target Web server) and other requests to the same Web page are downloaded within seconds.

The current 32-bit IP address is divided into four 8-bit segments (e.g., xxx.xxx.xxx.xxx). Groups of addresses are assigned to Internet users based on Class licenses. Table A-3 lists the various classes along with their address ranges and number of nodes available. Class A licenses are typically owned by Internet backbone providers such as AT&T (att.com) and UUNet (uunet.com). Most mid-sized U.S. corporations own Class C licenses.

Table A-3   IP Class Licenses

Class License	Address Range (networkID.nodeID.nodeID.nodeID)	Nodes Available
A	1.x.x.x through 127.x.x.x	16.8 million
B	128.0.x.x through 191.255.x.x	65,536
C	192.0.0.x through 223.255.255.x	256
D	Used for multicast and special projects	
E	Used for multicast and special projects	

All IP addresses are administered by the Internet Assigned Numbers Authority (IANA). The IANA is also responsible for the registration of any "unique parameters and protocol values" for Internet operation. These parameters and values may include port numbers, character sets, and Multipurpose Internet Mail Extensions (MIME).

■■■■■■■■■■■■■■■■■■
Visit the Internet Assigned Numbers Authority at:

IANA.org

Domain Name System (DNS)

The Domain Name System (DNS) is a set of protocols and services on a TCP/IP network that allows users to access other computers on the network using user-friendly names. A domain name is a meaningful and easy-to-remember "handle" for an Internet address. It's impractical to maintain a complete list of every domain name and IP address on each router or switch. Consequently, lists of domain names and IP addresses are distributed throughout the Internet in a hierarchy of authority. Most PCs connected to the Internet will have a DNS server within close geographic proximity that maps the domain names in each Internet request or forwards them to other DNS servers on the Internet that are able to match the request.

■■■■■■■■■■■■■■■■
Did you know...

"Page-jacking" or "cyber-jacking" is sometimes used to refer to the illegal practice of corrupting a DNS server and redirecting Internet requests to an imposter Web site.

Dynamic Host Configuration Protocol

Rather than assigning each PC on the network a unique static IP address, LAN administrators typically use Dynamic Host Configuration Protocol (DHCP) to dynamically assign each computer a free IP address as needed (i.e., when the computer boots up). This is an efficient way of assigning IP addresses and typically makes network management much easier.

Other Network Protocols

For reference purposes, Table A-4 lists some other network protocols that aren't needed by the Internet, but implement OSI layers 3 through 6.

Table A-4 Other Network Protocols

Vendor	Network Protocol
Apple Computers (apple.com)	AppleTalk.
Banyan Systems (banyan.com/epresence.com)	Vines.
Compaq (compaq.com/digital.com)	DECnet.
IBM (IBM.com)	Systems Network Architecture (SNA)
Microsoft Networking (microsoft.com)	Network Basic Extended Interface (NetBEUI), Network Basic Input/Output System (NetBIOS), and Server Message Block (SMB). Note that Remote Access Server (RAS) uses Asynchronous NetBEUI.
Novell NetWare (novell.com)	IPX (connectionless), SPX (connection oriented), Network Basic Input/Output System (NetBIOS), and Netware Core Protocols (NAP).
Siemens (siemens.com/siemens.de)	H1.

Routers and Switches ■■■■■

Data networks that operate on packet-based architectures (e.g., Internet Protocol - IP) are inherently less expensive to operate than traditional voice networks, which typically operate on circuit-switched networks. Circuit-switched networks are less efficient because a circuit-switched voice call requires a continuous signal between callers. This requires network capacity even during pauses in conversation. Data networks, on the other hand, break the signal into packets. No capacity is used during silences, so other traffic can use the network at the same time.

Routers are multi-protocol devices that provide connectivity between Local Area Networks (LANs). Routers are capable of forwarding and translating traffic in various protocols and are also responsible for selecting the paths that network traffic will follow. Due to the amount of processing required, the level of software intelligence needed to handle routing functions is relatively high compared to most switching devices found on a LAN. High-end routers are often used in LAN backbones and, in some cases, serve as the interface to a Wide Area Network (WAN).

Asynchronous Transfer Mode (ATM) switches are used in both WANs and LANs to collapse voice, video, and data onto the same network. ATM uses switches to establish a circuit from end to end, which guarantees a quality of service for that transmission. However, unlike telephone switches that dedicate circuits end to end, unused bandwidth can be appropriated whenever available. ATM switches are typically installed in the LAN backbone and represent the gateway between the LAN and WAN networks. ATM switches are usually deployed at a customer's site, but may also reside at the telco's central office. Many telcos that offer Internet service use ATM to support IP services, and ISPs often deploy ATM in their infrastructure to improve performance and scalability.

■■■■■■■■■■■■■■■■■
Did you know...

Asynchronous Transfer Mode should not be confused with the banking industry's use of ATM (Automated Teller Machine).

There are several important considerations that you should remember when selecting the hardware for your Web site test environment. Some network cards and modems have CPUs built in, while others rely on software (i.e., the host computer's CPU) to handle network protocols. In general, network cards and modems that have their own CPUs perform better than those that don't. They place less responsibility on the host CPU and transmit and receive data faster. However, devices with built-in CPUs usually cannot be upgraded and cost more than devices without CPUs.

Network Diagnostics   ■■■■■

Windows includes several diagnostic utilities (Table A-5) that you may find useful when troubleshooting your Web site. Each of these utility programs can be executed from a Windows MS-DOS prompt. In addition, NeoWorx (neoworx.com) sells a graphical Internet route-tracing tool called NeoTrace, which provides information similar to *ping* or *tracert*, but in a graphical format.

Table A-5   Windows/MS-DOS Network Utilities

File Name	Description
arp.exe	Used to view or modify the hardware/IP addresses of your local host and default gateway.
ping.exe	Used to ensure that a host computer you're trying to reach is actually operating.
route.exe	Used to view or modify the local routing table in a computer.
tracert.exe	Used to document the TCP/IP route that is being taken to access a remote host.
winipcfg.exe and ipconfig.exe	Used to display the TCP/IP configuration parameters for your computer.

Useful URLs ■ ■ ■ ■ ■

Table A-6 Useful Web Sites

Web Site URLs	Description of Services
IAB.org, IANA.org, ICANN.org, IEFT.org, IRTF.org, ISO.ch, and W3C.org	Information on the Internet Protocol (IP).
apple.com, banyan.com/epresence.com, compaq.com/digital.com, IBM.com, microsoft.com, novell.com, and siemens.com/siemens.de	Information on non-Internet protocols.

Appendix B – Further Reading

While there are currently hundreds of books available that seek to help designers and developers build Web sites and applications, there are very few resources dedicated to testing Web sites or applications. Until Web testing books become more plentiful, the following books may provide some additional background reading.

Web Testing

Making E-Business Work: A Guide to Software Testing in the Internet Age by Steve Marshall, Ryszard Szarkowski, Billie Shea
Newport Press Publications; ISBN: 0970133103

Testing Applications for the Web: Testing Planning for Internet-Based Systems by Hung Quoc Nguyen
John Wiley & Sons; ISBN: 047139470X

Web Performance/Reliability Testing

Blueprints for High Availability: Designing Resilient Distributed Systems by Evan Marcus, Hal Stern
John Wiley & Sons; ISBN: 0471356018

Capacity Planning for Web Performance: Metrics, Models, and Methods by Daniel A. Menasce
Prentice Hall; ISBN: 0136938221

Disaster Recovery Planning: Strategies for Protecting Critical Information Assets by Jon William Toigo, Margaret Romano Toigo
Prentice Hall; ISBN: 013084506X

Foundations of Service Level Management by Rick Sturm, Wayne Morris, Mary Jander
Sams; ISBN: 0672317435

Gain eConfidence by Segue Software
Segue Press; ISBN: N/A

Internet Performance Survival Guide by Geoff Huston, Vinton G. Cerf, Lyman Chapin
John Wiley & Sons; ISBN: 0471378089

Scaling for E-Business: Technologies, Models, Performance, and Capacity Planning by Daniel A. Menasce, Virgilio A. F. Almeida
Prentice Hall; ISBN: 0130863289

Web Performance Tuning: Speeding Up the Web by Patrick Killelea
O'Reilly and Associates; ISBN: 1565923790

Web Security

E-Commerce Security: Weak Links, Best Defenses by Anup K. Ghosh
John Wiley and Sons; ISBN: 0471192236

Hacking Exposed - Second Edition by Joel Scambray, Stuart McClure, George Kurtz
McGraw-Hill; ISBN: 0072127481

Hack Proofing Your Network: Internet Tradecraft by Syngress
Media (Editor), Ryan Russell
Syngress Media Inc; ISBN: 1928994156

Protocols for Secure Electronic Commerce by Ahmed
Sechrouchni, Mostafa Hashem Sherif
CRC Press; ISBN: 0849395976

Web Security by Amrit Tiwana
Digital Press; ISBN: 1555582109

Web Security: A Step-by-Step Reference Guide by Lincoln D.
Stein
Addison-Wesley Pub Co; ISBN: 0201634899

Web Security & Commerce (O'Reilly Nutshell) by Simson
Garfinkel, Gene Spafford
O'Reilly & Associates; ISBN: 1565922697

Web Usability

Designing Web Usability: The Practice of Simplicity by Jakob
Nielsen
New Riders Publishing; ISBN: 156205810X

Information Architecture for the World Wide Web by Louis
Rosenfeld, Peter Morville
O'Reilly & Associates; ISBN: 1565922824

International Programming for Microsoft Windows by David A.
Schmitt
Microsoft Press; ISBN: 1572319569

Usability Engineering by Jakob Nielsen
Morgan Kaufmann Publishers; ISBN: 0125184069

Web Navigation: Designing the User Experience by Jennifer
Fleming, Richard Koman
O'Reilly & Associates; ISBN: 1565923510

Web Site Usability: A Designer's Guide by Jared M. Spool
Morgan Kaufmann Publishers; ISBN: 155860569X

*Web Style Guide: Basic Design Principles for Creating Web
Sites* by Patrick J. Lynch, Sarah Horton
Yale University Press; ISBN: 0300076754

Testing Tools

*Automated Software Testing: Introduction, Management, and
Performance* by Elfriede Dustin, Jeff Rashka and John Paul
Addison-Wesley; ISBN: 0201432870

Software Test Automation: Effective Use of Test Execution by
Dorothy Graham, Mark Fewster (Preface) and Brian Marick
Addison-Wesley; ISBN: 0201331403

Testing Object-Oriented Systems: Models, Patterns, and Tools
by Robert V. Binder
Addison-Wesley; ISBN: 0201809389

Web Languages & Technologies

Cookies by Simon St. Laurent
Computing McGraw-Hill; ISBN: 0070504989

DHTML for the World Wide Web by Jason Cranford Teague
Peachtree Press; ISBN: 0201353415

HTML 4 for the World Wide Web by Elizabeth Castro
Peachtree Press; ISBN: 0201354934

Java for the World Wide Web by Dori Smith
Peachtree Press; ISBN: 0201353407

JavaScript for the World Wide Web by Tom Negrino and Dori
Smith
Peachtree Press; ISBN: 0201354632

Perl and CGI for the World Wide Web by Elizabeth Castro
Peachtree Press; ISBN: 020135358X

Platinum Edition Using HTML 4, XML, and Java 1.2 by Eric
Ladd and Jim O'Donnell
Macmillan Publishing Company; ISBN: 078971759X

TCP/IP Network Administration by Craig Hunt
O'Reilly & Associates; ISBN 9781565923225

VBScript for the World Wide Web by Paul Thurrott
Peachtree Press; ISBN 0201688921

Voice and Data Communications Handbook by Regis J. "Bud"
Bates, Donald Gregory
McGraw-Hill; ISBN 0070063966

Web Commerce Technology Handbook by Daniel Minoli, Emma
Minoli
McGraw-Hill; ISBN 0070429782

Web Design in a Nutshell by Jennifer Niederst
O'Reilly & Associates; ISBN 1565925157

XML Pocket Reference by Robert Eckstein
O'Reilly & Associates; ISBN: 1565927095

Web History

Inventing the Internet by Janet Abbate
MIT Press; ISBN: 0262011727

Weaving the Web: The Original Design and Ultimate Destiny of the World Wide Web by Its Inventor by Tim Berners-Lee and Mark Fischetti
Harper San Francisco; ISBN: 0062515861

General Testing

Software Testing in the Real World: Improving the Process by Edward Kit and Susannah Finzi (Editor)
Addison-Wesley; ISBN: 0201877562

Testing Computer Software by Cem Kaner, Hung Quoc Nguyen and Jack Falk
John Wiley and Sons; ISBN: 0471358460

Test Process Improvement by Martin Pol and Tim Koomen
Addison-Wesley; ISBN: 0201596245

Client/Server Testing

Client/Server Performance Tuning: Designing for Speed by Sid
Wise
Computing McGraw-Hill; ISBN: 0070711739

Client/Server Software Testing on the Desktop and the Web by
Daniel J. Mosley
Prentice Hall; ISBN: 0131838806

High-Performance Client/Server by Chris Loosley, Frank
Douglas
John Wiley & Sons; ISBN: 0471162698

Testing Client/Server Systems by Kelly C. Bourne
Computing McGraw-Hill; ISBN: 0070066884

Techniques

Orthogonal Arrays: Theory and Applications by A.S. Hedayat,
Neil J. A. Sloane and John Stufken
Springer Verlag; ISBN: 0387987665

*Queueing Networks and Markov Chains: Modeling and
Performance Evaluation With Computer Science Applications*
by Gunter Bolch et al.
John Wiley & Sons; ISBN: 0471193666

*The Art of Computer Systems Performance Analysis Techniques
for Experimental Design, Measurement, Simulation, and
Modeling* by Raj Jain
John Wiley & Sons; ISBN: 0471503363

*The Practical Performance Analyst: Performance-By-Design
Techniques for Distributed Systems* by Neil J. Gunther
McGraw-Hill; ISBN: 0079129463

e-Law

The Law of Electronic Commerce by Benjamin Wright, Jane K.
Winn
Aspen Publishers; ISBN: 1567069401

UML Notation

UML Distilled by Martin Folwer and Kendall Scott
Addison Wesley; ISBN 0201325632

Humor

The Dilbert Principle by Scott Adams
Harper Collins; ISBN 0887307876

Index

M

T